MAKING THE CASE FOR EQUALITY

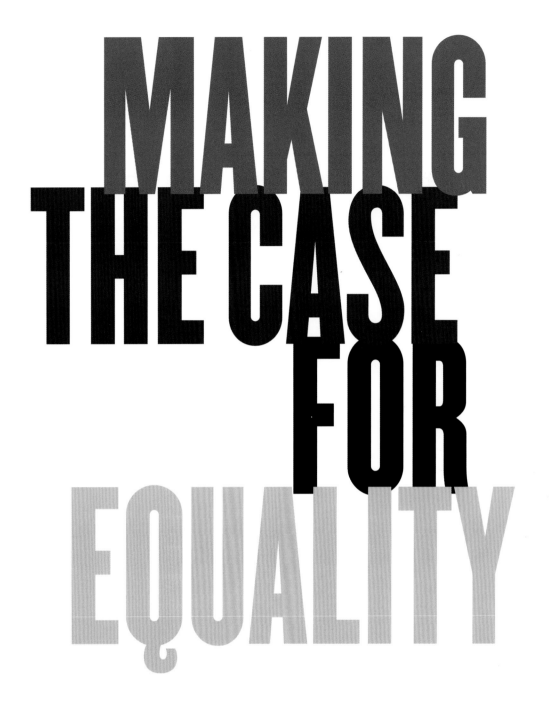

MAKING THE CASE FOR EQUALITY

50 YEARS OF LEGAL MILESTONES IN LGBTQ HISTORY

BY JENNIFER C. PIZER AND ELLEN ANN ANDERSEN

FOREWORD BY ROXANE GAY

AFTERWORD BY TREVOR WILKINSON

CONTENTS

7   ACKNOWLEDGMENTS

8   FOREWORD   By Roxane Gay

12   INTRODUCTION   FRAMING THE CASE

20   CHAPTER 1   WE'RE HERE, WE'RE QUEER, GET USED TO IT
WINNING THE RIGHT TO EXIST, BE SAFE, AND BE SEEN

40   INTERLUDE   A SKETCH OF THE LEGAL SYSTEM

42   CHAPTER 2   "THE GAY PLAGUE"
CONFRONTING STIGMA AND DISCRIMINATION BASED ON HIV/AIDS

68   CHAPTER 3   WORKING
SECURING EMPLOYMENT FAIRNESS

90   INTERLUDE   PUBLIC EDUCATION AND ENGAGEMENT

100   CHAPTER 4   BAD MEDICINE
CHALLENGING DISCRIMINATION IN HEALTH INSURANCE
AND MEDICAL CARE

118   CHAPTER 5   NOT JUST ROOMMATES
PROTECTING LGBTQ+ FAMILY RELATIONSHIPS

134   CHAPTER 6   LOVE UNITES US
WINNING THE FREEDOM TO MARRY

166   INTERLUDE   THE LONG ROAD TO MARRIAGE EQUALITY

CHAPTER 7   **STUDENT LIFE**
MAKING SCHOOLS SAFE AND WELCOMING FOR LGBTQ+ YOUTH

CHAPTER 8   **SEEKING SHELTER**
REDUCING DISCRIMINATION IN HOUSING AND LODGING

INTERLUDE   **THE LEGAL HELP DESK**

CHAPTER 9   **IMPERFECT INSTITUTIONS**
MANAGING IN AND REFORMING OUR LEGAL SYSTEMS

CHAPTER 10   **NEWS FROM THE FRONTLINES**
DEFENDING AGAINST ANTI-LGBTQ+ ATTACKS

CHAPTER 11   **ENVISIONING JUSTICE/CLAIMING OUR FUTURE**
By Kevin Jennings

AFTERWORD   By Trevor Wilkinson

276   ABOUT THE AUTHORS

278   INDEX

280   ENDNOTES

283   PHOTO CREDITS

ACKNOWLEDGMENTS

This book is the brainchild of Lambda Legal CEO Kevin Jennings and Monacelli Publisher Philip Ruppel. Many of Lambda Legal's staff provided invaluable assistance, with Senior Paralegal Jamie Farnsworth lead among them. Michael Green found and sourced the images, guided by his gift for visual storytelling. And we are grateful to Sarah Hanson, Brian Rosenkrans, and Chris DeCarlo for their beautiful artistic contributions. Our wonderful Monacelli team included Senior Editor Carla Sakamoto and Production Director Michael Vagnetti, with Phil Kovacevich and Shawn Hazen crafting the book's gorgeous design. We are especially grateful to Keith Fox, CEO of Phaidon, for his strong support of this project.

At this 50th Anniversary, special honor is due to our founder Bill Thom, and to E. Carrington ("Cary") Boggan and Michael Lavery, the courageous team who launched Lambda Legal at a time when most states made same-sex relationships a crime; when homosexuality and gender variance were equated with mental illness, instability, promiscuity, and pedophilia; and when being known or suspected to be LGBTQ+ was disqualifying for many jobs. Given the "moral turpitude" exclusions common for bar licensure, this was widely true for practicing law.

The volunteer attorneys who took the risk to affiliate with Lambda Legal and represent gay people in the early years included and depended on those willing to serve publicly as board members. In addition to Bill, Cary, and Mike, these included Rodney Eubanks, Nick Russo, and Shepherd Raimi. Some of our early board members died way too young from AIDS. Others who survived formed lifelong relationships with the organization. Richard Burns is one and, three decades later, played a key role as interim CEO.

Our earliest staff needed similar courage and commitment; they included Barbara Levy and Tim Sweeney, our first paid executive directors, and the Hon. Rosalyn ("Roz") Richter and Abby Rubenfeld, who led the legal work in the early and mid-1980s, respectively. A few staff have provided especially lengthy and influential leadership. Kevin Cathcart served as Executive Director for nearly a quarter century, taking the reins when AIDS-related hysteria and sodomy laws fueled stigma and leading us to nationwide marriage equality. Jon Davidson served as a supervising litigator for twenty-two years, thirteen as Legal Director. Before that, Beatrice Dohrn led the Legal Department during eight years of expansion. Leslie Gabel-Brett led the education team through the decade of marriage equality advocacy that culminated in the U.S. Supreme Court victory, with a strong majority of the American public having come to agree. She envisioned and edited *Love Unites Us*, Lambda Legal's book of essays by the movement lawyers and activists telling their inside stories of how the victory was won. And Stefan Johnson staffed and then led our Legal Help Desk for a remarkable twenty-four years.

As a whole, the half-century of progress recounted in this book is the achievement of hundreds of individuals, specifically including Lambda Legal's current staff—an extraordinary group of colleagues who we lift up with gratitude for their resilience and daily dedication to the ongoing fight for full civil rights for LGBTQ+ people and everyone living with HIV.

(opposite) Marchers in New York City carry a mile-long rainbow flag to celebrate the 25th anniversary of Stonewall, June 26, 1994.

(page 2) Paul Smith, Pat Logue, and Ruth Harlow outside the Supreme Court after arguing *Lawrence v. Texas*, March 26, 2003.

FOREWORD
ROXANE GAY

When I first came out, I was very young, and I knew very little but, as nineteen-year-olds are wont to do, I was confident I knew everything. It was, in many ways, a different time. The LGBTQ+ community was experiencing a measure of social acceptance, but it was not nearly enough. We had few civil liberties. We could not marry and those of us in long-term, committed relationships had no legal protections unless the couple had the resources to protect themselves with formal documents that only serve limited purposes anyway. In most states, we couldn't adopt children. The specter of the AIDS crisis loomed darkly. Coming out was a risky prospect more often than not. We recognized the hard-fought progress that had been made. We understood how far we had yet to go. We hoped more change would come.

In Lincoln, Nebraska, where I was living at the time, I would have never dared to hold a girlfriend's hand while walking down the street. Certainly, I was out and proud, but I understood the inherent risks of living my truth. Back then, marriage equality seemed like an impossible goal. In passionate discussions about queer liberation, I boldly declared that marriage was a heteronormative construct we should eschew, that we didn't need the government's sanction to love, that we could build families of choice and demonstrate commitment to those we loved without mimicking the relationships of the very people who were so willing to deny us the right to ours.

I married my wife Debbie in June 2020. It was during the height of the COVID-19 pandemic. We went to a business called Instant Marriage LA, in an office park in Encino, and FaceTimed our families as we exchanged vows. A few weeks later, we received our marriage certificate. It was striking that the moment we said, "I do," there was a new and satisfying gravity to our relationship. We were already committed but now there was a legal bond between us. Our marriage was recognized not only by our witnesses but the State of California and the country we live in. I was surprised by how much that meant to me, by how validating it was.

When I look back on myself, at nineteen, so convinced I was right about marriage while being so loudly wrong, I find myself wanting to be gentle with my younger self. Thirty years later, our community has made some of the progress we yearned for back in the 1990s and well before. We can serve in the military and yes, we can marry. We can adopt children in most places. We can love openly and freely in most places. We can work without fear of losing our jobs because of our sexual orientation or gender identity, in most places, thanks to the Supreme Court. We see versions of ourselves reflected in popular culture. And at the same time, we just endured four long years of unrelenting federal attacks during the Trump years and now are facing an alarming retraction of our rights by the U.S. Supreme Court and in several states. Now, more than ever, without unceasing advocacy to defend and advance our legal protections, progress will only ever be temporary.

I was born in 1974, and the '70s were a transformative decade for queer liberation. In 1969, the Stonewall Riots were a defining moment in the history of queer political activism and queer visibility.

Chairperson Sabrina Sojourner leads the Gay Freedom Parade in San Francisco, marking the 10th anniversary of Stonewall, June 24, 1979.

The LGBTQ+ community was no longer going to live in the shadows or live in shame. Companies started including sexual orientation as a protected characteristic. Activists organized and one such group was Lambda Legal, founded in 1973 by a group of lawyers who understood that one of the greatest weapons we wield in the fight for equality is changing the legal landscape. They fought and continue to fight so our community is afforded the same rights and liberties as anyone else. Over the past fifty years, Lambda Legal has taken on fights great and small—from allowing gay student groups to form at colleges and universities to striking down sodomy laws, to helping parents adopt their children and live free of the fear of losing them. They have helped people with HIV and AIDS receive much-needed healthcare and supported members of the LGBTQ+ community in the military who only wanted to serve. In addition to their litigation efforts, they have worked on policy and legislative reform, understanding that these strategies must work in concert.

The people of Lambda Legal have worked tirelessly because they understand we must protect ourselves to both make and sustain progress. There are critical fights ahead. Book banning is on the rise in far too many school districts and communities, and many of the banned titles are about LGBTQ+ life. Across the country, state legislators are attacking LGBTQ+ rights in unprecedented ways. In 2022, there were at least 155 anti-LGBTQ+ bills introduced in thirty-two states. Florida passed the "Florida Parental Rights in Education Act," a policy also known as "Don't Say Gay or Trans," in a thinly-veiled attempt to erase the LGBTQ+ community by forbidding the discussion of anything related to our community in certain grades. It is that kind of policy serving as the top of a very slippery slope, at the bottom of which is the complete eradication of our rights. As I write this, Lambda Legal's attorneys are in court making the case that it must be struck down.

Meanwhile, in Texas, state attorney general Ken Paxton tried to compile a list of trans people in the state, a terrifying prospect when you consider what he could do with such a list. At the direction of Governor Greg Abbott, the state's Department of Family and Protective Services set out to investigate and punish families who seek gender-affirming care for their trans children as child abusers. Lambda Legal's cases have blocked his pernicious crusade so far. But other states are following suit. And in at least a dozen, trans children are banned from school athletics if they want to participate as their true selves, rather than their sex assigned at birth. There are bathroom bills, yet again, which make it impossible for many trans kids to make it through the school day. In Virginia, as one of his first acts as governor, Glenn Youngkin established broad restrictions on the rights of trans children in all of the state's school districts.

We must also remember that in 2022, the Supreme Court overturned *Roe v. Wade* in the *Dobbs* decision. As part of his concurring opinion, Justice Clarence Thomas suggested that the Court should reconsider *Lawrence v. Texas* and *Obergefell v. Hodges*—landmark Lambda Legal victories abolishing sodomy laws and guaranteeing marriage equality. *Dobbs* was a painful reminder that truly, none of us are free until we are all free.

The Biden Administration has responded to some of these attacks by signing the Respect for Marriage Act into law to federally protect same-sex couples' marriages. But, unlike *Obergefell*, the Act only protects same-sex couples once they are married and does not require all states to issue marriage licenses without discrimination. Should *Obergefell* be overturned, same-sex couples in more than thirty states would again need to go elsewhere to celebrate and secure their relationships by marrying.

For every step forward toward queer liberation, there are powerful forces trying to pull us back into the closet, relegate us to living in shadows of shame, and eradicate our existences. But there is even more power in knowing we will not go back. We will not be erased. We will not be denied. We will not surrender our rights and freedoms. The efforts of Lambda Legal are needed now, more than ever, to help us hold that line.

Roxane Gay is a professor, writer, editor, and commenter. She is the author of the best-sellers *Bad Feminist* (2014), *Hunger* (2017), and *Difficult Women* (2017), as well as many highly praised short stories. She is a contributing opinion writer for *The New York Times* and the author of *World of Wakanda* for Marvel.

Celebrants outside the Supreme Court after the decision in *Obergefell*, which gave same-sex couples the right to marry anywhere in the United States, June 26, 2015.

T his book invites you to reflect on and celebrate Lambda Legal's fifty years of making the case for LGBTQ+ equality and freedom. It is not a complete catalog of our work. That would be impossible. In the past half century, Lambda Legal has litigated more than a thousand cases on behalf of tens of thousands of clients. We have drafted statutes, trained judges, published Know-Your-Rights toolkits, led awareness campaigns, and responded to at least a quarter million Legal Help Desk inquiries. And because this work is designed to change laws, empower the LGBTQ+ community, and deepen public understanding, its radiating effects have improved the lives of many millions.

To mark this historic occasion, we have selected a variety of cases that spotlight important moments in Lambda Legal's ongoing campaign for LGBTQ+ rights and against HIV stigma. These cases tell many tales. They connect the past to the present, showing how far the movement for LGBTQ+ equality and freedom has progressed, and how far it has left to go. They show how Lambda Legal's mission and strategic priorities have evolved in response to community needs and opportunities. They illuminate the promises and perils of impact litigation as well as the relationship between our cases and our education and policy work. And always, they demonstrate the power of our stories and storytelling in our movement's struggle for social change.

Marchers in New York's first Pride march, the Christopher Street Liberation Day March, on June 28, 1970, with the banner of the Gay Activists Alliance, which used the Lambda symbol to indicate lesbian and gay freedom.

A WORD ABOUT LANGUAGE

The language used to describe LGBTQ+ people has evolved greatly in the past fifty years, and our word choices reflect that. When we describe Lambda Legal's work in the 1970s and '80s, we use terms such as "gay rights," and "anti-gay" to match the language of the era. When we discuss our more recent work, or describe our community as a whole, we use the more current term LGBTQ+.

We include many of our biggest cases—cases that generated landmark rulings changing the face of American law—as well as cases that are less well-known, but that established important legal principles and/or brought attention to the many forms of stigma and discrimination LGBTQ+ people have faced during the past fifty years, including the dangerous, escalating attacks underway nationwide as this book goes to press at the end of 2023.

The scale and ferocity of these attacks are undeniably frightening, both because they often target some of the most vulnerable members of our community—LGBTQ+ youth, especially trans, nonbinary, and gender nonconforming youth—and because they threaten to roll back our hard-fought advances. There can be no mistaking the urgency to defend what we have won and to continue forward. We must protect and support those cruelly targeted by a blizzard of transphobic disinformation. We must oppose the notion that religious beliefs allow harmful violations of the law. We must fight for the right to autonomy in reproductive and other healthcare decision-making. And we must continue to challenge the marginalization of and elevated violence against LGBTQ+ people who are Black, Indigenous, and other people of color (BIPOC), who live with HIV and disabilities, and who endure family rejection, social stigma, and poverty at alarming rates.

(above) 1963 button from the collection of the National Museum of American History.

(right) Early Lambda Legal leaders (L-R): Michael Seltzer, Bill Thom, Rosalyn ("Roz") Richter, D. Nicholas ("Nick") Russo, and Michael Lavery.

Central Park during Christopher
Street Liberation Day, New York City,
June 27, 1971.

As frightening as these attacks are, they also are familiar. LGBTQ+ people have long been the targets of "moral panics," from the Lavender Scare of the 1950s to the AIDS hysteria of the 1980s to the extended frenzy over marriage equality.

We know how to defend and strategically advance despite daunting odds, in part because we have had brilliant teachers. Lambda Legal's founders were inspired by impact litigators—such as the NAACP Legal Defense and Educational Fund and the NOW Legal Defense and Education Fund—who drove positive change in other civil rights movements. Our work draws from and builds on the innovative strategies used to challenge race-based segregation, sex-based job requirements, and many other forms of institutionalized discrimination.

We also have outstanding partners. We collaborate often with other legal organizations working for LGBTQ+ rights and to end HIV stigma, including the American Civil Liberties Union, GLBTQ+ Legal Advocates and Defenders, Human Rights Campaign, National Center for Lesbian Rights, Transgender Law Center, and Transgender Legal Defense and Education Fund. We work regularly with partners and allies in other national, and state, and local organizations, elected officials, and scholars. These deep and enduring relationships are a signal of strength of our civil rights movement and are why we are so confident we will maintain our forward progress despite the ferocious opposition of current times.

(above) Marchers in New York City's Pride parade respond to the stigma surrounding HIV/AIDS in the epidemic's early years, June 26, 1983.

(right) *San Francisco Chronicle*, June 27, 2013

Gay Liberation Front "Gay-In"
during the first Christopher Street
Liberation Day, June 28, 1970.

Finally, we have the accumulated wisdom that comes with long experience. Over the past fifty years, we have played a key role in every major public policy area affecting LGBTQ+ and HIV-positive people. In the following pages, we lay out ten of those areas, sharing examples of the ways we have used storytelling and strategic advocacy to accomplish profound change.

In Lambda Legal's earliest years, it was an all-volunteer organization often on the brink of insolvency and operating from founder Bill Thom's apartment. Fifty years in, it has nearly one hundred staff based in six offices across the nation and is the largest legal advocacy organization in the United States dedicated to advancing and protecting the civil rights of LGBTQ+ and HIV-positive people.

This book pays tribute to the thousands upon thousands of people who have powered Lambda Legal's growth. It honors the clients who have stepped forward to fight back against injustice, sometimes at great personal cost. It honors the staff who have challenged the irrational and often cruel actions of governments and private institutions with brilliance and determination. And it honors the generous board members, donors, and volunteers who have made the work possible.

(above, left) Pin from the 1993 March on Washington, which called on President Bill Clinton to honor his campaign pledge to end the ban on military service by lesbian, gay, and bisexual people based on its anti-sodomy rule.

(right) (L-R) Richard Burns and Urvashi Vaid with Lambda Legal's newly appointed Executive Director Kevin Cathcart, June 1992.

Lambda Legal's mission has been and remains the pursuit of full civil rights for our community through test case litigation, policy development and legislative lawyering, and public education. One of our biggest problems always has been how fear keeps us closeted—silent and invisible—allowing often defamatory fictions about us to be spread. Representation requires calling out these lies and telling the truth. We do this with our clients' testimony, by showing that misguided policies are harming real people, by debunking junk pseudoscience, and by demanding justice. Here is the story of Lambda Legal's first half-century making the case for LGBTQ+ equality and freedom.

(above) Donna Gottschalk–lesbian, feminist, activist, photographer, artist–at the first Christopher Street Gay Liberation Day March in New York City, June 28, 1970.

(right) Lambda Legal at New York Pride, 2023.

CHAPTER 1

WE'RE HERE, WE'RE QUEER, GET USED TO IT

WINNING THE RIGHT TO EXIST, BE SAFE, AND BE SEEN

When Lambda Legal opened its doors in 1973, it confronted a world in which one of the biggest challenges facing LGBTQ+ people was the government itself. People who were perceived as LGBTQ+ were targeted by police wielding a range of laws that punished them for daring to exist. Some—like prohibitions on certain same-sex intimate activity (often called "sodomy") and cross-dressing—were directly aimed at LGBTQ+ people. Others—like prohibitions on loitering and disorderly conduct—could apply to everyone but were used in discriminatory ways against LGBTQ+ people.

From the outset, Lambda Legal has understood the importance of dismantling laws and practices that punish people for simply living authentically and openly, causing harm to no one. That's why we made the elimination of sodomy laws a key priority and why we continue to confront police misconduct. It's also why we challenge laws that seek to remove rights from LGBTQ+ people and why we're fighting to ensure that governments issue identity documents that accurately reflect a person's gender identity. But before we could do anything, we had to fight for our own right to exist.

(opposite) Sign during a San Francisco demonstration against the June 1986 U.S. Supreme Court ruling upholding Georgia's sodomy law, *Bowers v. Hardwick*.

(page 20) Activists from the Gay Liberation Front, Gay Activists Alliance, Radical Lesbians, and others march down 7th Avenue on August 29, 1970, to protest police harassment of gay New Yorkers.

WINNING THE RIGHT TO EXIST

In *re Thom* (1972-1973)

When attorney Bill Thom first conceived of a law firm dedicated to advancing gay rights,[1] he knew there would be problems. For one thing, as he put it "[e]veryone was in the closet in those days and it was very hard to find 'out' lawyers, or firms that would work on gay issues," especially because attorneys at that time could be disbarred if their homosexuality became known. However, he didn't expect that Lambda Legal would become its own first client.

In New York, nonprofit law firms have to show that they have a "benevolent or charitable purpose." To make sure that Lambda Legal's petition for incorporation met these guidelines, Bill copied the successful petition of the Puerto Rican Legal Defense and Education Fund nearly word-for-word, changing only the name and the community to be served.[2]

But according to the three-judge panel that reviewed the petition in 1972, working to advance gay rights and provide legal representation to lesbians and gay men was "neither benevolent nor charitable." If lesbians and gay men had trouble finding lawyers, that was simply a matter of lawyers' "personal tastes" in clients.

Undaunted, Bill appealed the ruling, arguing that Lambda Legal's right to exist was protected by the U.S. Constitution. The First Amendment, he argued, protects the right of all Americans to speak out and form organizations. And the equal protection clause of the Fourteenth Amendment means that the government must treat "similarly situated groups" (like Puerto Ricans and gay people) similarly. In July 1973, New York's top court reversed the decision of the three-judge panel, ordering it to process Lambda Legal's incorporation papers, which the panel did, begrudgingly, on October 18, 1973.

Bill Thom deposited $25 into a bank account and installed a second phone line in his apartment. Lambda Legal was open for business. The calls for help began pouring in.

> ### Homosexual Legal Aid Group Set Up
> The formation of a fund to provide free legal counsel for homosexuals was announced by William J. Thom, a lawyer in New York City. Mr. Thom said the group, the Lambda Legal Defense and Education Fund, was designed to aid homosexuals in the same way that similar organizations assist blacks, Puerto Ricans and members of other minority groups. He added that the fund was expected to be in operation by the end of the year.

BEHIND THE SCENES

"We had absolutely no money. I wrote Lambda on a Band-Aid and stuck it on my apartment mailbox so we wouldn't miss business mail—that was Lambda's first official sign. There was no budget for advertising or promotion, but somehow, in a very short period it became known that there was a group that would help with legal issues, and we started getting inquiries."
—Bill Thom

(left) Bill Thom's Manhattan apartment building, Lambda Legal's first office.

(opposite, top) Lambda Legal Staff celebrating Pride in Chicago, circa 1994.

(opposite, bottom) Judicial campaign ad for Bill Thom in *The New York City News: Newsmagazine for the Gay and Lesbian Community*, September 6, 1984.

"By being out, we changed the world. We changed attitudes and hearts and minds. Ask yourself: where would we be if Bill Thom and others had not been willing to put their names on a piece of paper with the word 'gay'?"[3]

—ROZ RICHTER, EXECUTIVE DIRECTOR OF LAMBDA LEGAL, 1980-1983

MAY IT PLEASE THE COURT

Bill Thom went on to become New York City's first openly gay judge. He was the first of several Lambda Legal alumni to join the bench. Former executive director (1980-1983) Roz Richter enjoyed a thirty-year career as a judge in New York, making history in 2009 when she and a colleague became the two first lesbians to be appointed to the appellate courts in New York. Patricia (Pat) Logue, who played many vital roles during her years at Lambda Legal (1993-2007), spent the next twelve years as a trial court judge in Illinois. And Jane Morrison, former director of the Southern Regional Office (1997-2000), has been repeatedly reelected to her position as a trial court judge in Fulton County, Georgia, since first winning office in 2012. She was among the first openly LGBTQ+ judges in Georgia.

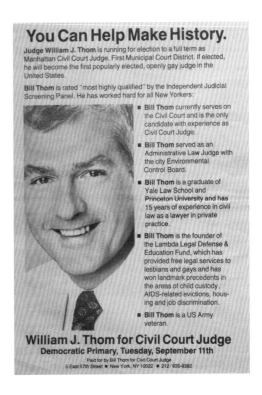

You Can Help Make History.

Judge William J. Thom is running for election to a full term as Manhattan Civil Court Judge, First Municipal Court District. If elected, he will become the first popularly elected, openly gay judge in the United States.

Bill Thom is rated "most highly qualified" by the Independent Judicial Screening Panel. He has worked hard for all New Yorkers:

■ Bill Thom currently serves on the Civil Court and is the only candidate with experience as Civil Court Judge.

■ Bill Thom served as an Administrative Law Judge with the city Environmental Control Board.

■ Bill Thom is a graduate of Yale Law School and Princeton University and has 15 years of experience in civil law as a lawyer in private practice.

■ Bill Thom is the founder of the Lambda Legal Defense & Education Fund, which has provided free legal services to lesbians and gays and has won landmark precedents in the areas of child custody, AIDS-related evictions, housing and job discrimination.

■ Bill Thom is a US Army veteran.

William J. Thom for Civil Court Judge
Democratic Primary, Tuesday, September 11th

Paid for by Bill Thom for Civil Court Judge
5 East 57th Street ■ New York, NY 10022 ■ 212/935-9382

ENDING SODOMY LAWS

Bowers v. Hardwick (1983-1986)

It has never actually been illegal to be LGBTQ+ in the United States. If that sounds odd given the history of government persecution, it is because sodomy laws were used to justify discrimination against LGBTQ+ people in realms ranging from family law to military service to immigration. The problem, though, was that sodomy laws were rarely enforced; hardly anyone was actually arrested for private, consensual, same-sex intimacy. That's what made *Bowers v. Hardwick* seem like a perfect test case: Michael Hardwick had literally been arrested *in his own Atlanta bedroom* for having sex with another man.

When the ACLU of Georgia sued on Michael's behalf, Lambda Legal realized the case's potential and created the Ad Hoc Task Force to Challenge Sodomy Laws, bringing the small community of gay and lesbian rights litigators into one room to develop a unified legal strategy. This work paid off when, in 1985, the Eleventh Circuit Court of Appeals ruled that the state's sodomy law violated the constitutional right of privacy. One year later, though, the Supreme Court overturned that decision, holding in a devastating 5–4 decision that Georgia's law was legal and calling the claim that LGBTQ+ people had any right to sexual privacy "at best, facetious."

Hardwick placed a major roadblock in front of the LGBTQ+ rights movement, but our intracommunity organizing proved invaluable. The Ad Hoc Task Force morphed into the Litigators' Roundtable in the aftermath of *Hardwick* and became a key mechanism for Lambda Legal and our movement partners to develop and coordinate legal strategies. The Roundtable—now called the National LGBT Litigators' Roundtable—continues to serve that function today.

BEHIND THE SCENES

"When I started at Lambda in January 1983, there was no coordination among the few legal groups then in existence and the various individuals doing LGBT rights work. I am very proud to have created the Roundtable to address that lack of coordination. It originally was called the Ad Hoc Task Force to Challenge Sodomy Laws, because that was an important emphasis back when our private consensual behavior was still criminal in many states. And it has lasted many decades and still serves an important purpose. Back in the '80s to now—Lambda has led the way."
—Abby Rubenfeld, Legal Director (1983-1988)

Gay·Love

it's the real thing

(right) Andy Humm, long-time community leader and journalist, at an April 30, 1976 demonstration when the notoriously anti-gay U.S. Supreme Court chief justice Warren Burger spoke at NYU.

GET THE GOVERNMENT OUT OF OUR BEDROOMS!

G.P.U. of N.Y.U.

> "The cop stood there for like . . . thirty-five seconds while I was engaged in mutual oral sex. When I looked up and realized he was standing there, he *then* identified himself. He said I was under arrest for sodomy. I said, 'What are you doing in my bedroom?'"[4]

—MICHAEL HARDWICK

Jork Times

Weather: Partly sunny and mild today, light, variable winds; mostly cloudy tonight. Partly cloudy, humid tomorrow. Temperatures: today 75-80, tonight 67-70; yesterday 61-80. Details, page C9.

SDAY, JULY 1, 1986

60 cents beyond 75 miles from New York City, except on Long Island

30 CENTS

HIGH COURT, 5-4, SAYS STATES HAVE THE RIGHT TO OUTLAW PRIVATE HOMOSEXUAL ACTS

Privacy Law And History

60 Years of Expansion Interrupted by Ruling

BY LINDA GREENHOUSE
Special to The New York Times

WASHINGTON, June 30 — With its decision today that there is no constitutionally protected right to engage in homosexual conduct, the Supreme Court interrupted the expansion of the concept of privacy on which it embarked more than 60 years ago.

News Analysis

The 5-to-4 majority drew a sharp line of demarcation between those choices that are fundamental to heterosexual life — whether and whom to marry, whether to conceive a child, whether to carry a pregnancy to term — and the decision to engage in homosexual acts.

The heterosexual choices fall within the "zone of privacy" that the Court has defined, with greater or lesser clarity, in dozens of cases. The line stretches back to a pair of decisions in the mid-1920's that gave parents the right to make basic choices about their children's education, and more recently includes rulings on contraception and abortion.

No Resemblance to Precedents

Writing for the majority today, Justice Byron R. White canvassed those precedents and then observed, "We think it evident that none of the rights announced in those cases bears any resemblance to the claimed constitutional right of homosexuals to engage in acts of sodomy that is asserted in this case."

Arguments to the contrary, Justice White said, were "insupportable" and "facetious."

For reasons why the

Associated Press
Associate Justice Byron R. White, who wrote the majority opinion.

Thomas Stoddard, executive director of a homosexual advocacy group, said of ruling, "It's a major disaster from our point of view."

DIVISION IS BITTER

Dissents Assail Ruling's Refusal to Extend the Privacy Guarantee

By STUART TAYLOR Jr.
Special to The New York Times

WASHINGTON, June 30 — A bitterly divided Supreme Court ruled 5 to 4 today that the Constitution does not protect homosexual relations between consenting adults, even in the privacy of their own homes.

The Court held that a Georgia law that makes it a crime for anyone to engage in oral or anal sex could be used to

Excerpts from opinions, page A18.

prosecute homosexual conduct between men or women.

The majority said it would not rule on whether the Constitution protected married couples and other heterosexuals from prosecution under the same law. Justice John Paul Stevens, however, said in a dissent that such laws were "concededly unconstitutional with respect to heterosexuals" under the reasoning of previous Supreme Court rulings.

Weakens Legal Position

The decision is unlikely to curb the growing visibility of homosexuality as a fact of daily life in America, but it weakens the legal arguments of homosexual activists against various forms of discrimination.

This does not necessarily mean it would allow discrimination against homosexuals in other contexts. However, both homosexual groups and their opponents agreed the ruling would slow the advancement of homosexual rights. [Page 18.]

shift from the national level to

The issue presented is whether the Federal Constitution confers a fundamental right upon homosexuals to engage in sodomy, and hence invalidates the laws of the many States that still make such conduct illegal. . . . Proscriptions against that conduct have ancient roots. . . . to claim that a right to engage in such conduct is "deeply rooted in this Nation's history and tradition" or "implicit in the concept of ordered liberty" is, at best, facetious.

--Justice Byron White

Lawrence v. Texas (1998-2003)

Hardwick's outcome meant that sodomy challenges would not win in the federal courts anytime soon. Lambda Legal and our Roundtable colleagues decided to attack sodomy laws state by state instead, a strategy that began producing positive results in the '90s. Then, in 1998, we were asked to join a case with eerie similarities to *Hardwick*: John Lawrence and Tyron Garner had been arrested in John's Houston home and charged with violating Texas's "Homosexual Conduct" law. We recognized that the time was ripe to return to federal court.

We had many decisions to make. Should we just argue that Texas's law violated the equality rights of same-sex couples by explicitly targeting them, but not different-sex couples? Or should we argue more broadly that the government has no business telling consenting adults what intimate conduct is allowed in the privacy of their own homes? The constitutional right to privacy must mean at least that much.

In the end, we argued both. And this time, we won! On June 26, 2003, the Supreme Court ruled 6–3 that sodomy laws violate the Constitution's guarantees of privacy and equal protection. John and Tyron, the majority wrote, were "entitled to respect for their private lives. The State cannot demean their existence or control their destiny." It had taken nearly thirty years and unprecedented intra-community cooperation, but Lambda Legal had dismantled a key justification for anti-LGBTQ+ discrimination.

a place male was going ... he was armed with a gun. Officers met the reporter who directed officers to the upstairs apartment. Upon entering the apartment and conducting a search for the armed suspect, officers observed the defendant engaged in deviate sexual conduct namely, anal sex, with another man.

(above, right) A copy of the original police report of John and Tyron's arrest, September 17, 1998.

(above, left) Community members celebrate our landmark U.S. Supreme Court victory in *Lawrence v. Texas* outside Houston City Hall on June 26, 2003.

"*Bowers* was not correct when it was decided, and it is not correct today. It ought not to remain binding precedent. *Bowers v. Hardwick* should be and now is overruled."

—U.S. SUPREME COURT JUSTICE ANTHONY KENNEDY, *LAWRENCE V. TEXAS*

Tyron (L) and John (R)
celebrate their victory.

ANATOMY OF A CASE *Lawrence v. Texas* (1998-2003)

"I called my friend Suzanne Goldberg. I knew that we needed constitutional law experts."

–MITCHELL KATINE

"Suzanne and I both knew immediately that the charges against them—for consensual sodomy in a private home—could tee up a strong challenge to *Bowers v. Hardwick* and its sweeping endorsement of sodomy laws."

–RUTH HARLOW, LEGAL DIRECTOR (2000-2003)

SEPTEMBER 17, 1998

John Lawrence and Tyron Gardner are arrested in John's home and charged with violating the Texas Homosexual Conduct law. Houston attorney Mitchell Katine learns of the arrest and contacts Lambda Legal's Suzanne Goldberg.

"I was standing next to our local counsel as an outsider—a Lambda Legal lawyer from New York City, not expecting to say much. But the prosecutor read from the police report that an officer had seen Tyron and John engaging in oral sex. I had to jump in with a correction: 'Excuse me, your honor, it was anal sex.' We know that faithfulness to the facts, including about sexuality, is part of what's needed to reduce anti-gay stigma."

–SUZANNE GOLDBERG, OUR INITIAL ATTORNEY ON THE CASE

HARRIS COUNTY CRIMINAL COURT

DECEMBER 22, 1998

With Suzanne and Mitchell by their side, John and Tyron plead "no contest," are found guilty, and fined. This sets up the case for appeal.

"We needed to expose *Bowers* as resting on a toppling tripod with three illusory legs: first, a false history that mistakenly painted anti-gay laws as age-old and innate to Western civilization; second, a false assumption that gay sexual intimacy had no connection to family relationships; and third, an erroneous sense within the *Bowers* majority that sodomy laws did not matter much (despite their ubiquitous use as the excuse for anti-gay policies and decisions), because they were rarely enforced as a direct matter."

–RUTH HARLOW

TEXAS COURT OF APPEALS

NOVEMBER 3, 1999

Ruth Harlow argues the case before a 3-judge panel of the Texas Court of Appeals, which rules 2-1 against the law.

MARCH 15, 2001

The full Texas Court of Appeals reverses our victory without hearing argument. We ask Texas' highest criminal court to hear the case, but it refuses.

JUNE 26, 2003

The Supreme Court overturns
Bowers v. Hardwick, ruling 6-3
that anti-sodomy laws violate the
constitutional right of personal
liberty.

"What *Lawrence* does is
finally declare that moral
disapproval is not a
legitimate state interest.
It clearly says that gay
people must be treated just
like everyone else."[6]

–PAT LOGUE

"I used to say, as the case
was proceeding, that we were
doing this for our children.
Now, I have two 20-year-olds
and they and their friends
live in a much better world."[7]

–MITCHELL KATINE, IN 2022.

MARCH 26, 2003

Oral arguments before the U.S.
Supreme Court.

"When I argued the *Lawrence*
case, the pressure felt
enormous—not just because of
the importance of the case
but also because so many
people had worked so hard
to get us to this point!
I did have the advantage
that I really knew the Court
and the Justices knew me.
That helped."

–PAUL SMITH

"We wanted the court to
understand the devastating
impact of these laws—that
was the hearts and minds of
the case."[5]

–PAT LOGUE

JULY-DECEMBER 2002

We invite seasoned Supreme
Court litigator Paul Smith and his
firm Jenner & Block to join our
petition for U.S. Supreme Court
review, which the Court grants on
December 2.

"If I had argued the case
I would have been seen as
an activist lawyer from
a special interest group.
[Paul was well known to
the justices and] the
living example of a very
accomplished, openly
gay man."

–RUTH HARLOW

(opposite) Suzanne Goldberg
speaks to reporters after
the Harris County Criminal
Court judge found John,
left, and Tyron, right, guilty,
December 22, 1998.

(above) Lambda Legal's team
after oral arguments before the
Supreme Court. (L-R): Susan
Sommer, Mitch Katine, Paul
Smith, Ruth Harlow, and Pat
Logue, March 26, 2003.

31

CHALLENGING POLICE MISCONDUCT

The job of the police is to enforce the law. Unfortunately, prejudice and intolerance sometimes make the police themselves a threat to law-abiding LGBTQ+ people. *Brandon v. Richardson* and *Calhoun v. Pennington* are examples of Lambda Legal's ongoing work to challenge police misconduct.

Brandon v. Richardson (2000-2001)

Brandon Teena, a young transgender man in Nebraska, was raped and beaten one night in 1993 by his girlfriend's brother and a friend. They told him they would kill him if he went to the police. When, terrified, he did report the crime to Falls City Sheriff Charles Laux, he was brutalized again. Laux subjected Brandon to graphic and degrading questioning and referred to him as "it." Rather than protecting Brandon, Laux told the rapists that Brandon was pressing charges. A few days later, Brandon's attackers found and killed him. His heartbroken mother sued Laux for negligence, wrongful death, and intentional infliction of emotional distress. She won damages, but the award was dramatically reduced on appeal, adding further insult to her devastating loss. We entered the case, and argued to the Nebraska Supreme Court that Sheriff Laux needed to be held accountable for both his abusive treatment and his reckless disclosure of Brandon's plans and whereabouts to his rapists. In 2001, the Nebraska Supreme Court agreed, ruling that Laux's conduct was "extreme and outrageous, beyond all possible bounds of decency, . . . atrocious and utterly intolerable in a civilized community."

Brandon's story became the basis for a compelling documentary and the 1999 Oscar-winning film *Boys Don't Cry*.

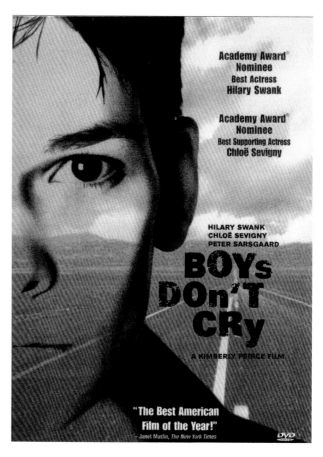

(above, left) Richardson County Sheriff Charles Laux Sr.

(left) Brandon Teena

"Brandon Teena was the first transgender man I ever knew existed due to the film *Boys Don't Cry*. I was moved by his search for love, connection, and survival in small town Nebraska, a search not unlike mine, a decade later, in rural Colorado. But I was also deeply saddened and enraged to discover that Brandon's experience of abuse by law enforcement officials was endemic of trans people's experience with institutions ostensibly meant to 'serve and protect.'"

—CARL CHARLES, SENIOR ATTORNEY

[V]iolence motivated by prejudice and hatred . . . hurts us all. Anybody who thinks that in the world of today and tomorrow, that he or she can hide from the kind of poison that we see in various places in our country, is living in a dream world. Whether we like it or not, our futures are bound together, and it is time we acted like it.

- President William J. Clinton, at the November 10, 1997, White House Conference on Hate Crimes.

Crime

AP/WIDE WORLD PHOTOS

Just prior to her murder, Teena Brandon (*left*) dated Lana Tisdel.

HEARTLAND HOMICIDE

Small-town Nebraska life was fine for a 21-year-old man—until everyone discovered he was actually a woman

By Ingrid Ricks

Teena Brandon had nowhere else to turn the night of Dec. 31, 1993, when she took refuge at the small farmhouse that her friend Lisa Lambert was renting just outside Humboldt, a town of 1,000 people in southeastern Nebraska. Opinion in the area had turned against her—and she knew her life might be in danger.

Two weeks earlier Brandon, 21—a transsexual who had successfully passed as a male in the nearby town of Falls City,

MARCH 8, 1994

(left) *The Advocate*, March 8, 1994

(above) Brandon and his girlfriend Lana Tisdel in 1993.

Calhoun v. Pennington (2009-2015)

Calhoun v. Pennington highlights both the threat that police misconduct continues to pose to LGBTQ+ people and its entrenched nature. In 2009, dozens of Atlanta police officers, many in SWAT gear, descended on the Atlanta Eagle, a gay bar. They detained and searched everyone, then entered all the patrons' IDs into a police database. The patrons were forced to lie face down on the floor, in spilled beer and broken glass for up to two hours, while being subjected to slurs and threats of violence. In the end, not a single patron was charged with a crime. It was pure intimidation and abuse with a badge.

Representing nineteen of the bar patrons, Lambda Legal filed a federal lawsuit against the City of Atlanta and the Atlanta Police Department (APD), arguing that the raid was an unconstitutional search and seizure that also violated many state laws. After a federal court ruled that our clients had been

unlawfully detained and arrested, we negotiated a consent order requiring the APD to overhaul its procedures, including ending warrantless stop and frisk searches, requiring police to identify themselves and permit public videotaping of police activity, and improving police training. That should have been enough. However, the APD repeatedly violated the consent order, forcing us to return to court to enforce it. In 2015, a federal judge held the city and the APD in contempt for failing to comply with the consent order. In the end, Atlanta paid out millions of dollars for the abusive misconduct of its police force.

LITTLE BLACK BOOK

This One Can Keep You *Out* of Trouble

A B C D E F G H I J K L M

Lambda Legal Defense and Education Fund, Inc.

GA VOICE

3.19.10 | Vol. 1, Issue 1 | SPEAKING OUT

THE FIGHT CONTINUES

Focus shifts to federal court in battle over gay bar raid
Page 4

GENERAL ASSEMBLY
What shocked new lesbian lawmaker Simone Bell. Page 6

CHELSEA'S BIG 'BANG'
Chelsea Handler tour tops March events.
Page 28

DEBUT ISSUE

(left) *Calhoun* was the lead story in the March 19, 2010, issue of the *Georgia Voice*. Simone Bell (lower left), then in Georgia's General Assembly, later was our Southern Regional Director.

(above) Lambda Legal's *Little Black Book* (1992)—a guide for dealing with police harassment, entrapment, and other abusive policing practices.

(above, right) *Calhoun* plaintiff Chris Daniels

"Because our clients stood up against the injustice done to them, the Atlanta Police Department will be a better force for good in the community."

–BETH LITTRELL, ONE OF OUR ATTORNEYS ON *CALHOUN V. PENNINGTON*

(above) Lambda Legal staff attorney Beth Littrell (center) flanked by plaintiffs David Thomas (left) and Thomas Hayes.

(left) Thomas Hayes and Mark Danak, two of our plaintiffs in *Calhoun*, outside the Atlanta Eagle bar.

STOPPING ANTI-GAY INITIATIVES

Romer v. Evans (1992–1996)

LGBTQ+ people have had their civil rights put to a popular vote more than any other group of Americans. Efforts in the 1970s to use the ballot box to take away rights from lesbians and gay men were largely responses to new local laws protecting city and county workers from job discrimination based on sexual orientation. Many of the activists spearheading these repeal efforts became part of the newly coalescing conservative Christian Right and, in the 1980s, campaigns to repeal gay rights laws through popular votes became routine. (None of the measures addressed gender identity, a telling indicator of the pervasive invisibility of trans people at that time.) As the '80s turned into the '90s, anti-gay crusaders ramped up their use of ballot campaigns and added a new twist: not just repealing existing protections but trying to prevent the passage of future ones. Lambda Legal and other LGBTQ+ rights litigators were sometimes able to block proposed ballot measures on technical grounds, but our ability to do so varied from state to state.

The most consequential of these campaigns happened in Colorado, where in 1992 voters passed Amendment 2, changing the state constitution to block all existing local gay rights laws and require that any future protections be passed at the state level.[8] This new hurdle was designed to make it extremely difficult for LGBTQ+ people to address discrimination. Working with the ACLU and the Colorado Legal Initiatives Project, we sued to prevent Amendment 2 from taking effect, on behalf of the cities of Denver, Boulder, Aspen, and eight individuals. After eight days of testimony, the trial judge agreed that Amendment 2 was unconstitutional. Colorado appealed the ruling all the way up to the U.S. Supreme Court, losing at every step and generating an historic, pro-LGBTQ+ decision. Amendment 2, the Supreme Court said, was "born of animosity" and designed to make gay men, lesbians, and bisexuals unequal to everyone else. Our victory established that people are entitled to equal protection of the laws regardless of sexual orientation and despite popular notions of morality. It removed a potent weapon from the steadily growing anti-gay movement.

(above) Lesbian and gay community demonstration for new civil rights bill in Sheridan Square, New York City, on May 10, 1978.

(right) Former Colorado Supreme Court justice and our co-counsel for plaintiffs in *Romer v. Evans*, Jean Dubofsky argues the case to the Colorado Supreme Court on May 26, 1993.

"We must conclude that Amendment 2 classifies homosexuals not to further a proper legislative end but to make them unequal to everyone else. This Colorado cannot do. A State cannot so deem a class of persons a stranger to its laws."

—U.S. SUPREME COURT JUSTICE ANTHONY KENNEDY, *ROMER V. EVANS*

(top) John Miller and Bob Bixler hold tight while listening to speeches during a rally on October 9, 1995, the night before the U.S. Supreme Court arguments in *Romer v. Evans*.

(above) "No on 2" pin as produced by the 1992 campaign against Colorado's Amendment 2.

(left) Widespread calls to boycott Colorado followed voters' passage of Amendment 2.

(above) Plaintiffs, attorneys, and supporters who challenged Amendment 2, after oral arguments to the U.S. Supreme Court, October 10, 1995.

SECURING ACCURATE IDENTITY DOCUMENTS

Legal documents verifying identity are an inescapable feature of modern society, required for many different tasks including driving, starting a job, traveling abroad, and applying for public benefits like Medicare and Medicaid. And because many identity documents have gender markers, they pose problems for transgender, intersex, nonbinary, and gender-diverse Americans, whose gender identity and presentation do not match the gender marker on their IDs. They are, in essence, "outed" every time they start a new job, take a flight, or otherwise do things that require a government ID. Making this problem worse, identity documents are produced by many different government agencies, which may have vastly different requirements and processes for changing gender markers—if they allow changes at all. Here are two examples of our work in this area. (We cover recent attacks on accurate identity documents in Chapter 10.)

Campos v. Cohen (2021-2022)

In 2021, we challenged North Carolina's policy making "sex reassignment surgery" a precondition for changing gender markers on birth certificates, because not everyone is eligible, desires, or can afford such surgery. Our client, Lilith Campos, had employer-provided health insurance that excluded gender affirming surgery. (We talk more about insurance exclusions in Chapter 4.) We argued, among other things, that the surgery requirement was invasive and discriminatory, violating the right to liberty and medical autonomy. In June 2022, North Carolina settled the suit, agreeing to remove the surgery requirement.

Zzyym v. Blinken (2014-2021)

Dana Zzyym, an intersex and nonbinary U.S. Navy veteran, applied for a passport in 2014, asking that their gender be marked as X rather than M or F. We stepped in when the U.S. State Department denied Dana's application, launching what would become a six-year odyssey to win Dana an accurate passport. After we prevailed in court three times, the State Department finally changed its policy. In October 2021, Dana became the first American to hold a passport with an X gender marker.

"It was outrageous and dehumanizing that I was denied a birth certificate just because I didn't have surgery. We should all agree that everyone deserves accurate and accessible identity documents that allow us to go through life and run errands with safety, dignity, and respect."

—LILLITH CAMPOS

(opposite, top left) Dana Zzyym portrait from the cover of a 2016 issue of *Outfront* magazine.

(opposite, right) Passport with X gender marker.

"I almost burst into tears when I opened the envelope, pulled out my new passport, and saw the 'X' stamped boldly under 'sex' . . . It took six years, but to have an accurate passport, one that doesn't force me to identify as male or female but recognizes I am neither, is liberating."

—DANA ZZYYM

BEHIND THE SCENES

"When we filed *Zzyym* in 2015, no state offered gender-neutral ID documents, and many thought winning was unlikely. But Dana trusted Lambda Legal to tell their story as an intersex and nonbinary veteran forced to lie to obtain an essential ID and travel document, and our victory brought a cascade of state law changes as well as the end of the State Department's discriminatory passport policy."
—Paul Castillo, our attorney on *Zzyym*

INTERLUDE. A SKETCH OF THE LEGAL SYSTEM

STRUCTURE OF THE COURTS

The United States has a dual court system, consisting of one federal court system and 50 state court systems. They all share the same basic structure, except that the smallest states don't have intermediate courts of appeal.

The federal courts are arranged regionally. Every state has a least one District Court, which feeds into one of twelve Circuit Courts. There is a separate Federal Circuit Court of Appeals for certain federal law cases.

TRIALS AND APPEALS IN THE FEDERAL COURTS

Most cases start out at the District Court and are heard by one judge. Either the judge or a jury determines the facts, and then the judge applies legal principles to decide the outcome.

At the appeals level, cases are heard by three-judge panels selected from the full court (the Ninth Circuit has 29 judges!). These panels review the legal reasoning of the district judge. Losers of a panel decision can ask for a full court review; the full court is more likely to review a case when the issues are controversial.

Losers at the appeals level may ask the U.S. Supreme Court to hear the case, but review is unlikely. The Supreme Court typically hears fewer than 5% of these petitions.

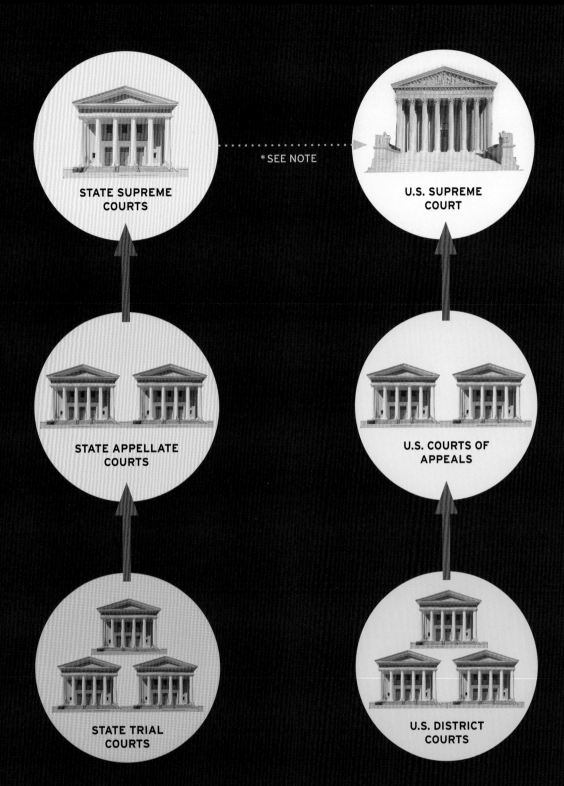

* SEE NOTE

STATE SUPREME
COURTS

U.S. SUPREME
COURT

STATE APPELLATE
COURTS

U.S. COURTS OF
APPEALS

STATE TRIAL
COURTS

U.S. DISTRICT
COURTS

STATE V. FEDERAL CASES

Some categories of cases are usually the domain of state courts and others the domain of federal courts. For example, family law is usually governed by state law, while immigration law is federal. But sometimes a case may be heard in either court system (often because the case involves both state and federal laws). For example, a case could include a federal healthcare discrimination claim and a state insurance claim.

*NOTE: The U.S. Supreme Court can hear a case from a state court if it asks a "federal question." Federal questions involve the U.S. Constitution, federal laws, or the U.S. government. Otherwise, state supreme court decisions are final. We used this feature in our right-to-marry cases. Early on, our cases relied strictly on state constitutions, keeping them safe from U.S. Supreme Court review.

"THE GAY PLAGUE"

CONFRONTING STIGMA AND
DISCRIMINATION BASED ON HIV/AIDS

The emergence of the AIDS epidemic in the 1980s devasted the LGBTQ+ community.[9] From 1981 to 1990, more than 100,000 Americans died of complications related to AIDS, the majority of them gay and bisexual men between the ages of 25 and 44.[10] Lambda Legal found itself confronting an avalanche of requests for help from people whose committed relationships were being ignored during their times of crisis, and who were encountering AIDS-related discrimination in all directions—healthcare, housing, employment, immigration, and insurance coverage. And because the disease was so closely associated with gay men, opponents of gay and lesbian rights began invoking AIDS to justify their anti-gay biases and behaviors. AIDS was used as a pretext to prevent lesbians and gay men from forming gay rights groups, working with the public, and retaining custody and visitation with their children. Not surprisingly, AIDS was also used as a justification for sodomy laws. As former executive director Tim Sweeney explained in 1985, "There is no question that AIDS now puts a veneer over the top of every civil rights issue I see."

To add further heartbreak to public abuse, the AIDS epidemic drove home the precarious position of same-sex couples, given their lack of legal ties to one another. Hospitals could legally withhold medical information from a same-sex partner and could prevent visitation. The legal relatives of people who died without a will could exclude same-sex partners from funeral arrangements and inheritance. Surviving partners found themselves evicted and sometimes homeless when the lease to an apartment was only in their beloved's name. It was, in short, a nightmare wrapped around another nightmare.

(opposite) ACT-UP demonstrators in 1987 protest for increased government involvement in the fight against AIDS.

(page 42) Robert Robinson and David Armedariz embrace during protest against Orange County, California Board of Supervisors' rejection of an anti-discrimination ordinance to protect people with AIDS, June 20, 1989.

RESPONDING TO THE CRISIS

Lambda Legal responded to the outpouring of need by incorporating AIDS-related litigation into our mission and creating the AIDS Project. In 1983, we litigated the first AIDS discrimination lawsuit in the country, successfully preventing a New York City co-op building from evicting Dr. Joseph Sonnabend, who treated patients with AIDS.[11] By the mid-'80s, as the epidemic and its related discrimination devastated the community, a third of our cases concerned AIDS. By 1989, AIDS litigation comprised nearly half of our docket.

Ironically, the disease that generated so much demand for our services also powered our capacity to respond. Mainstream foundations that had previously shied away from supporting gay rights donated money for our AIDS-related work. In addition, bequests and memorial donations began flowing in, another awful indicator of the epidemic's toll. One such bequest, by Bon Foster, funded the establishment of our regional office in Chicago in 1993.

The sheer crush of calls for help related to HIV and AIDS began to taper off in the 1990s, coinciding with medical advances and improved access to care, but HIV and its effects have not gone away. Nearly 1.2 million people in the United States were living with HIV in 2021 (the last year for which comprehensive data is available),[12] and HIV-related discrimination persists. Here are a few highlights from Lambda Legal's four-decade fight to eliminate HIV-related stigma and protect the rights of all people living with HIV.

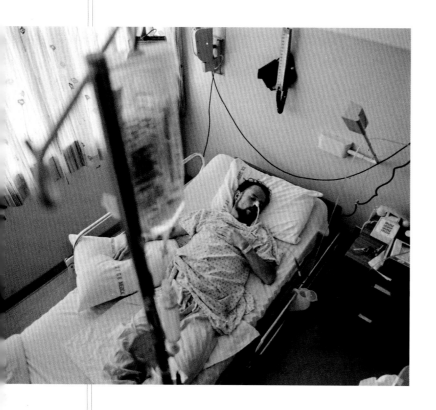

(above) Deotis McMather asleep in bed at San Francisco General's AIDS ward. After being diagnosed with AIDS, he had returned to his apartment where all of his belongings had been thrown out onto the street, circa 1983.

(above, right) Medical staff of San Francisco General Hospital's AIDS ward, 1987-1988

BEHIND THE SCENES

"Early 1983 was the very beginning of awareness about HIV/AIDS and the devastation it was already wreaking on our community. I am proud that Lambda saw the significance of the HIV epidemic and jumped right in. The *AIDS Legal Guide* we produced in 1984 was the first comprehensive guide to litigating HIV/AIDS-related issues in the world."
—Abby Rubenfeld, Legal Director (1983-1988)

RARE CANCER SEEN IN 41 HOMOSEXUALS

Outbreak Occurs Among Men in New York and California —8 Died Inside 2 Years

By LAWRENCE K. ALTMAN

Doctors in New York and California have diagnosed among homosexual men 41 cases of a rare and often rapidly fatal form of cancer. Eight of the victims died less than 24 months after the diagnosis was made.

The cause of the outbreak is unknown, and there is as yet no evidence of contagion. But the doctors who have made the diagnoses, mostly in New York City and the San Francisco Bay area, are alerting other physicians who treat large numbers of homosexual men to the problem in an effort to help identify more cases and to reduce the delay in offering chemotherapy treatment.

The sudden appearance of the cancer, called Kaposi's Sarcoma, has prompted a medical investigation that experts say could have as much scientific as public health importance because of what it may teach about determining the causes of more common types of cancer.

First Appears in Spots

Doctors have been taught in the past that the cancer usually appeared first in spots on the legs and that the disease took a slow course of up to 10 years. But these recent cases have shown that it appears in one or more violet-colored spots anywhere on the body. The spots generally do not itch or cause other symptoms, often can be mistaken for bruises, sometimes appear as lumps and can

(top) Viewing the first unveiling of the NAMES Project AIDS Memorial Quilt in Washington, DC, October 11, 1987.

(above) *New York Native* issue no. 17, July 27-August 9, 1981

(right) *The New York Times*, July 3, 1981

ACCESS TO HEALTHCARE

Many of Lambda Legal's early HIV/AIDS cases concerned discrimination by healthcare providers and insurance companies. In 1988, for example, we compelled a rehabilitation program to admit an HIV-positive man, winning the first federal court ruling that HIV/AIDS discrimination violated laws prohibiting discrimination on the basis of disability.[13] In 1990, we forced one of New York's largest insurers, Empire State Blue Cross/Blue Shield, to cover the costs of a bone marrow transplant to Thomas Bradley from his twin brother, to slow Thomas's HIV.[14] Tragically, however, the insurer's delays had allowed Thomas's HIV to advance, and he was no longer able to have the procedure. (His story became the basis for one of the first television movies to tackle AIDS: *My Brother's Keeper*, starring John Lithgow.) Then, in 1998, we sued Mutual of Omaha for placing arbitrary caps on HIV-related treatment that it didn't impose for other serious illnesses like cancer. Our federal trial court victory established that the Americans with Disabilities Act (ADA) made such discriminatory treatment illegal.[15] A divided appeals court erased our victory, however, using language obviously inconsistent with the ADA's text and purpose. Shortly after the decision was final, though, the insurance giant announced plans to lift the special restrictions on AIDS-related coverage. It was a breakthrough that influenced the rest of the market.

Court Orders Blue Cross to Pay For Transplant in an AIDS Case

By BRUCE LAMBERT

A New York City man suffering from an AIDS infection won a court order yesterday requiring Empire Blue Cross Blue Shield to pay for a bone-marrow transplant from his identical twin.

The man's doctors say the procedure, estimated to cost up to $150,000, is his only hope of survival. The insurer had argued that it did not have to pay for the transplant because it was still an experimental treatment for AIDS.

The case illustrates the legal hurdles AIDS patients sometimes face in getting coverage for newly developing treatments, and the skepticism of insurance companies about therapies they do not accept as standard.

The patient, Thomas J. Bradley, 46 years old, of Rego Park, Queens, won a preliminary injunction yesterday from Justice Elliott Wilk of the New York State Supreme Court in Manhattan. Mr. Bradley, a popular elementary school teacher in the Bayport-Blue Point district on Long Island, has gained widespread support for his cause from administrators, staff members, students and parents.

Twin Eager to Cooperate

Empire Blue Cross said it would await Justice Wilk's written opinion before deciding whether to appeal.

The patient's lawsuit was filed jointly by Mark Scherzer, a private lawyer who has specialized in AIDS insurance cases, and Evan Wolfson, staff attorney for Lambda Legal Defense and Education Fund, a national gay-rights organization based in Manhattan.

Mr. Bradley lives with his brother, Robert, who is not infected with the AIDS virus and says he is eager to cooperate in the transplant. As a twin, he is an ideal donor, and testing has shown his marrow matches his brother's.

In the planned operation at Johns Hopkins Oncology Center in Baltimore, radiation would be used to destroy the remainder of Thomas Bradley's depleted and infected immune system.

Then his blood system would be [in]... with marrow drawn from his br[other's] hip bones in hope of regenerat[ing] and uninfected immune syste[m.]

Bone marrow transplant[s] other immune illnesses [like] leukemia, breast cancer a[nd] anemia. But it has been a[pplied to] six AIDS cases so far. Th[ree] be doing well, according t[o] for Mr. Bradley. Two p[atients] died, although not because [of the opera]tion, and one of the two wa[s declared] free of the AIDS virus. The [fourth is] still in treatment, too early [for a prog]nosis.

After the court decision, Mr. [Bradley] said he felt a sense "of profo[und re]lief." But he added that he wo[uld not] "rest easy till I'm in a bed at Joh[ns] Hopkins."

"If Blue Cross appeals, that alarms me," he said. "As the testimony showed, I don't have that much time. If they hold out they're only going to harm me."

When he decided to go forward with his suit, Mr. Bradley recalls fearing the reaction of his pupils and their parents. But the children took to the streets gathering "over a thousand signatures" at supermarkets on a petition calling for Blue Cross to pay for his operation.

"These people will hold a special place in my heart," Mr. Bradley said.

Jockey's Remains Identified

LONG BRANCH, N.J., July 31 (AP) — Body parts that washed up in a garbage bag at Seven Presidents Park beach have been identified as the remains of a New York jockey. Crews removing timber and other waste from beaches on Thursday discovered the bag, which contained a head, arms and legs. The Monmouth County authorities used fingerprints to identify the dead man as Pedro Ortega, 26 years old, of the Bronx, an apprentice jockey who rode at New York's Acqueduct and Belmont Park race tracks.

"Mutual of Omaha has known for a long time that there is no legitimate, financial reason to treat its policyholders with AIDS differently than everybody else. But the company stood by what it knew was an unfair, unjustified policy, while policyholders like our plaintiffs feared that potentially life-saving treatments would be cut off."

—HEATHER SAWYER, OUR ATTORNEY ON *DOE V. MUTUAL OF OMAHA*

(left) August 1, 1990, *The New York Times* article about the Bradley brothers and the case.

(opposite) Tom and Bob Bradley

(opposite, inset) Poster for the 1995 CBS TV movie about the Bradley Brothers starring John Lithgow as both brothers.

48

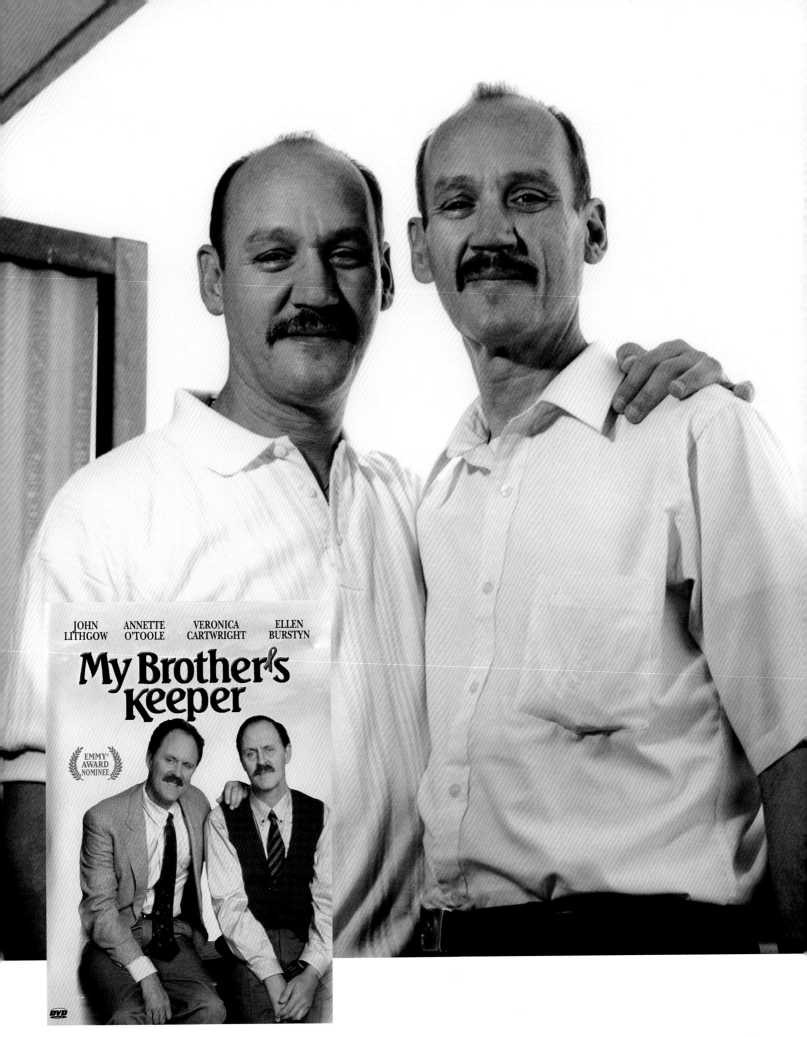

JOHN LITHGOW   ANNETTE O'TOOLE   VERONICA CARTWRIGHT   ELLEN BURSTYN

My Brother's Keeper

EMMY AWARD NOMINEE

DVD

Cook County AIDS Ward Excludes Women.
15 Beds Are Empty.

DISCRIMI...

AND CHILDREN
...LING THROUGH
...CKERS OF OUR
...LTHCARE SYSTEM!

At Cook County Hospital, neither the Women and Children with AIDS Project...
funding of support services, No...
...ed all the ful...
...ated all fif...
...

Women and children with AIDS are falling through the cracks of our public healthcare system.

Women are Dying.

ACT UP CHICAGO

NATIONAL AIDS ACTIONS FOR HEALTHCARE

FIGHTING WORKPLACE DISCRIMINATION

Cusick v. Cirque du Soleil (2003-2004)

One of the persistent problems faced by people living with HIV has been workplace discrimination. In one consequential case, we represented Matthew Cusick, who was fired in 2002 from his job as a Cirque du Soleil gymnast because he had HIV. We filed an employment discrimination claim with the EEOC,[16] arguing that Matthew's HIV status posed no health or safety threat and that he was protected by the ADA. When the EEOC agreed that Cirque had likely violated the ADA, Cirque decided to settle. It paid Cusick a then record-setting sum of $560,000, initiated companywide training, and altered its worldwide employment policies concerning people living with HIV. We launched an extensive public education campaign around the case, which drew support from medical experts, sports teams, and celebrities like Nathan Lane and Bebe Neuwirth.

BEHIND THE SCENES

"I was the brand-new HIV Project Director when Matthew Cusick sought our help. I remember my conviction that we needed to take his case. The discrimination was so blatant and the excuses were science-defying—that he might endanger co-workers and even the audience at Cirque du Soleil. We did a major public education campaign around the case to teach the truth about HIV. Our outreach drew public support from doctors, performers, celebrities, and sports teams—including the San Francisco Fog rugby club, which bragged that its players enjoyed one of the bloodiest sports around, and nonetheless recognized that HIV discrimination is wrong on and off the field."
—Hayley Gorenberg, our attorney on *Cusick*

(previous spread) In an ACT-UP protest in Chicago that ran from April 20-23, 1990, women created an AIDS ward in the street to condemn Cook County Hospital's refusal to admit women with AIDS to the AIDS ward.

(right) Coverage of the case in the *Los Angeles Times*, January 31, 2004.

LOS ANGELES TIMES   THE STATE

Cirque du Soleil Offers to Rehire Acrobat Fired Over Having HIV

The circus will draft an anti-bias policy after a federal panel's finding sets the stage for lawsuit.

By LEE ROMNEY
Times Staff Writer

SAN FRANCISCO — Cirque du Soleil will offer to rehire an acrobat fired last year because he is HIV-positive. The circus also plans to draft an anti-discrimination policy with help from the San Francisco Human Rights Commission that protects the rights of all qualified HIV-positive athletes to perform, company and commission officials said Friday.

Cirque announced its decision to rehire 32-year-old Matthew Cusick in a brief statement shortly after the U.S. Equal Employment Opportunity Commission determined there was reasonable cause to believe that Cirque had discriminated against Cusick because of his disability.

The determination sets the stage for a federal lawsuit against the circus if mediation through the federal panel fails.

But a Cirque spokeswoman

HIV transmission during an accident were infinitesimal.

"We're basically saying there are no restrictions now for anyone with HIV at Cirque," spokeswoman Renee-Claude Menard said. "It's been a learning process.... We're very confident now that the risks are minimal."

Cusick, 32, voluntarily disclosed his HIV status to doctors during a four-month training period with the circus, known worldwide for its aerial acrobatics and surreal beauty. The doctors cleared him as healthy and able to perform, and Cirque offered him a contract as an acrobatic "catcher" in the Las Vegas production of "Mystere." But officials abruptly terminated his contract days before he was to begin, telling him that he posed a risk to other performers as well as the audience.

Menard said Cirque will offer Cusick the same job when it begins mediation in the coming weeks.

In addition to the federal complaint, the case triggered protests at Cirque performances in San Francisco, Los Angeles and Costa Mesa, as well as a separate investigation by the San Francisco Human Rights Commission, which alleged discrimination by the company on city-owned land. AIDS activists

could jeopardize decades of public education to remove the stigma of HIV in the workplace.

Cusick expressed relief at the commission's finding, but said that neither he nor his attorney had been told of the job offer or the company's change of policy.

"I'm very excited that the EEOC is standing behind me on this," said Cusick, who watched a lifelong dream evaporate last year when he was fired and has been slowly rebuilding his personal training business in Maryland. "I hope that no one else will have to go through the same thing that I've gone through over the past year or year and a half."

Cusick's attorney, Hayley Gorenberg of the gay civil rights organization Lambda Legal, said the finding "clearly supports what we were saying about discrimination."

In addition to a job as a former, Gorenberg said, she believes Cusick is due damages for what he has suffered, as well as assurances that "Cirque has the proper policies and training so they don't visit this kind of discrimination on anybody else."

Larry Brinkin, lead negotiator with the San Francisco Human Rights Commission's HIV division, confirmed Friday that Cirque has agreed to do exactly that. The commission's complaint against the circus for discrimination alleged HIV-posi-

of soul-searching discussions, Brinkin said.

Several company vice presidents and a Cirque attorney met for three hours with commission negotiators last month. "We tried to tell them that their understanding of the risk was simply incorrect," said Brinkin, whose staff gathered medical information on behalf of the circus. "They were very interested.... I could see minds being changed as I spoke."

Brinkin said Cirque Vice President Marc Gagnon will return to San Francisco on Tuesday to begin drafting a written anti-discrimination policy. "I can clearly say that they are reversing their position, and that all of the positions at Cirque du Soleil, including the position that Matthew was [hired to perform], are definitely open to people with HIV. That's what we needed to hear in San Francisco."

Cirque's admission that it fired Cusick due to his HIV status prompted concern from people across the country, including Los Angeles City Atty. Rocky Delgadillo, who wrote to company officials offering the legal expertise of the city's AIDS/HIV discrimination unit — the first of its kind in the country.

On Friday, the unit's supervising attorney, David Schulman, expressed "appreciation" that Cirque has educated itself and turned around on this is-

(right) Matthew's case hit a nerve nationwide, so much so that *The Advocate* featured him on the cover, as captured by celebrity photographer Blake Little.

ACTIVISTS' NEW PLAN TO CRACK MARY CHENEY

The national gay & lesbian newsmagazine

The Advocate

www.advocate.com
APRIL 13, 2004

MARRIAGE
BREAKTHROUGHS
& BREAKDOWNS

GAVIN RULES

FREEDOM TO MARRY

SAN FRANCISCO STILL DEFIANT

WINTER 2004

GAYS IN SPORTS
HOW THEY'RE WINNING THE GAME

Gymnast **Matt Cusick** takes on
Cirque du Soleil's anti-HIV discrimination

Out at the Athens Olympics ◦ Dueling Gay Games

LAMBDA|UPDATE
CIVIL RIGHTS NEWS FROM LAMBDA LEGAL

Target: HIV Discrimination

Inside:

CIRQUE DU SOLEIL
BATTLE HEATS UP

THE GOVERNMENT'S
HIV POLICY PROBLEM

SPOTLIGHT ON
LAMBDA LEGAL'S
AIDS PROJECT

ENDING NURSING
HOME BIAS

Lambda
LEGAL

"The way they treated me, it was like I was a piece of trash."[17]

—MATTHEW CUSICK

Taylor v. Rice (2003-2008)

The U.S. Foreign Service and the Department of Defense (DOD) continued to discriminate against employees and job applicants with HIV long after the rest of the federal government had adopted fair workplace practices. We've successfully pushed back against both. Lorenzo Taylor, a trilingual Georgetown graduate who had easily passed the rigorous application process to become a Foreign Service Officer, was denied employment in 2003 solely due to his HIV status, which did not affect his ability to work. We sued, because the federal Rehabilitation Act[18] prohibits the federal government from discriminating against people with disabilities. When the Foreign Service tried to get the case dismissed, the DC Circuit refused, saying that Taylor had presented "more than enough" evidence to go to trial. In 2008, two weeks before the trial's start date, the Foreign Service folded and adopted new and non-discriminatory hiring guidelines.

Harrison v. Austin (2018-2022) and *Roe and Voe v. Austin* (2018-2022)

In *Harrison v. Austin*[19] and *Roe and Voe v. Austin*[20], both filed in 2018, Lambda Legal teamed up with the Modern Military Association of America to represent a trio of servicemembers with asymptomatic HIV who were challenging two DOD policies. Army National Guard Sgt. Nick Harrison, a combat veteran, had been denied an officer's commission, based on a DOD policy that prevented people with HIV from being commissioned as officers or deploying overseas. (It also prevented people living with HIV from enlisting, but that was not at issue in this case.) The two plaintiffs in *Roe and Voe*, who remained anonymous to protect their medical privacy, were airmen who had been discharged from the Air Force under a Trump-era policy known as "Deploy or Get Out," which mandated the discharge of any servicemembers unable to deploy overseas—as all HIV-positive servicemembers were under the first policy. The two cases were heard together, and, in April 2022, a federal judge concluded that both policies were discriminatory, unconstitutional, and based on outdated science, ordering the DOD to end them. In response, the DOD issued a new policy ending its restrictions on the deployment and promotion of people with asymptomatic HIV.

HIV-positive man fights legal battle to join Foreign Service

Department of State lawyers contend making accommodations for employees fighting HIV would be costly, interfere with work duties

By Ann Rostow Contributing Writer

Lorenzo Taylor has spent his career working for the U.S. government in various capacities since 1979.

The 50-year-old Georgetown graduate speaks three languages, and has spent nearly a decade coordinating international exchange and cultural affairs programs for the United States Information Agency. In the course of his assignments, Taylor has traveled around the world, from Brazil to Russia to Zimbabwe to China.

A few years ago, Taylor applied for his dream job, a post in the Foreign Service. After breezing through the difficult tests, he was offered a position, subject to a routine medical exam.

But the exam was anything but routine. Since 1986, the Foreign Service has flatly rejected any candidate who is HIV-positive, as is Taylor, who was diagnosed in 1985.

But in the 15 or so years since his sero-conversion, Taylor had remained asymptomatic. His medical treatment consisted of checkups twice or three times a year, and a combination of drugs.

Lorenzo Taylor speaks three languages and has traveled

(left) *Dallas Voice*, May 5, 2006

"People with HIV do not have to surrender to stigma, ignorance, fear, or the efforts of anyone, even the federal government, to impose second-class citizenship on us. We can fight back. Now people like me who apply to the Foreign Service will not have to go through what I did."

—LORENZO TAYLOR

"This is a landmark decision . . . because they put science ahead of stigma—and that's a very important thing for those of us living with HIV."[21]

—NICK HARRISON

Wilkins v. Austin (2022-ongoing)

Despite the explicit, forceful court ruling in *Harrison* and *Roe and Voe*, the DOD kept its ban on enlistment. So, to mark Veterans Day in 2022, we filed *Wilkins v. Austin* on behalf of Isaiah Wilkins and two anonymous plaintiffs. Isaiah, who had served in the National Guard, was admitted to the U.S. Military Academy's Preparatory School at West Point only to be rejected after a standard medical exam revealed his HIV status. Natalie Noe's story is similar. She was rejected from the Army Reserves when her HIV test was positive. Carol Coe, a transgender lesbian woman, had previously served in the U.S. Army, where she contracted HIV. (She stayed on duty because prior to Trump's "Deploy or Get Out" policy, the military did not discharge people based solely on HIV status.) Carol left the military in 2013 to access gender-affirming care. She now wishes to return to the military but cannot because of the enlistment ban. With *Wilkins v. Austin*, we hope to finally end the military's outdated and unconstitutional treatment of people living with HIV.

"I'm a strong, capable person and living with HIV has no bearing on my ability to serve. It's still my dream to serve my country, and I won't give up on that dream."

–ISAIAH WILKINS

"The existing policy is out of step with science and unlawfully excludes people living with HIV from performing as members of the U.S. military. A positive HIV status alone has no effect on a person's ability to safely serve."

–KARA INGELHART, OUR LEAD ATTORNEY ON *WILKINS*

UNITED STATES DISTRICT COURT
FOR THE EASTERN DISTRICT OF VIRGIN
Alexandria Division

ISAIAH WILKINS, CAROL COE,
NATALIE NOE, and MINORITY
VETERANS OF AMERICA,

Plaintiffs,

v.

LLOYD AUSTIN III, in his official capacity
as Secretary of Defense, and CHRISTINE
WORMUTH, in her official capacity as
Secretary of the Army,

Defendants.

Civil Action No. 22-

COMPLAINT FOR DECLARATORY AND INJU

Plaintiffs Isaiah Wilkins, Carol Coe, Natalie Noe, and M
("Plaintiffs"), by and through their attorneys, hereby bring this a
injunctive relief against Lloyd Austin III, in his official capacit
Christine Wormuth, in her official capacity as the Secretary of
challenging current military policies that discriminate against
immunodeficiency virus (HIV).

STATEMENT OF THE C

1.   For more than thirty-five (35) years, the mil
service of people living with HIV. Military regulations cur
with HIV from joining the Armed Forces and for decades
of members diagnosed with HIV while in service. The ti
Court, citing modern medical facts, issued a permanent
restrictions on the deployment and commissioning of s

1

The Complaint in *Wilkins v. Austin,* as filed on November 10, 2022.

HOUSING DISCRIMINATION

Franke v. Parkstone Living Center (2009-2010)

Lambda Legal's first AIDS case (*Sonnabend*) was, in essence, about housing discrimination. We remain committed to rooting out this invidious practice. In *Franke v. Parkstone Living Center* we represented Dr. Robert Franke, a retired university provost and minister, who moved into an assisted living facility in Little Rock, Arkansas, in early 2009 to be closer to his daughter. Just one day after he moved in, the facility abruptly ejected him because of his HIV status. We argued that this action was clearly illegal under the Fair Housing Act, the ADA, and several Arkansas laws. Parkstone asked the judge to dismiss the case, saying that it was not only entitled but required to evict Dr. Franke, because Arkansas law listed HIV as a communicable disease, and that made him a threat to other residents as a matter of law. The judge disagreed and said Parkstone would have to prove that he was actually dangerous. Parkstone settled the case rather than try to defend its position at trial.

Dr. Franke and his daughter were invited to participate in a conference on HIV and aging at the White House in 2010, and his case was incorporated into staff training materials at other independent living facilities. Dr. Franke passed away in 2011, leaving the world richer for his presence.

"He was an educator through and through. He never had any desire to draw attention to himself— or his medical condition—but he was willing to do whatever was necessary to make his terrible experience a teachable moment."

–SCOTT SCHOETTES, OUR ATTORNEY ON *FRANKE*

(right) The order of events for the White House Meeting on HIV & Aging Agenda, held on October 27, 2010.

(opposite) Sara and Robert Franke

White House Meeting on HIV and Aging Agenda
Eisenhower Executive Office Building
October 27th, 2010
8:30am-Noon

8:30am — Welcome/ Meeting Purpose

Jeffrey S Crowley, Office of National AIDS Policy
Gregorio Millett, Office of National AIDS Policy, Centers for Disease Control & Prevention

8:45am — Epidemiological Overview/ Clinical Considerations & Challenges

Amy Justice, Yale School of Medicine and West Haven VA Healthcare System

15 minute Q&A

9:15am — Community Panel 1: Raising Awareness about Older Populations with HIV

ABC Brothers & Sisters Clip

Moderator: Sean Cahill, Gay Men's Health Crisis
Panelists: Ronald Johnson, AIDS Action
Jane P. Fowler, HIV Wisdom for Older Women
Joanne Keatley, Center of Excellence for Transgender Health University of California, San Francisco
Carolyn Massey, New Samaritan Baptist Church

15 minute Q&A

10:00am — Federal Perspectives

Moderator: Christopher Bates, HHS Office of HIV/AIDS Policy
Panelists: Maggie Czarnogorski, Veterans Administration
Carl Dieffenbach, National Institutes of Health
Jonathan Mermin, Centers for Disease Control &Prevention
Allison Nichol, Department of Justice
David Rust, Social Security Administration

10:50am — Community Panel 2: Getting Ahead of the Curve: Identifying and Tackling Important Issues

Moderator: Cornelius Baker, AED Center on AIDS & Community Health and the National Black Gay Men's Advocacy Coalition

Panelists: Michael Adams, Services and Advocacy for Gay, Lesbian, Bisexual & Transgender Elders
Dorcas Baker, John Hopkins Local Performance Site PA/Mid-Atlantic AIDS Education and Training Center
Steven Manley, HIV Health Services Planning Council of San Francisco
Scott Schoettes, Lambda Legal
Ken South, The American Academy of HIV Medicine
Daniel Tietz, AIDS Community Research Initiative of America

20 minute Q&A

11:50am — Next steps

Kathy Greenlee, HHS Administration on Aging
Jeffrey Crowley, Office of National AIDS Policy

Noon — Adjourn

DISCRIMINATION IN PUBLIC ACCOMMODATIONS

Briteramos v. King of Kuts (2018-2019)

In October of 2017, 34-year-old Nikko Briteramos contacted Lambda Legal's Help Desk. He had just been turned away from a Los Angeles barbershop, King of Kuts, due to his HIV status. One of the barbers had recognized him and told the proprietor that he is HIV-positive. The proprietor then refused to buzz Nikko's hair.

We sued on Nikko's behalf in federal court because denying service based on a person's HIV status violates the federal Americans with Disabilities Act and California's civil rights law. In addition to financial damages for Nikko, we sought a public apology from the shop owner and asked that he stand with us for some public education about the lack of danger from HIV and the need to end day-to-day discrimination in barber shops, beauty salons, and other public places. While pursuing the lawsuit, we also joined with the Black AIDS Institute to produce an educational video and send Nikko on a "Cut the Stigma" tour of historically Black colleges and universities to spread the word that, today, HIV is both easily treatable and becomes untransmittable thanks to prevention medications. The campaign aimed to inform and reduce HIV stigma in majority Black settings, such as the neighborhood barbershop where Nikko was turned away.

Disappointingly, the proprietor of King of Kuts declined to participate. The following summer, however, the federal court entered judgment in Nikko's favor.

"Black people living with HIV are often confronted with discrimination due to stigma and misinformation in public places of importance within our community. The barbershop is a sacred social space, where Black Americans debate social, cultural, and political ideas. HIV discrimination destroys those safe spaces."

—STEFAN JOHNSON, OUR THEN-LEGAL HELP DESK DIRECTOR AND MEMBER OF THE TEAM REPRESENTING NIKKO BRITERAMOS.

(right) Nikko Briteramos

"It was important for us to get involved in Nikko's case because there's no way to end the AIDS epidemic if we're not fighting bigotry, discrimination, and bias. As a Black organization, we have to be ever vigilant in confronting injustice. It is a part of our survival."

–PHILL WILSON, FOUNDER AND THEN-CEO OF THE BLACK AIDS INSTITUTE

(below) Nikko and Lambda Legal's Scott Schoettes with "Cut the Stigma" campaign partners at Southern University, 2020.

HIV AND PUBLIC PROGRAMS

Doe v. A.J. Boggs Co. (2018-2023)

People living with HIV who have low or very low incomes can be especially vulnerable to social stigma and discrimination when their receipt of medical or other services through public programs results in a release of their private medical information. A careless government contractor caused this problem in 2016 in California. The A.J. Boggs Company had a state contract to manage the state's AIDS Drugs Assistance Program (ADAP). Close to 100 people were enrolled when each person's private medical information, including their HIV-positive status, was publicly released contrary to California law and the contract's requirements. We filed a class action lawsuit under California's HIV-privacy law to establish that this right is important. After seven years of litigation to enforce the company's duty to compensate those made vulnerable by its negligence, we reached a settlement that awarded $4,000 to each class member (close to the statutory maximum). We crafted the settlement to pay out over time to avoid making class members ineligible for the ADAP program on which they depend. We were gratified when only a handful of the first batch of checks distributed were returned as undeliverable— a satisfying delivery rate because the impacted population is more likely than the general population to experience changes of address. We were even more gratified because class members reached out to thank us and express how much both the financial award and the vindication meant to them.

HIV DECRIMINALIZATION

During the early years of the AIDS epidemic, many states passed laws criminalizing actions that could potentially expose another person to HIV. As the Centers for Disease Control and Prevention notes, these laws are bad public policy for several reasons: they don't reflect current scientific understanding of how HIV is transmitted, they increase stigmatization and reduce disclosure, they deter people from testing and seeking treatment, and they treat HIV differently from other communicable diseases. They also are used disproportionately against communities of color. Yet, as of 2022, half the states still have HIV criminalization laws, with sentences ranging from less than a year to life imprisonment. Lambda Legal is working to dismantle these unjust laws. *Rhoades v. Iowa* and *Roe v. Precythe* illustrate this work.

Rhoades v. Iowa (2012-2014)

Nick Rhoades, a gay Iowan living with HIV, was sentenced in 2008 to 25 years in prison and lifetime registration as a sex offender because of a one-time sexual encounter in which he used a condom and did not, in fact, transmit HIV to his partner. Lambda Legal fought the case all the way to the Iowa Supreme Court which, in 2014, set aside Nick's conviction, noting that there had been great strides in the treatment and prevention of HIV since the law was passed, and that Nick's undetectable viral count meant he could not transmit HIV. Shortly after the decision, Iowa modernized its law to limit HIV criminalization to the intentional or reckless transmission of HIV to an unaware person. This change was the product of an intensive coalition effort in which we were deeply involved. Two years later, we played a key role in a successful coalition effort to update California law to limit criminal penalties based on a person's HIV status to only those people with the criminal intent to transmit HIV or who commit a sexual assault. Public health experts supported these changes because they increase people's willingness to get testing and treatment for HIV, and to discuss their HIV status with sexual partners. We continue to work state-by-state with community partners and elected officials for the modernization of HIV criminalization laws, efforts that dovetail with our work to end the criminalization of sex work, which is discussed below.

Nick Rhoades

California Senate Bill 982 says:

HAVE SEX-GO TO JAIL.

No kidding. SB 982, brought to you by former L.A. police chief, Republican Senator Ed Davis and the Traditional Values Coalition, would make it a felony for people with HIV to have sex, *even protected sex,* or share needles without "disclosing" their status.

Under SB982, disclosure is not just stating that you are HIV+, it is a major educational undertaking, which includes explaining how HIV is transmitted, and that HIV can lead to AIDS. This bill mandates that people living with the disease become the educators and take all responsibility for their partner's activities -- if your partner is not safe, you could go to jail!

Maybe you feel people with HIV should disclose their status. Maybe you believe it when someone tells you they are HIV-. Maybe you believe in AIDS predators. If so, **READ ON:**

This bill operates under the false assumptions that 1) people with HIV and AIDS actively and intentionally seek to spread the virus, and 2) that HIV transmission occurs intentionally rather than negligently, and 3) that criminalization will stop the spread of HIV.

Does this scare you? It should!

Do something. ACT UP LOS ANGELES

BEHIND THE SCENES

"The *Rhoades* case put the sex lives of the LGBTQ community and people affected by HIV front and center before the Iowa Supreme Court. We won because we talked frankly about sex in a way that persuaded the court to re-examine its outdated assumptions about how HIV is transmitted through sexual activity. Our victory helped to amplify the important public health research proving that effective HIV treatment eliminates the risk of transmission, a message that endures today through the U=U (Undetectable=Untransmittable) public health campaigns.
—Christopher Clark, our attorney on *Rhoades*

(top) Activists participating in the "We Can End AIDS" March on July 24, 2012, in Washington, DC, during the International AIDS Conference.

(above) 1991 ACT-UP/LA poster. ACT-UP (the "AIDS Coalition To Unleash Power") was founded in 1987 to fight the epidemic through dramatic grassroots protests and advocacy.

(right) HIV criminalization laws enacted decades ago vary in severity and continue to be enforced in many states.

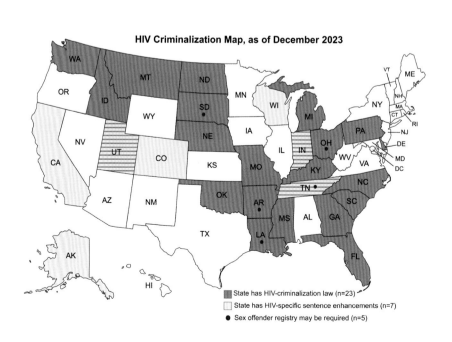

HIV Criminalization Map, as of December 2023

■ State has HIV-criminalization law (n=23)
□ State has HIV-specific sentence enhancements (n=7)
● Sex offender registry may be required (n=5)

Roe v. Precythe (2023-ongoing)

Our efforts to decriminalize HIV are not limited to law reform. We also are working to change prison policies that subject inmates to additional punishment due to their HIV status. In *Roe v. Precythe*, we represent Jane Roe, a transgender woman living with HIV who was imprisoned by the Missouri Department of Corrections ("MDOC"). Because of her HIV status, Ms. Roe was placed in solitary confinement for more than six years without meaningful review. MDOC deemed her "an immediate and long-term danger to other offenders" despite the fact that her viral counts are suppressed by medication that makes it virtually impossible for her to transmit HIV.

Simply because of her HIV status, Ms. Roe was wrongfully denied the benefits of services and programs offered to others incarcerated at the facility. But the harm went beyond that. The severe physical and psychological harms associated with solitary confinement are well-documented.

In fact, the United Nations Special Rapporteur on Torture has determined that solitary confinement lasting beyond 15 days constitutes torture or cruel, inhumane, and/or degrading treatment in violation of international human rights law.

Two years after Ms. Roe's release, we joined with the MacArthur Justice Center to sue MDOC on her behalf, charging that the institution's policy is unconstitutional and discriminates against people living with HIV in violation of the Eighth and Fourteenth Amendments of the U.S. Constitution, the Americans with Disabilities Act, and the federal Rehabilitation Act. We argue that MDOC's policy lacks any consideration of modern medicine and fails to make individualized assessments. The lawsuit, which is ongoing as this book goes to press, seeks an end to the discriminatory policy, monetary damages, and other relief.

(above) *The Kansas City Star,* June 29, 2023

(right) A solitary confinement cell, known as the Bing, at New York City's Rikers Island.

ADVOCACY FOR SEX WORK DECRIMINALIZATION

Lambda Legal has long recognized that LGBTQ+ people participate in street economies including sex work due to family rejection, truncated educational opportunities due to bullying, employment and housing discrimination, and other barriers to economic security. For LGBTQ+ youth and transgender women of color in particular, sex work often is a means of survival for a limited time or longer, and criminalization has many harsh effects. It empowers law enforcement to harass people actually or perceived to be engaged in this work, including to extort sex, money, and other things from people targeted. It increases vulnerability to violence and compromises health by limiting the ability to insist on condom use and other ways of reducing transmission of HIV and other sexually transmitted infections. Criminal laws that keep this work in the shadows also reduce workers' ability to negotiate for their physical safety and thus increase risks of trafficking. Moreover, when prosecuted for sex work, LGBTQ+ people face shockingly high rates of physical and sexual abuse in custody, while also losing chances to access resources and opportunities.

Consequently, in 2015, we joined Amnesty International's resolution supporting the human rights of sex workers and calling for both decriminalization of sex work and action to prevent exploitation of sex workers and sexual exploitation of children. Since then, we have joined with advocates in multiple states to pursue diverse legal changes, including in California, Illinois, Maryland, New York, and the District of Columbia, as well as in Congress.

"We remain committed to honoring Lambda Legal's rich history of HIV/AIDS advocacy and serving long-term survivors, while also focusing on the needs of the populations most affected by HIV today: Black people, women, individuals with substance dependence, sex workers, and transgender folks."

–JOSE ABRIGO, HIV PROJECT DIRECTOR

(left) Cartoon by Ingrid Mouth for the 10th Biennial San Francisco Bay Area Sex Worker Film and Arts Festival, 2019.

(above) Marchers protesting recent police raids that closed many strip clubs on Bourbon Street in New Orleans, February 1, 2018.

(right) Positive Women's Network USA has organized the National Day of Action to End Violence Against Women Living with HIV since 2014.

VIOLENCE AGAINST WOMEN LIVING WITH HIV

Women living with HIV experience disproportionately high rates of interpersonal violence. We advocate to increase public awareness of the need to end HIV-related social stigma, which fuels this violence. This advocacy has included supporting the National Days of Action to End Violence Against Women Living with HIV, created by our frequent partners at the Positive Women's Network USA. Together, we also highlight the ways in which gender identity and gender expression often intersect with race, ethnicity, socio-economic class, age, disability, and other aspects of identity, and can compound the effects of inequality. This is why living with HIV so often is predictive of violence by family members, police, service providers, and members of the public. Ending this vulnerability is necessary for both community survival and community health.

CHAPTER 3

WORKING

SECURING EMPLOYMENT FAIRNESS

Employment is a survival need, all the more so because more than half of all Americans access healthcare through the workplace. Unfortunately, discrimination and harassment have been pervasive for LGBTQ+ employees. Calls to Lambda Legal's Help Desk show the scope of the problem: workplace issues are consistently one of the top concerns. This chapter explores three facets of our efforts to secure fair and equitable workplaces: our fight to overturn the military bans on LGB and T servicemembers, our work to protect employees in the absence of a nationwide law explicitly prohibiting anti-LGBTQ+ discrimination, and our push to persuade federal courts that the sex discrimination ban in the existing employment non-discrimination law (called "Title VII") covers discrimination on the basis of sexual orientation and gender identity.

(opposite) Lesbian and gay rights demonstration, Albany, New York, 1971.

(page 69) Barbara Gittings in a white shirt, Ernestine Eckstein fourth in line, at the third White House picket, October 23, 1965.

THE RIGHT TO SERVE

As the largest employer in the nation (indeed, the world!), the military has long been a key battleground for equal opportunity. Military policy on LGBTQ+ servicemembers has evolved substantially in the past fifty years, in no small part because of Lambda Legal's work.

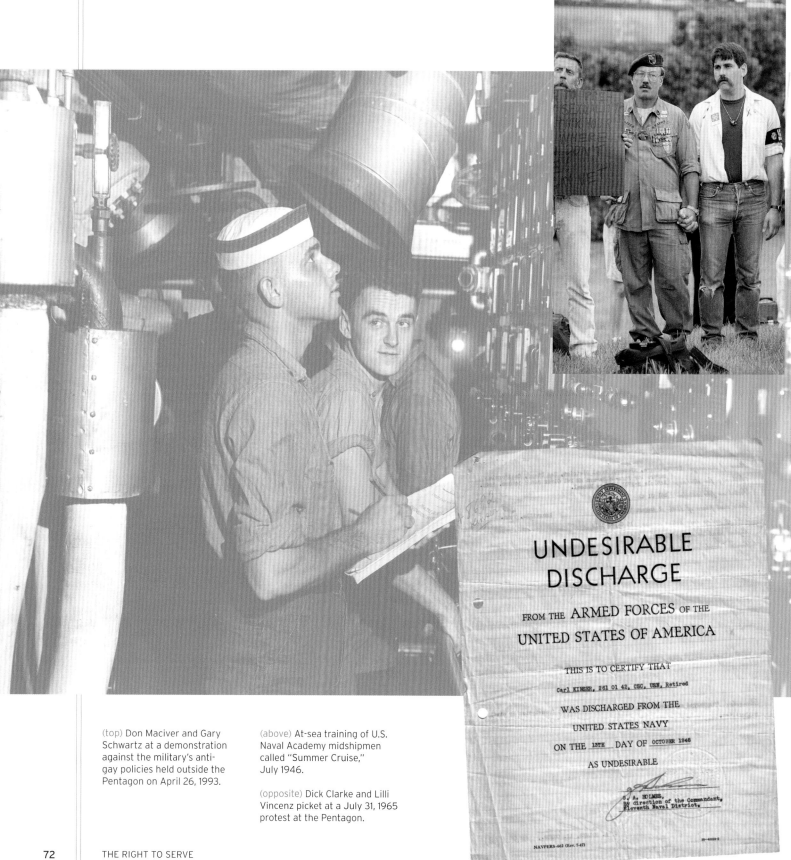

(top) Don Maciver and Gary Schwartz at a demonstration against the military's anti-gay policies held outside the Pentagon on April 26, 1993.

(above) At-sea training of U.S. Naval Academy midshipmen called "Summer Cruise," July 1946.

(opposite) Dick Clarke and Lilli Vincenz picket at a July 31, 1965 protest at the Pentagon.

BEFORE DON'T ASK, DON'T TELL

Matlovich v. Secretary of the Air Force (1976-1980) and *Berg v. Claytor* (1976-1981)

In the 1970s, homosexuality was seen as both a mental illness and a crime by the military. Dishonorable discharge was the norm for anyone known or suspected to be gay or lesbian, although there was a vague "extenuating circumstances" exception letting the military selectively retain servicemembers otherwise subject to discharge.

Two of Lambda Legal's earliest cases were on behalf of gay men challenging their discharges. In 1975, Technical Sergeant Leonard Matlovich came out in a letter to his commanding officer. The highly decorated Air Force veteran did so because he wanted to be open about who he really was, and to bring the first test case challenging the military's ban. The Air Force promptly began discharge proceedings.

Unlike Sgt. Matlovich, Ensign Vernon "Copy" Berg did not set out to prove a point about the military. He just fell in love. After graduating from the U.S. Naval Academy, he and his partner moved into an off-base apartment in Italy, where he was stationed. Naval intelligence spied on the couple for months before dishonorably discharging Copy in 1976.

Both men were represented by Cary Boggan, one of Lambda Legal's cofounders. He won a measure of justice for both men, although not the sweeping victory they had hoped for. In 1978, the D.C. Circuit consolidated the two cases and heard them together, ultimately ruling that both discharges were unfair because the military had not explained why neither man met the extenuating circumstances requirement. Ens. Berg, whose discharge the Navy upgraded to honorable, was prepared to exit litigation at this point, but Sgt. Matlovich persisted, seeking reinstatement. After the Air Force repeatedly failed to explain what "extenuating circumstances" meant, a federal court ordered Matlovich reinstated. And because their cases were joined, the decision affected Berg as well. The Air Force ultimately settled the case by promoting Matlovich then giving him an honorable discharge and a financial payout. Negotiations between the Navy and Copy Berg took a bit longer, but ultimately, Berg received a financial payout as well. In 1981, the Pentagon reiterated its discharge policy but announced that all future discharges would be honorable.

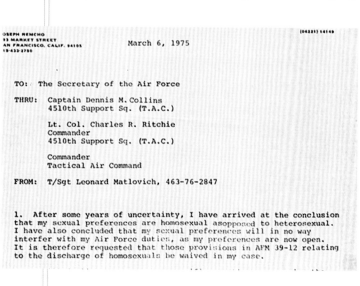

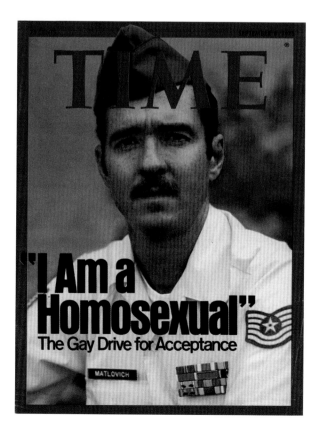

NEVER AGAIN
6 JULY 1943

NEVER FORGET
22 JUNE 1988

A GAY VIETNAM VETERAN

WHEN I WAS IN THE MILITARY
THEY GAVE ME A MEDAL FOR KILLING TWO MEN
AND A DISCHARGE FOR LOVING ONE.

GET OFF MY SHIP

ENSIGN BERG VS. THE U.S. NAVY

E. LAWRENCE GIBSON

"The best ever account of the intrigue and shenanigans behind the scenes in the military. A stunning story made all the more poignant by the candor and nobility of its writing."
C.A TRIPP
AUTHOR OF THE HOMOSEXUAL MATRIX

ILLUSTRATED BY VERNON E. BERG III

BEHIND THE SCENES

When Leonard Matlovich and Copy Berg came to Lambda Legal for assistance in 1976, we could only afford to underwrite one of their cases. The Board of Directors opted to support Berg's case, while Cary Boggan graciously offered to represent Matlovich pro bono, so long as Leonard could cover some of the costs of the appeal. Sadly, all three of these pioneering crusaders against the military's anti-gay policies died in their forties from complications related to AIDS.

(opposite, right) Sgt. Leonard Matlovich in his Air Force uniform.

(opposite, left) Memo from Leonard to his commanders requesting a waiver of the military's anti-gay policy.

(above) Leonard's gravestone in the Congressional Cemetery, Washington, DC.

(above, left) Cary Boggan

(above, right) Ens. Copy Berg

(above) 1978 paperback edition of Copy's memoir

BEFORE DON'T ASK, DON'T TELL

Cammermeyer v. Perry (1991-1997)

We brought several more legal challenges over the years, including *Cammermeyer v. Perry*. In 1992, National Guard Colonel Margarethe "Grethe" Cammermeyer became the highest-ranking officer to be discharged for being gay after she refused to lie about her sexuality when asked during a routine security clearance interview. Her twenty-five-year military record was extraordinary, earning her a Bronze Star for her work as a combat-hospital nurse in Vietnam and many other honors. Col. Cammermeyer was, in short, living proof of the irrationality of the military's position on lesbian, gay, and bisexual servicemembers. We sued on her behalf, arguing that the military's policy was based on nothing but prejudice. In 1994, a federal judge agreed, ruling that Grethe had been discharged based solely on irrational prejudice in clear violation of her constitutional rights.

By the time *Cammermeyer* was decided, a new military policy, referred to as "Don't Ask Don't Tell" (DADT), had taken effect (see below), which blunted the impact of the ruling. But she was reinstated to her position as Chief Nurse of the Washington State National Guard and served under DADT until she retired in 1997, her very presence undermining the new policy's supposed rationale.

(left) Grethe Cammermeyer receiving a Bronze Star in 1968 for her meritorious service at an evacuation hospital in Vietnam.

(above) Former Lambda Legal attorney Mary Newcombe and Col. Cammermeyer planning her case.

(right) *The New York Times*, May 31, 1992

National Report
The New York Times

Dismissed From Army as Lesbian, Colonel Will Fight Homosexual Ban

By TIMOTHY EGAN
Special to The New York Times

TACOMA, Wash., May 30 — Having served 14 months in a war zone in Vietnam, given birth to four sons and worked daily with some of the most fragile American war veterans, Col. Margarethe Cammermeyer has seen her share of pain and torment.

But there was a moment Thursday afternoon, at the Washington National Guard headquarters just south of here, that broke her heart. After nearly 27 years in the military, Colonel Cammermeyer, the chief nurse of this state's guard, was discharged because she is a lesbian.

She wept, as did the man who was forced to dismiss her, Maj. Gen. Gregory P. Barlow, the commander of the Washington National Guard.

But this is not the end of Colonel Cammermeyer's involvement with the Federal Government. She said she would challenge her dismissal in Federal court, and her lawyers have expressed the hope that her case may ultimately overturn the 49-year ban on homosexuals in the military.

Reiterating Policy

The Army refused on Friday to comment on Colonel Cammermeyer's case beyond reiterating its policy that regards homosexuality as "incompatible with military service." Defense Secretary Dick Cheney has said he has no plans to change the policy, though he has dismissed one reason cited against homosexuals, that they pose a security risk, "as something of an old chest-

the Nazis after they invaded her native Norway in World War II. After coming to America, she joined the Army in the early 1960's, was awarded a Bronze Star for her tour in Vietnam and in 1985 was chosen from among 34,000 candidates nationwide as the Veterans Administration's Nurse of the Year. While rising to the rank of chief nurse in the Washington Army National Guard, she got her doctorate in nursing at the University of Washington.

Her record was without blemishes, guard officials say. What derailed her career goal of becoming the nation's chief military nurse was a security clearance question that she was asked

> 'I'm not a threat,'
> a high-ranking
> nurse says of her
> homosexuality.

three years ago. After she applied for admission to a war college, Colonel Cammermeyer went through an extensive background check. Asked by a Pentagon official during a personal interview if she was a homosexual — something she said she had never been quite sure of for the last 10 years — Colonel Cammermeyer answered yes, without hesitation.

all alike," she said. "If people can see the sameness of me to you, then perhaps they won't have the walls that makes it so they have to hate us with out a cause."

The issue was fanned again on Friday when Ross Perot, the undeclared independent candidate for President, told Barbara Walters in an interview on the ABC News program "20/20" that he would not allow homosexuals to serve in certain Cabinet posts.

"It will distract from the work to be done," Mr. Perot said. He also indicated that he would not seek to overturn the ban on homosexuals in the military.

After Colonel Cammermeyer heard Mr. Perot's comments, she said, "I was frightened by them, really frightened."

'Based on Ignorance'

Officially, the military lists seven reasons for keeping homosexuals out of the service. These have to do with problems of morale, recruitment, discipline and privacy, among other factors.

"I'm not a threat," Colonel Cammermeyer said. "This is a regulation that is truly based on ignorance more than prejudice, but the two go hand in hand."

While Colonel Cammermeyer may not have the support of Mr. Cheney, her immediate commander in chief, Gov. Booth Gardner of Washington, has fully backed her.

"The Army and the United States of America are senselessly losing an outstanding individual who is eminently qualified to continue serving in the Washington National Guard," said Mr. Gardner a Democrat

> "I never thought I'd have to choose between being honest and serving my country. I didn't think I'd lose my military career because of prejudice and hate."[22]

—GRETHE CAMMERMEYER

(above) Poster for the 1995 Emmy-winning television movie based on Grethe's memoir, *Serving in Silence*, starring Glenn Close as Grethe and Judy Davis as her spouse, Diane Divelbess.

BEHIND THE SCENES

"I was representing Grethe in front of the board convened to adjudicate her discharge. We were eager to cram as much evidence into the record as possible. Our third witness was Larry Korb, a former assistant deputy at DOD. I worked hard to prepare my direct examination, knowing that Larry, a wonderful guy, was a talker, something lawyers dread in trial and deposition testimony. Sure enough, he ignored all my cues and prepared questions, which, in a flash of desperate inspiration, I ditched and urged the board members, all colonels in the Army National Guard, to ask Larry anything they wanted. Larry was superb, answering questions about personal feelings as well as military concerns until the individual board members were satisfied. We always knew the board would have to discharge Grethe, but we were elated with the testimonial record we later were able to present to the court."

—Mary Newcombe, our attorney on *Cammermeyer*

THE RISE AND FALL OF DON'T ASK, DON'T TELL

Able v. United States of America (1994-1998)

While campaigning for president in 1992, Bill Clinton pledged to end the military's anti-gay policy if elected. Once in office though, he found himself outmaneuvered by members of Congress and senior military leadership who staunchly favored retaining the ban. In July 1993, he announced a compromise designed to appease all sides: lesbian, gay, and bisexual people could serve in the military, so long as their sexuality stayed under wraps. Coming out—an act of speech—would be treated as dischargeable conduct. The policy came to be known as "Don't Ask, Don't Tell" (DADT).[23]

Together with the ACLU, we filed the first test case to challenge DADT, on behalf of Lt. Colonel Jane Able and five other active service members. DADT, we argued, violated our clients' free speech and equal protection rights, served no legitimate military interest, and was impermissibly based on the presumed prejudices of heterosexual servicemembers. In 1994, the federal trial judge agreed, striking down DADT as unconstitutional. However, this ruling was overturned by the Second Circuit. DADT, the court said, was "necessary to unit cohesion and the military mission." Prejudice had won. Bigotry had become its own defense.

By 2010, the military had discharged more than 13,000 people under DADT, at a cost of nearly $200 million.[24] Amid growing calls for repeal, including from some high-ranking military officials, Congress finally ended DADT. The new policy, which took effect on September 20, 2011, allowed lesbian, gay, and bisexual people to serve openly.[25]

(above) Plaintiffs in *Able* leave the federal court in Brooklyn, NY on March 16, 1995. (L-R) Lambda Legal attorney Beatrice Dohrn, Army Reserve Sgt. Stephen Spencer, Navy Seaman Werner Zehr, Army Reserve Capt. Kenneth Osborn, and Navy Cmdr. Richard Von Wohld.

BEHIND THE SCENES

"I argued the *Able* case before a three-judge panel of the Second Circuit. Then, as now, our cases were fought over bathroom fears! Amidst the insistent questions about how it would work for there to be gay men in military bathrooms and showers (as if there weren't already), I felt a flash of feminist rage. All the way to middle age, these three straight white men had been able to maintain the belief that they were in complete control of when and where they might be sexually objectified. Not for a moment could I or my women friends and colleagues have even entertained such a notion!"

—Beatrice Dohrn, our lead attorney on *Able*

(above) Protesting against "Don't Ask, Don't Tell," New York City, July 20, 1993.

(right) President Clinton speaks to U.S. troops two months before his announcement of the "Don't Ask, Don't Tell" policy, May 5, 1993.

TRANSGENDER MILITARY SERVICEMEMBERS

Karnoski v. Trump (2017-2021)

In 2016, after extensive studies concluded that transgender people could serve well and without incident, the Obama administration announced that transgender people would also be permitted to serve openly, effective July 1, 2017. However, on July 26, 2017, President Trump rejected that policy in a series of tweets, followed by a formal memorandum. Lambda Legal immediately sued to stop the new ban, as did the other major LGBTQ+ legal groups. Every single lawsuit succeeded, allowing transgender people to begin enlisting while the ban was being litigated. For the next three years, LGBTQ+ rights litigators kept the proposed ban tied up in court,

essentially running out the clock on the Trump presidency. In early 2021, the incoming Biden administration reversed the Trump-era ban and opened military service to transgender people.

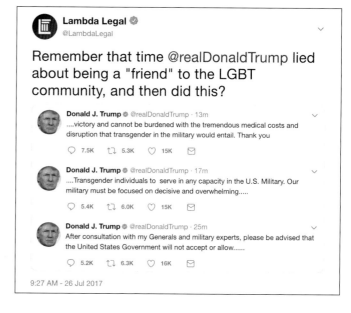

(top) Protest in New York's Times Square against President Trump's anti-transgender military directive, July 26, 2017.

(above) Plaintiff Staff Sgt. Cathrine Schmid speaking to reporters about *Karnoski* with Peter Renn at left.

"President Trump's government kept pursuing every avenue to prevent courageous and qualified transgender people from serving our country. And courts across the country kept swatting his policy down. It was discriminatory and dangerous and there was no defensible reason to resurrect it."

–PETER RENN, OUR LEAD ATTORNEY ON *KARNOSKI*

"All of the trans people that are being impacted by this military ban, we don't just go home every day and disappear into the ether. We have families, and we have hobbies, and we have hopes and aspirations for our careers that are being impacted by this really insidious and problematic and unfounded legal assertion that trans people are less than because of their identity."[26]

–RYAN KARNOSKI

(above) Protest against Trump's anti-trans military service ban at the White House on July 26, 2017.

(right) *Karnoski* plaintiff Navy Petty Officer Megan Winters

ENFORCING EQUAL OPPORTUNITY POLICIES

Congress has never passed a bill explicitly protecting LGBTQ+ people from discrimination in the workplace, and prior to our gradual success persuading courts to interpret existing federal law favorably and the U.S. Supreme Court's 2020 ruling in *Bostock v. Clayton County* (see below), protection against anti-LGBTQ+ discrimination in employment varied with geography. Our ability to bring job discrimination cases depended heavily on whether state or local governments had anti-discrimination laws that protected LGBTQ+ workers. We therefore prioritized actions to put teeth in those laws, so that protections on the books were meaningful in real life. Here are two examples of this work.

Grobeson v. City of Los Angeles (1996-2007)

When Mitchell ("Mitch") Grobeson was hired by the Los Angeles Police Department (LAPD) in the 1980s, he was the first and only out officer on the force. In 1988, after enduring unrelenting harassment and dangerous lack of backup, he quit his job and sued the LAPD and the City of Los Angeles, pointing to a city ordinance prohibiting job discrimination based on sexual orientation. Mitch settled the case in 1993 and rejoined the LAPD, only to face retaliation from supervisors for alleged "unauthorized recruiting" of lesbians and gay men to join the force and for wearing his uniform without permission at Pride and AIDS awareness events. In 1996, Mitch sued again, this time with Lambda Legal in his corner. Settlement discussions took over a decade, but in the end, we secured sweeping changes in the city's employment practices.

"I always felt that making it possible for law enforcement officers to be open about who they are is essential to long-lasting reform. We will never end anti-LGBTQ police misconduct until we eradicate the prejudice that too often flows from the police seeing our community as 'them' rather than part of the 'us' that is the force."

–JON DAVIDSON, OUR ATTORNEY ON *GROBESON*

(opposite, top) Sgt. Mitch Grobeson at the Los Angeles Christopher Street West Pride parade on June 12, 1994.

(opposite, right) In 1999, Mitch wrote *Outside the Badge*, a detective story based on his experience as an LAPD officer.

SGT. MITCH GROBESON
L.A.P.D.'s First Open Gay

City of Los Angeles

RICHARD J. RIORDAN
MAYOR

CITY HALL
LOS ANGELES, CALIFORNIA 90012
(213) 847-2489

OFFICE OF THE MAYOR
September 8, 1994

Executive Directive No. 4 - Riordan Series

TO: THE HEADS OF ALL DEPARTMENTS OF CITY GOVERNMENT

SUBJECT: SEXUAL ORIENTATION

In 1979, the City of Los Angeles adopted Ordinance No. 152,458 (Municipal Code 49,70) which established and defined the City's intent to promote and maintain a working environment free from discrimination on the basis of sexual orientation. Specifically, the ordinance protects gays, lesbians, bisexuals, and heterosexuals from discrimination in employment, housing, business establishments, city facilities and services, and education. In keeping with this ordinance, the City's Affirmative Action Program specifically prohibits discrimination on the basis of sexual orientation. In 1992, the State of California also passed legislation prohibiting discrimination based on actual or perceived sexual orientation. Recently, the City Council adopted a Policy on Sexual Orientation Discrimination in Employment (attached) that reaffirms its commitment on this topic.

It is the policy of the City of Los Angeles that discrimination in the workplace on the basis of an individual's sexual orientation is unacceptable and will not be tolerated. An appointing authority shall not consider an applicant's or employee's known or presumed sexual orientation in any pre-employment or employment action or decision, including but not limited to background checking, testing, hiring, assigning, training, transferring, upgrading, promoting, compensating, disciplining and discharging.

It is the policy of the City that prompt and appropriate action be taken to deter and punish sexual orientation discrimination. Therefore, it shall be the responsibility of all Department Managers to take necessary steps, including appropriate disciplinary action, to ensure and maintain a working environment free from sexual orientation discrimination. The policy shall prohibit, as a form of discrimination, the creation of or contribution to a hostile, intimidating, threatening, offensive, or abusive work environment on the basis of an individual's known or presumed sexual orientation. This includes written, spoken, graphic or demonstrative

OUTSIDE THE BADGE

Mitchell Grobeson

Dunbar v. Foot Locker (2004)

In places without inclusive anti-discrimination laws, we had to get creative, drawing on an array of laws and policies. In *Dunbar v. Foot Locker*, for instance, we represented Kevin Dunbar, a gay man who had suffered severe anti-gay harassment at the hands of his co-workers and supervisors at several Foot Locker locations in South Carolina. When he reported the harassment to his district manager, it got worse. Kevin was shuffled from one store location to another and was ultimately fired. South

Carolina had no laws protecting LGBTQ+ people from job discrimination, but Foot Locker had company-wide anti-harassment and anti-discrimination policies. So in 2004, we sued Foot Locker—a Fortune 500 company—for breach of contract, because the company was violating the promises in its own policies. The company settled the case a few months later, paying Kevin an undisclosed amount and agreeing to overhaul its training and reporting procedures to address anti-gay harassment.

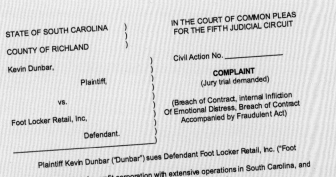

CREATING A PRODUCTIVE WORK ENVIRONMENT

@FootLocker, we *Play to Win* by demonstrating our core values of *Team Work* and *Leadership* in our interactions. We embrace diversity and are expected to treat everyone with dignity, respect, trust and fairness.

✔ **FOOT LOCKER APPROVED:** We are committed to maintaining an inclusive work environment where all associates demonstrate leadership by making others feel welcome and free to be themselves. Valuing our differences and recognizing how those differences allow us to make meaningful contributions to the team, drives our elite performance. We are all responsible for preserving a work environment of mutual respect free from discrimination, harassment, bullying, illegal drugs, and inappropriate or excessive use of alcohol, or other behavior that can create an offensive or hostile environment.

WE KNOW GAME by...

> Considering the potential impact of our conduct on each other.

> Behaving like a pro and never engaging in (or allowing) behavior that is threatening, humiliating, intimidating, abusive, or could interfere with a team member's work performance.

> Demonstrating leadership by respecting others and never making inappropriate comments, offensive jokes, or sexual advances, or taking any other actions that could create a hostile work environment.

> Using good judgment where alcohol is served, either at Company-sponsored functions or where we are represent Foot Locker.

(opposite, left) The Complaint in *Dunbar* as filed on June 29, 2004.

(above) Foot Locker's updated policy

(right) Kevin Dunbar

10 Foot Locker Code of Business

85

LITIGATING TITLE VII

Bias against LGBTQ+ people is often rooted in gender stereotypes about how women and men should present themselves and behave, including who should form romantic relationships with whom. Title VII of the Civil Rights Act of 1964 bans sex discrimination in the workplace, but for decades courts rejected the argument that discrimination based on sexual orientation or gender identity is a form of sex discrimination covered by Title VII. Intent on convincing federal judges to expand their understanding of sex discrimination and to reverse earlier decisions, Lambda Legal and other members of the Litigators' Roundtable began hunting for cases with facts that showed the connection between anti-LGBTQ+ discrimination and gender stereotypes. The plan was to build a body of favorable lower court decisions and then seek a nationwide ruling from the Supreme Court. *Glenn v. Brumby* and *Hively v. Ivy Tech* illustrate this strategy.

Glenn v. Brumby (2008-2011)

Vandy Beth Glenn was fired from her job as a legislative editor for the Georgia Legislature in 2007, after she announced her plan to transition. Her supervisor admitted he did so because he found it "unnatural" and "unsettling to think of someone dressed in women's clothing with male sexual organs inside that clothing." Our argument that Vandy Beth's firing was based on sex discrimination was adopted by the Eleventh Circuit in 2011, which observed that a person is considered transgender "precisely because of the perception that his or her behavior transgresses gender stereotypes." *Glenn* marked the first time a federal appeals court held that anti-transgender bias is a form of sex discrimination, a major breakthrough.

(left) Lambda Legal attorney Greg Nevins with Vandy Beth, who returned to her job in the Georgia Legislature following our victory in her case.

"I am asking for just one thing: to be given my job back. I love that job, I can do it well, and I never want another transgender person to experience the discrimination I've endured."

—VANDY BETH GLENN

(above) Testifying before Congress in support of the Employment Non-Discrimination Act (ENDA), a federal bill, in 2009.

(left) The National Trans Visibility March along Pennsylvania Avenue in Washington, DC, on September 28, 2019.

Hively v. Ivy Tech (2015-2017)

It took another six years until Lambda Legal persuaded a federal appeals court to adopt similar reasoning in a case involving sexual orientation. Kim Hively, who had worked for fourteen years at Ivy Tech Community College in South Bend, Indiana, as an adjunct professor, was fired after a coworker saw her kiss her female partner in the school parking lot. Kim filed a Title VII complaint in 2013, but a trial court dismissed her case. Lambda Legal took it on appeal, and in 2017 the Seventh Circuit, hearing the case as a full court, ruled that discrimination based on sexual orientation is a form of sex discrimination. The court said that Hively's sexuality represented "the ultimate case of failure to conform to the female stereotype," and that her claim was "no different from the claims brought by women who were rejected for jobs in traditionally male workplaces, such as fire departments, construction, and policing."

The Second Circuit Court of Appeals relied on *Hively* when deciding in *Zarda v. Altitude Express* that anti-gay bias was sex discrimination. These three cases paved the way for the U.S. Supreme Court's landmark decision in *Bostock v. Clayton County* (2020), which held that Title VII protects LGBTQ+ employees from discrimination. *Bostock* ultimately secured the nationwide employment protections that Congress has yet to confirm.

> "[A]n employer who fires an individual for being homosexual or transgender fires that person for traits or actions it would not have questioned in members of a different sex. Sex plays a necessary and undisguisable role in the decision, exactly what Title VII forbids."
>
> **—U.S. SUPREME COURT JUSTICE NEIL GORSUCH,** ***BOSTOCK V. CLAYTON COUNTY***

BEHIND THE SCENES

Greg Nevins was our lead attorney in this area. When arguing to the Second, Seventh, and Eleventh Circuits, Greg's core message to the judges was simple and compelling: "How can discrimination against someone in an interracial relationship be illegal, but discrimination against someone in a same-sex relationship not be?"

(opposite) Kim Hively with Greg Nevins

INTERLUDE. PUBLIC EDUCATION AND ENGAGEMENT

Our mission has always included education. It's right there in our name: Lambda Legal Defense and Education Fund. This reflects our general theory of social change:

First, ignorance and fear are two of the greatest stumbling blocks to equality and freedom for LGBTQ+ and HIV-positive people. We've seen this again and again. Fear that LGBTQ+ people are dangerous to children. Panic that people living with HIV will infect those around them. Assumptions that LGBTQ+ and HIV-positive people will weaken the military. Worries that same-sex couples will destroy marriage. Anxieties that transgender people (especially women) are threats to cisgender women and girls. Our opposition capitalizes on these beliefs to paint us as dangerous, and we cannot achieve equality and freedom without defusing them.

Second, while judges are trained to "think like lawyers," they are as human as anyone else, and their understanding of the law is unavoidably colored by their understanding of the world around them. So, we center education in our litigation.

Third, litigation can be a powerful way to educate, both in and out of court, by showing that misguided policies are harming real people. And for purposes of social change, losing in court can be as powerful as winning (though we always aim to win) if our clients' stories touch the hearts of policymakers and the general public. But for this out-of-court education to happen, people must hear our clients' stories. Our job includes amplifying their voices.

Fourth, fear and ignorance plague our own community as well, keeping us closeted and conditioning us to accept injustice. A community that knows its rights is a community more able to exercise them.

In other words, education is central to everything we do, and our audiences include judges, lawmakers, and other government officials; reporters, academics, and other thought leaders; community leaders including clergy; the general public; and our own beloved community.

Here's a look into the many ways we do this.

PUBLICATIONS

LGBTQ+ people and people living with HIV remain extra vulnerable in our legal system. Many of the rights others take for granted are—or have been—denied to us, and bias often makes it harder to exercise the rights we do have. We have had to make innovative use of existing rules to create new protections, while pushing to end the exclusions. All of this makes for ongoing change and confusion, which is why we produce know-your-rights toolkits and fact sheets. Many of these, like our

Suit Over Death Benefits Asks, What Is a Family?

By TAMAR LEWIN

married, so because of their sexual orientation, they're denied the benefits that spouses get, even though, where there's a death, they have the same needs as any other family that's lost a wage-earner.''

Experts say private employers have been reluctant to expand benefit packages to include domestic partners, the public sector private sec- a spokes- fit Re-

NBC NEWS Teen wins right to wear 'Jesus Is Not a Homophobe' T-shirt to school

rick Couch can wear his "Jesus Is Not a H... without fear of being suspended...

SAY GAY!
SAY LESBIAN!
SAY TRANS!
SAY BISEXUAL!

LAMBDA LEGAL

Lambda Legal

making the case for equality

LOVE UNITES US

WINNING THE FREEDOM TO MARRY

MARRIAGE EQUALITY MATTERS

MARRIAGE EQUALITY MATTERS

TRANSGENDER RIGHTS TOOLKIT

A LEGAL GUIDE FOR TRANS PEOPLE AND THEIR ADVOCATES

Lan

LIVE

MARRIAGE EQUALITY & LGBTQ+ RIGHTS

KEVIN JENNINGS
Lambda Legal
Chief Executive Officer

FLYING SOLO
A TRANSGENDER WIDOW FIGHTS DISCRIM...

#DontEraseUs

QUEER JUSTICE

50 YEARS OF LAMBDA LEGAL AND LGBTQ RIGHTS

Lambda Legal

OUTSERVE

STAND WITH TRANSGENDER SERVICE MEMBERS, RECRUITS AND THEIR FAMILIES

FLYING SOLO

Trans Youth Are Suing to Block Louisiana's Ban on Gender-Affirming Care

teenVOGUE

Plaintiffs argue the ban violates...

Take the Power and *Crisis Care* toolkits, inform our community about their rights and/or provide legal resources in times of crisis. Others, like *Creating Equal Access to Quality Health Care for Transgender Patients* explain the need for and offer model policies. We also publish research reports, legislative language, and our legal briefs. These inform policymakers and other advocates. Examples of our publications are peppered throughout the chapters of this book.

"What kind of long-range vision do you have for your future and that of your loved ones? Have you taken the necessary legal and financial planning steps to protect that vision? The *Take the Power* toolkit includes questions to help you find out how prepared you really are—and what you should start thinking about now."
—Judi O'Kelley, former Southern Regional Director

AWARENESS CAMPAIGNS

Our litigation usually grabs the headlines, but it rarely happens in isolation. Instead, it often complements our awareness and advocacy campaigns. Our work to end marriage discrimination is a prime example. The Marriage Project developed creative campaigns to build support for the freedom to marry. Evan Wolfson used the Marriage Resolution to gather support from public figures, including civil rights heroes such as Coretta Scott King, Congressman John Lewis, and Gloria Steinem, along with hundreds of civil rights groups, civic leaders, celebrities, businesses, and congregations nationwide. National Freedom to Marry Day was launched in 1998 on February 12 (Abraham Lincoln's birthday), right

before Valentine's Day, to link the themes of equality and love. It was celebrated annually with dozens of events nationwide.

The Freedom to Marry Coalition convened a national table of organizational leadership and facilitated state-by-state political organizing and public education, in the process establishing a 50-state network of marriage equality activists. In California, for example, we partnered with community-based and allied groups, such as the clergy-led California Faith for Equality, and groups doing outreach in communities of color, such as the Latino Equality Alliance and the Jordan-Rustin Coalition.

The largest of those groups was API Equality-LA, which created a lively LGBTQ+ presence throughout Southern California's diverse Asian American communities and filed amicus briefs joined by scores of Asian American bar associations and community and religious groups.

In Iowa, our five-year-long statewide organizing campaign transformed public awareness while our litigation advanced to its Iowa Supreme Court triumph (see Chapter 6). And in Illinois, the ILove campaign helped drive passage of the marriage bill we drafted for our legislative champions. These campaigns, and others like them, did the vital work of paving the way for the legal and legislative advances that ultimately secured the freedom to marry.

(opposite, left) (L-R): Marc Solomon of Freedom to Marry, Rev. Eric P. Lee, President/CEO of the Southern Christian Leadership Conference–Los Angeles, and Ron Buckmire of the Jordan/Rustin Coalition responding to the California Supreme Court's Prop 8 decision, May 26, 2009.

(opposite, right) (L-R): Rev. Dr. Neil G. Thomas and Rev. Dr. Jonipher Kūpono Kwong of California Faith for Equality.

(above, right) API Equality-LA contingent in the Golden Dragon Parade in Chinatown, Los Angeles, January 28, 2012.

(below) Jim Bennett performs "The Church of Hamballs" at *The Moth Radio Hour* on October 18, 2019.

BEHIND THE SCENES

One of the comments we would hear over and over is, "If you really want the hearts and minds of Iowans, you need to ride RAGBRAI (an annual, weeklong bike ride across Iowa)." You can listen on *The Moth* to former Midwest Regional Director Jim Bennett's side-splitting story of how the Lambda Legal team spearheading the awareness campaign in Iowa rode RAGBRAI. The story is called "The Church of Hamballs."

VISIBILITY AND COMMUNITY ENGAGEMENT

As LGBTQ+ people, our invisibility and small numbers can make us vulnerable. When others don't see and know us, we can be demonized for reactionary purposes. The answer has been coming out, telling our stories, and organizing to be visible. Here are some examples.

PRIDE!

We join dozens of Pride marches and festivals annually so more community members will know to look to us for information and potential help, and to share the empowerment that comes with legal victories.

(clockwise from above) Los Angeles (2008), Atlanta (2005), Dallas (2023), Chicago (2017), New York (2019), Los Angeles (2008)

Regional Leadership

Lambda Legal's regional structure with dedicated regional staff is unique among our movement colleagues. We opened our Western office (in Los Angeles) in 1990, then our Midwest office (Chicago, 1993), our Southern office (Atlanta, 1997), our South Central office (Dallas, 2002), and our DC office (2017).

Our regional teams help to build our community partnerships. For example, our longest serving regional director, Shedrick ("Rick") Davis, was a regional leader long before he joined us and draws on his network to boost our advocacy. In 2005, for instance, we provided friend-of-the-court support in litigation to overturn a devastating court decision that had erased the legal ties between thousands of LGB parents and their children. We and NCLR filed a brief in the California Supreme Court supporting families with LGBTQ+ members. Rick's network allowed us to highlight the often-overlooked needs of gay dads by including Southern California's Pop Luck Club as a client. The resulting victory brought immense relief.

Our regional offices are also sites of community engagement. Our Midwest leadership has built public support across the region. Shelly Skeen, who leads in our South Central region, rallies public support against the floods of discriminatory legislation there. Our team in Washington, DC, engages, with all parts of the federal government as well as nearby state and local governments. And Michael Shutt leads our presence across the Southern region, a similarly challenging area these days. Recently, he hosted *Queer Justice: 50 Years of Lambda Legal and LGBTQ+ Rights*, our traveling exhibition, at the National Center for Civil and Human Rights in Atlanta. We created this exhibition with The American LGBTQ+ Museum, drawing from this book. It launched in fall 2023, and we added content for each city to which it traveled.

(clockwise from above) Rick Davis and sons Terrance and William; Shelly Skeen; (L-R) Judge and founding Southern Regional Director Jane Morrison, Vandy Beth Glenn, Tim'm West of the National Center for Civil and Human Rights, and Lambda Legal's Dani Alexander-Burk; Michael Shutt; former Midwest Regional Directors Mona Noriega and Jim Bennett with plaintiffs Pat Ewert and the late Vernita Gray.

Podcasts and Films

We are always attuned to new ways to amplify our clients' stories. In recent years, we've added podcasts and films to our repertoire. The *Making the Case* podcast, developed by Erika Kramer and hosted by Alex Berg, debuted in 2022, with each of the ten episodes featuring a behind-the-scenes look at the strategies and challenges behind a case or set of cases.

We've also made short films that have brought the voices of our clients directly to audiences. In Chapter 6, we discuss our film about Robina Asti's case, *Flying Solo: A Transgender Widow Fights Discrimination*, which was screened widely to critical acclaim in 2014. The film caught the attention of NPR reporters, who featured Robina, then 94 years of age, in a special program on transgender family members which won a Peabody Award for excellence in broadcasting.[27] Here are two more examples of short films with impact.

I Believe in Me: Fighting for Trans Rights in Prison

Donisha McShan was paroled to The H Group, a halfway house in Marion, Illinois, to finish her sentence and receive substance abuse counseling. But The H Group insisted on treating her as a man, forcing her to room with men, confiscating any items they considered "feminine," and threatening her with a return to prison if she did not agree to present as a man. She called our Help Desk in 2014, and we contacted The H Group on her behalf, informing them that they were violating both state and federal law. The H Group immediately reversed course and began treating Donisha with the respect she deserved. We then produced a short film to tell her story, which premiered in fall 2014 and was shown at film festivals in the U.S. and England.

Dishonored in Death: Jack's Story

John (Jack) Zawadski and Bob Huskey were a devoted couple for 52 years who lived in Mississippi. As Bob's health began to fail, Jack moved him to a nursing home and pre-arranged funeral services. But when Bob died, the funeral home refused to collect his body after learning he had been married to Jack, citing religious objections and saying they did not "deal with their kind."

(left to right) Donisha McShan, Jack Zawadski

Struggling with grief and needing to move his husband's body immediately, Jack scrambled to find another option, only to learn the nearest alternative was ninety miles away. We represented Jack against the funeral home and, although he passed away before we secured a settlement for his estate,[28] Jack's story did not end there. The film and our other advocacy resonated widely, even reaching the U.S. Supreme Court. Justice Sotomayor discussed Jack's story in her blistering dissent in *303 Creative v. Elenis* (see Chapter 10), along with other Lambda Legal cases, to emphasize the prevalence and cruelty of religiously motivated anti-LGBTQ+ discrimination.

**A TRIBUTE TO
MARCO CASTRO-BOJORQUEZ**

In his day job, Marco Castro-Bojorquez was a community educator for our Western Region, advancing family acceptance of LGBTQ+ young people and HIV prevention, especially within Latinx families. His off-hours passion was making documentary films to amplify the voices of these families. *El Canto del Colibrí* [The Hummingbird's Song], a 2015 feature-length film, explored the relationships between Latino immigrant fathers and their LGBTQ+ family members through the fathers' stories of immigration, social oppression, faith, machismo, dealing with their children coming out, and acceptance of LGBTQ+ people within Latinx families. Shortly before Marco's sudden death in 2021, he was honored by his hometown in Sinaloa, Mexico, for his vision, advocacy, and films.

LAMBDA LEGAL'S PROJECTS

We sometimes put a brighter spotlight on the urgency of an issue or the needs of a population by creating a project to facilitate our education and public engagement work. Our very first one was the AIDS Project (now the HIV Project), which quickly became a clearinghouse for information about litigation and legislation. Among other things, the AIDS Project staff published a quarterly *AIDS Update* with legal news, created tool kits for people living with HIV, testified in legislative hearings, and created awareness and engagement campaigns. The AIDS Project was so successful that it became a model for future projects, like the Marriage Project and the Law and Policy Project. We discuss two of our current issue-focused projects—The Youth in Out-of-Home Care Project and the Fair Courts Project—in Chapter 9. Here we discuss two that are population-focused: Proyecto Igualdad and the Nonbinary and Transgender Rights Project.

Proyecto Igualdad

We created Proyecto Igualdad in 2002 to enhance our work within and for Latinx communities. Proyecto staff have produced Spanish-language know-your-rights materials, conducted community events and trainings in Spanish and English, and facilitated the Spanish language work of the Help Desk. Proyecto leadership has collaborated with the National Hispanic Bar Association on inclusive policies; hosted a Latino Institute at the National LGBTQ+ Task Force's Creating Change conference; and partnered with diverse Latinx organizations on ways to support their LGBTQ+ community members. A program called "Transforming the Margins" focused on the immigrant experience and family acceptance of LGBTQ+ Latinos. And Proyecto has boosted our advocacy to advance the rights of LGBTQ+ people in Puerto Rico and LGBTQ+ Latinx immigrants and refugees to the United States (see Chapter 9).

BEHIND THE SCENES

"Discussing LGBT issues using a bilingual approach can be essential for reaching communities filled with cultural intersections. Whether we were born in the United States and have immigrant parents, or identify as Latino, Hispanic or bicultural—we tell the real story of support for LGBT people within the Latino community. Bilingual education supports the conversation, and we emphasize core values that all families share—the importance of familial bonds and that love is the bridge from hesitance to acceptance."
—Francisco Dueñas, former director of Proyecto Igualdad

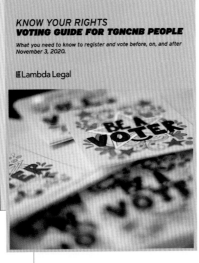

The Nonbinary and Transgender Rights Project

The need for focused advocacy to protect transgender people became obvious as the century turned. Our work against transphobic abuses (such as *Brandon v. Richardson*, see Chapter 1) revealed the vast public ignorance about gender dysphoria and gender diversity. It also showed the extreme violence directed at people considered gender nonconforming. At the same time, rising support for "gay rights" brought proposals to exclude gender identity from proposed legislation in order to win protections for LGB people, which we and our partners vigorously opposed. We launched the Transgender Rights Project in 2005 to expand our public engagement work and strengthen our advocacy, and to support our trans and nonbinary colleagues. Its directors and dedicated staff have published informational guides, conducted trainings, and served as internal and external experts as trans-and-nonbinary rights advocacy has grown to roughly 70% of our legal program work, some of it pushing for greater equality and some defending against vicious attacks (see Chapter 10 for more).

"I send all my love to fellow nonbinary and trans folks in this really difficult time. As these forces are seeking to erase and silence us, I'm honored to be a part of this community that's fighting back. Thank you for being visible and speaking out. And to allies, there has never been a time that I've been alive when we have needed your support and your voice more. So, thank you, thank you, thank you.

—SASHA BUCHERT, NONBINARY AND TRANSGENDER RIGHTS PROJECT DIRECTOR

CHAPTER 4

BAD MEDICINE

CHALLENGING DISCRIMINATION IN HEALTH INSURANCE AND MEDICAL CARE

Lambda Legal believes that everyone should be able to access healthcare without fear that their sexual orientation or gender identity will provoke discrimination, harassment, or denial of care. The unfortunate reality, though, is that LGBTQ+ people face widespread barriers to culturally competent and equitable care. Some of these barriers are due to bias and ignorance among healthcare workers. Others are structural, caused by laws, practices, and policies that limit who can get health insurance and what that insurance covers. Still others come from the tensions between so-called "religious freedom" protections and equality guarantees.

Lambda Legal has been deeply invested in the struggle for healthcare fairness since the early years of the AIDS epidemic. We've confronted doctors and other healthcare workers who have provided substandard care to LGBTQ+ and HIV-positive people and have worked to raise awareness of discrimination in the healthcare system. We've pushed for domestic partnership policies that allow unmarried couples to insure each other and their children. We've tangled with insurance companies that refuse to cover medically necessary care. And we've fought back against religiously based refusals of service. Here's a look into our work.

Healthcare reform advocates
march in Washington, DC,
October 22, 2009.

RAISING AWARENESS OF HEALTHCARE BARRIERS

In 2009–2010, Lambda Legal conducted the first-ever nationwide survey of the experiences of LGBTQ+ and HIV-positive people in our healthcare system. The results were shocking. Over half of LGB and more than two-thirds of transgender and gender non-conforming (GNC) people who took the survey said their experiences included being denied needed healthcare, being subject to physical or verbal abuse by healthcare workers, and/or being blamed for their own health problems. Low-income and non-white people were even more likely to experience discriminatory and substandard care. Over one-quarter of LGB people and about three-quarters of trans and GNC people also said they feared being treated differently because of being LGBTQ+. Our 2012 report, *When Health Care Isn't Caring*, received widespread notice and has been cited frequently since its publication. More recent studies continue to find that LGBTQ+ people face significant barriers to getting adequate, respectful care and that many delay necessary care because of it.[29]

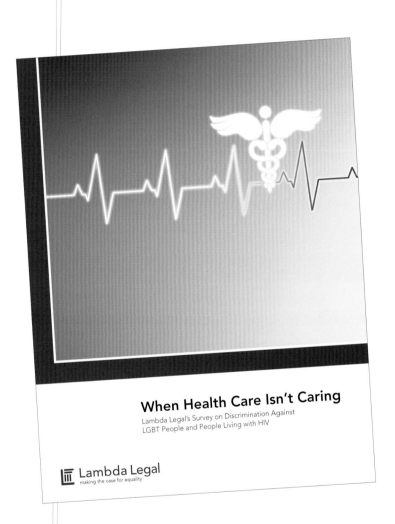

When Health Care Isn't Caring
Lambda Legal's Survey on Discrimination Against
LGBT People and People Living with HIV

Lambda Legal
making the case for equality

"The results of this survey make clear that the system is broken when it comes to healthcare for many LGBT people and those living with HIV. No one should be turned away or face discrimination when they are sick or seeking medical care."

—BEVERLY TILLERY, CO-AUTHOR OF
WHEN HEALTH CARE ISN'T CARING

Table 1: I was refused needed health care

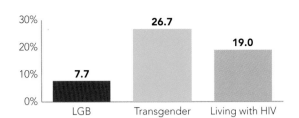

Table 2: Health care professionals refused to touch me or used excessive precautions

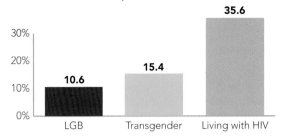

Table 3: Health care professionals used harsh or abusive language

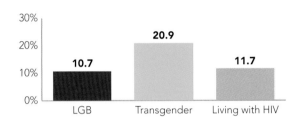

Table 4: Health care professionals blamed me for my health status

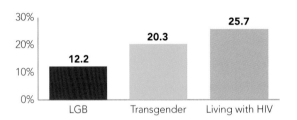

Table 5: Health care professionals were physically rough or abusive

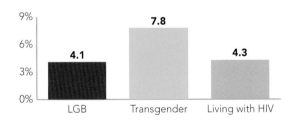

Table 6: Fears and concerns about accessing health care

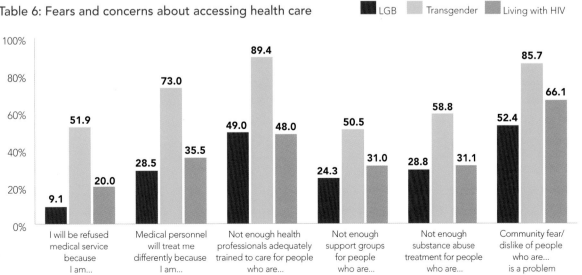

FIGHTING FOR FAMILY COVERAGE IN HEALTHCARE BENEFITS

One of the peculiarities of the U.S. healthcare system is that roughly half the population gets health insurance through the workplace, either directly as an employee or indirectly as a legally recognized family member of an employee. Before marriage equality, this system harmed workers in committed same-sex relationships. Because they could not marry their partners, they could not provide them with health insurance. And because they were denied family coverage, they effectively got paid less than similarly situated employees who could marry. Domestic partner (DP) benefits offered a partial solution. In workplaces with DP benefits, unmarried employees could add their domestic partners to their health insurance, although the cost of that coverage was treated as taxable income to the employee, unlike for married employees.

Lambda Legal advocated for the expansion of domestic partner benefits, despite their limitations, both because this approach helped to fill an immediate community need and to educate about the needs of families headed by same-sex couples. Here are two cases that illustrate our fight for family healthcare coverage.

Diaz v. Brewer (2008-2014)

When Arizona passed a law in 2008 restricting healthcare coverage to legal spouses and children—overturning a short-lived expansion of benefits to include domestic partners—we sued immediately to keep the partner benefits in place. Our clients were eight state employees who relied on the family coverage; clients like Joseph Diaz, whose long-term partner Ruben Jimenez had diabetes and high cholesterol, and Beverly Seckinger, whose long-term partner Susan Taunton had asthma and could only work part-time while she cared for her elderly mother. Neither Ruben nor Susan could find individual insurance because of their health conditions.[30]

The State of Arizona argued that our case should be dismissed but in 2010 we persuaded the federal trial court to keep the benefits in place during litigation. Unhappy, Arizona appealed this ruling, but the Ninth Circuit Court of Appeals determined that our clients likely had a constitutional right to equal compensation, an important recognition of same-sex couples' equality. Arizona then asked the Supreme Court to hear the case, which it declined to do, and the case returned to the trial court. At that point, we asked to turn our lawsuit into a class action and in December 2013 the court did so. (A class action is a case brought on behalf of a larger group

of people who have the same claim.) While *Diaz v. Brewer* was still in progress, marriage equality was expanding rapidly, and on October 17, 2014, it became the law in Arizona thanks to our *Majors v. Jeanes* case. Marriage equality effectively ended the need for *Diaz v. Brewer*, but it had done its job. For more than four years, the lawsuit had forced Arizona to continue providing essential health coverage to the domestic partners of state workers.

> "Arizona tried everything it could to eliminate the family health coverage for lesbian and gay state employees. But thanks to our injunction, they were assured that their families' insurance would not be stripped away while they fought for the equal pay for equal work that they always deserved."
>
> —TARA BORELLI, OUR LEAD ATTORNEY ON *DIAZ V. BREWER*

(clockwise from top left) Tracy Collins and Diana Forrest; Susan Taunton and Beverly Seckinger; Stephen Russell and Scott Neeley; Keith Humphrey and Robert Klay; Sue Shapcott and Carrie Sperling; Ruben Jimenez and Joseph ("Bob") Diaz; Corey Seemiller and Karrie Mitchell with their daughter.

Golinski v. U.S. Office of Personnel Management (2008-2013)

Same-sex couples were able to marry in California between June and November 2008 thanks to our state court litigation.[31] During that time, Karen Golinski married her partner, Amy Cunninghis. She then tried to add her wife to her employer-provided health plan, in the same way that newly married straight people do. But even though Karen lived in California, she worked for the federal government (as a lawyer for the Ninth Circuit, in fact). At the time, the Defense of Marriage Act (DOMA) prohibited the U.S. government from honoring same-sex couples' marriages for any purpose, including healthcare benefits. Citing DOMA, the U.S. Office of Personnel Management (OPM) refused to process Karen's healthcare enrollment form. Lambda Legal then sued on her behalf. The OPM was represented by the Department of Justice (DOJ), which speaks for the federal government in court.

As the case was proceeding, the legal landscape suddenly shifted. The Obama administration announced it would no longer *defend* DOMA against constitutional attacks but would continue to *enforce* DOMA as long as it was the law. We updated our Complaint to argue that DOMA was unconstitutional, and the same DOJ that had opposed us suddenly became our ally. In 2012, the federal trial court agreed with us that DOMA violated Karen's right to equal protection of the laws and issued a sweeping order striking it down.

When a group of Republican lawmakers appealed the ruling to the Ninth Circuit (Karen's workplace!), DOJ took the unusual step of asking the Supreme Court to hear the case immediately. *Golinski*, DOJ thought, was an excellent vehicle for deciding DOMA's constitutionality. Reflecting the careful coordination among LGBTQ+ legal groups, *Golinski* joined three separate challenges to DOMA awaiting possible Supreme Court review: two by New England-based GLAD and one by the ACLU. The Supreme Court eventually chose to hear the ACLU case, *U.S. v. Windsor*, and in June 2013 struck down a key part of DOMA in a landmark ruling. (We talk more about DOMA in chapter 5.) Citing *Windsor*, the Ninth Circuit then dismissed the government's appeal in *Golinski*, ending the case.

> "When I first put in my paperwork to add Amy to my health insurance, she and I joked that we were going to try, but hoped we wouldn't have to 'make a federal case out of it.' We laugh quite a bit about that now, two and a half years and a federal lawsuit later."
>
> **—KAREN GOLINSKI**

(opposite) Amy Cunninghis and Karen Golinski

FIGHTING FOR EQUITABLE INSURANCE COVERAGE

Esquivel v. Oregon (2010-2013)

Decades ago, Lambda Legal fought against exclusionary and substandard insurance coverage for HIV-related health conditions. More recently, we've been fighting against policies that exclude gender-affirming care for transgender people. In *Esquivel v. Oregon*, we represented Alec Esquivel, who sought insurance coverage for a hysterectomy as part of his gender transition. His doctor had determined it was medically necessary in part because of Alec's heightened risk for uterine and ovarian cancer. As a clerk for the Oregon Court of Appeals, Alec was covered by the state's health plan, which routinely covered hysterectomies. But in 2010, he was denied coverage based on the insurance plan's exclusion of transition-related care. We stepped in to administratively appeal the denial. When the appeal was rejected in 2011, we sued the State of Oregon, arguing that its own anti-discrimination law prohibited it from denying insurance coverage based on gender identity. Confronted with our lawsuit, Oregon agreed in 2013 to change its coverage to include all medically necessary care relating to gender transition.

Since *Esquivel*, Lambda Legal has been systematically challenging longstanding bans on gender-affirming care for people held in government custody and in public employee health insurance and Medicaid programs. We also have been litigating against newly imposed bans on gender-affirming care as a shocking rush of states have moved to impose them. We discuss this more in Chapter 10.

"My doctor has determined that this procedure is necessary for me. Other people who work here and who need this very same procedure get the coverage they need, why shouldn't I?"

—ALEC ESQUIVEL

Alec talks with the media outside the Marion County Courthouse in Salem, Oregon, after we filed *Esquivel*, June 21, 2011.

BEHIND THE SCENES

"The *Esquivel* case was cutting-edge in 2010. It was significant to have a plaintiff like Alec, who was also an attorney, bravely share the intimate details of his healthcare needs to bring empathy and understanding about the discrimination that transgender people face. It was also powerful for me, as an openly transgender attorney, to represent Alec. It was the beginning of an era where trans people could not only speak for themselves but could direct our transgender rights work."
—Dru Levasseur, one of our attorneys on *Esquivel*

FIGHTING BACK AGAINST RELIGIOUS REFUSALS TO PROVIDE HEALTHCARE

Opponents of LGBTQ+ rights frequently invoke religious beliefs as justification. This poses a particular problem in healthcare, since many healthcare institutions have religious affiliations, as do many employers who offer healthcare coverage. Because the First Amendment guarantees the free exercise of religion, some providers have argued that they have a constitutional right to refuse to provide care when doing so conflicts with their beliefs. Lambda Legal has been pushing back against these arguments because religious rights have limits and must be reconciled with patients' rights to equal treatment. Here are two windows into this work.

Benitez v. North Coast Women's Care Medical Group (2002-2009)

Guadalupe ("Lupita") Benitez and her partner, Joanne Clark, had been together for nearly a decade when they were ready to start their family. Lupita learned she had a common infertility condition so, starting in 1999, she spent a year receiving treatment from the one in-network clinic available through her health plan: the North Coast Women's Care Medical Group. Unfortunately, her treating physicians were conservative Christians who, for religious reasons, would provide testing and medication for Lupita, but not the intrauterine insemination she needed. Her physicians routinely performed this procedure for heterosexual patients.

The lawsuit Lupita filed against North Coast Women's Care in 2000 was initially dismissed. We helped get it reinstated and then joined the case to argue that religion did not give Lupita's doctors the right to ignore California's civil rights law. In August 2008, after years of litigation that ran up and down the California courts, the California Supreme Court ruled unanimously that religious beliefs do not exempt a for-profit medical clinic's physicians from their duty to treat LGBTQ+ patients without discrimination. In 2009, North Coast Women's Care settled the case.

Talking Points for Benitez

1. **Lesbians and gay men are entitled to the same access to health care as everyone else.**
   Lupita Benitez's doctor provided her with infertility treatment for 11 months, but then – at the critical and brief moment when she needed a particular treatment – the doctor refused to treat her, simply because Lupita is a lesbian.

   Bigotry and discrimination have no place in health care facilities.

2. **This health care provider's discrimination forced Lupita to scramble to find a doctor who wasn't in her health care plan and to pay thousands of dollars out-of-pocket, all while in an incredibly vulnerable and precarious state.**
   While on hormones as part of her infertility treatment, Lupita was forced to scramble to quickly find a doctor who could treat her while she was still in the short window of time for the treatment. She was traumatized at being "dumped," and had no choice but to find a new doctor who wasn't in her employer's health care plan, costing her several thousand dollars.

3. **Personal religious beliefs do not release doctors or other medical professionals from their duty to provide treatment to their patients in a non-discriminatory manner.**
   Lupita's doctors are entitled to hold any personal religious beliefs they choose. But they do not have a right to refuse medically-appropriate treatment to a patient based on what they claim are personal religious beliefs about particular groups of people. Doctors are legally and ethically obligated to provide health care to patients based on their medical condition, not their identity. Doctors' personal religious beliefs don't lessen that at all.

4. **When women choose to bring children into their family, they are exercising their most basic personal rights – and their freedom of choice doesn't change based on whether they are lesbian, married or single.**
   These doctors weren't being asked to provide unusual services to Lupita – this is a core part of their jobs as OB/GYN physicians.

   All people have the right to choose to start a family, and doctors who have decided to make their living by offering these services to the public do not get to pick and choose who can be a family.

[Talking Points-Benitez.FINAL.doc]

(left) Lupita speaks to media with partner Joanne Clark (L), just after Jenny Pizer (R) argued her case before the California Supreme Court.

(above) Jenny's talking points for reporters

(opposite) Jenny and Joanne flank Lupita, joined by legal team (L-R) Al Gross, Seph McNamara, and Lee Fink, May 28, 2008.

C.P. v. Blue Cross/Blue Shield of Illinois (2020-ongoing)

Patricia Pritchard, a nurse employed by a Catholic hospital in Washington State, included her fifteen-year-old transgender son in her family healthcare plan. He had been receiving medically necessary gender-affirming care for three years without incident, when suddenly coverage for some of his care was denied. Blue Cross Blue Shield of Illinois (BCBSIL), which operates nationwide and administered the hospital's insurance plan, said that any care "for or leading to gender reassignment surgery" would no longer be covered, even though the same procedures—such as hysterectomies and breast augmentation—would be covered for cisgender patients. When pressed for an explanation, BCBSIL said that the Catholic hospital had made the decision based on its religious beliefs, and BCBSIL was simply following its customer's wishes.

We represent Patricia and her son Casey in a federal lawsuit arguing that BCBSIL's exclusion of gender-affirming care violated the Affordable Care Act's (ACA's) ban on sex discrimination. BCBSIL, in turn, argued that gender identity discrimination is not sex discrimination and that, even if it is, a federal law called the Religious Freedom Restoration Act (RFRA) allows it. Our response? While the hospital was religious, BCBSIL wasn't, and shouldn't be allowed to hide behind the shield of religion.

In late 2022, the federal trial court agreed with us. Drawing on the Supreme Court's 2020 decision in *Bostock* (see Chapter 3), the court ruled that (1) discrimination based on gender identity is sex discrimination and (2) BCBSIL must comply with the ACA when it administers health plans. Even better, the court agreed to turn the case into a class action, which means it covers the nearly 400 plans nationwide that BCBSIL administers.

"This is a victory for the many hundreds of transgender people who have been or were likely to be denied medically necessary gender-affirming care because of Blue Cross Blue Shield's administration of these discriminatory exclusions."

—OMAR GONZALEZ-PAGAN, OUR LEAD ATTORNEY ON C.P.

"My son and all other transgender youth deserve the ability just to be themselves and to thrive. That's all we ask."

—PATRICIA PRITCHARD

(right) Casey with Patricia at his high school graduation, 2023.

REPRODUCTIVE RIGHTS ARE AN LGBTQ+ ISSUE

Lambda Legal has always been a staunch supporter of reproductive rights. We've coordinated with reproductive and LGBTQ+ rights groups to file amicus briefs in reproductive rights cases. We've worked closely with pro-choice administrations at both the federal and state level to defend access to reproductive care and we've worked to limit the damage caused by hostile administrations. The reasons for our involvement are simple. First, LGBTQ+ people need access to the full gamut of reproductive healthcare, from medically assisted insemination to abortion. Second, the ability to control whether, when, and how to have children is central to the autonomy, dignity, and equality of anyone who can become pregnant, no matter their sexuality or gender identity. Third, LGBTQ+ rights and reproductive rights share the same legal foundation: freedom and equality regarding intimate, personal decision-making. The erosion of rights in one area threatens the other. Supreme Court Justice Clarence Thomas made this connection explicit in his concurring opinion in *Dobbs v. Jackson Women's Health Organization*, the 2022 decision that overturned *Roe v. Wade*. The Supreme Court, he said, should now revisit *Lawrence v. Texas* and *Obergefell v. Hodges*. Fourth, many of the courageous health clinics that provide full reproductive care also provide wellness care and gender-affirming care for LGBTQ+ people. We say: reproductive justice is health justice is LGBTQ+ and HIV+ justice.

BEHIND THE SCENES

"The tactics politicians are taking to deprive TGNCNB[32] people of gender-affirming healthcare are from a playbook I know all too well from my time in the reproductive rights space. The same people who brought about the downfall of *Roe* are seeking to criminalize gender-affirming care by using sham science and religious dogma to further a patriarchal version of society rooted in religious extremist notions of mandatory gender norms."
– Kristine Kippins, Deputy Legal Director for Policy

(above, left) Marchers in support of abortion rights in the San Francisco Pride parade, June 26, 2022.

(above, right) Cartoon by David Horsey, *Seattle Times* cartoonist, February 10, 2023.

(opposite) Protest against Florida abortion bans, April 8, 2023.

CHAPTER 5

NOT JUST ROOMMATES

PROTECTING LGBTQ+ FAMILY RELATIONSHIPS

In 1986's *Bowers v. Hardwick*, the Supreme Court held that the right to privacy did not encompass same-sex intimacy because the majority saw "no connection between family, marriage, and procreation" (which *were* seen as protected by the right of privacy) and what it called "homosexual activity." Throughout our history, Lambda Legal has fought to change practices, policies, and perceptions positioning LGBTQ+ people as outside of—and dangerous to—families, and to give families headed by LGBTQ+ people the legal tools to protect themselves. Our work started out as two different streams: one to protect parent-child relationships and the other to protect relationships between committed adult partners. The fight for marriage equality brought these streams together (see Chapter 6). Here's a look into our family work over the years.

(opposite) Illinois residents and Lambda Legal plaintiffs Daphne Scott-Henderson and Ryan Cannon-Scott and their children, Sonnet, Autumn, and Sebastian.

(page 118) Robert and Michael— with Eryn on piggyback —in 1983 photo for a *Life* magazine story on gay fathers. Michael and Robert were together for more than forty years, raised four children, and married in 2011.

PROTECTING PARENT-CHILD RELATIONSHIPS

In the 1970s, Lambda Legal received more requests for help from lesbian and gay parents fighting to retain custody and visitation than any other legal issue. Our goal in these early cases was to convince courts that homosexuality does not disqualify people from parenting. It was a hard slog and we failed more often than we won because we had to work against the entrenched misperception that gay people abuse children or that exposure to gay people makes children gay themselves. Over time, judges increasingly came to understand that homosexuality had nothing to do with parental fitness. Our cases helped, and so did the emergence of studies showing lesbian and gay parents were raising resilient, well-adjusted children.

Guardianship of Lydia M. Ramos (2002)

By the 1990s, the rising number of lesbian partners raising children together in planned families revealed a crucial disconnect between these evolving family structures and existing laws: in these families, only one parent had legal ties to the couple's children. *Guardianship of Lydia M. Ramos* highlights why this matters. Lydia Ramos was at work one day when she got a call from the San Bernadino County coroner telling her that Linda Rodriguez, her beloved partner of fourteen years, had died in a car accident. Linda was the birth mother to the couple's twelve-year-old daughter (named Lydia,

after her other mother). Right after the memorial service, Linda's homophobic relatives took the couple's daughter away from Lydia and cut off all communication, something they were able to do because Lydia and "Little Lydia" were not legally related. Lydia only got her daughter back after we went to court and convinced a judge that Linda's relatives were depriving the girl, already traumatized by the death of one mother, of her other mother, and two older siblings.

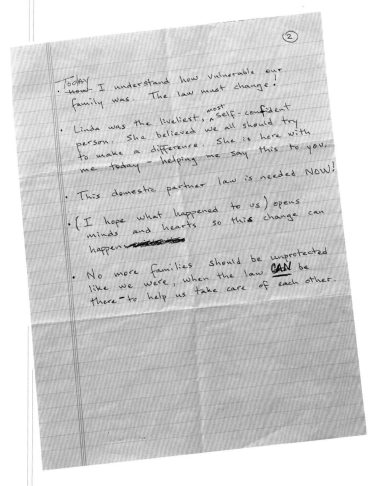

(left) Lambda Legal attorney Jenny Pizer wrote out Lydia's ideas for her testimony in support of AB 205 while they flew to Sacramento for an April 1, 2003 bill hearing.

"It took over ten days to get Linda's body from the coroner. He wouldn't give it to me, so I had to track down the father who had abandoned her. As soon as Linda's relatives saw that, they assumed I had no rights at all and took our daughter. I was ready to lose my mind. Lambda Legal got back my child, and my sanity."[33]

—LYDIA S. RAMOS

(opposite) Lita or "Little Lydia," Lydia, and Sajhili Ramos, October 2002

Alison D. v. Virginia M. (1988-1991)

Just as distressingly, when some same-sex couples broke up, the "legal" parent denied that their ex had ever been a parent at all. This is precisely what happened in 1991's *Alison D. v. Virginia M.* After several years together, Alison and Virginia decided to have a child together in 1980, agreeing that Virginia would be the one to carry the pregnancy. When the couple separated in 1983, Virginia allowed Alison to visit with their son regularly for the first few years before abruptly stopping all contact in 1986. After trying and failing to work things out with Virginia, Alison came to us. We sued for visitation on her behalf, fighting all the way up to New York's highest court—incongruously called the Court of Appeals—without success. Even though the Court of Appeals found that Alison had "nurtured a close and loving relationship with the child," it ruled that only a person related by biology or adoption qualified as a parent. Alison, the court said, was a "biological stranger" to her son and therefore ineligible for visitation rights.

(right) Alison D. (2nd from right) next to then-legal director Paula Ettelbrick, center. Also shown (L-R) are former public education coordinator Penny Perkins, Dale Rosenberg from Center Kids, and former board member, Noemi Masliah.

(below) *The New York Times* article about the *Alison D.* case, May 3, 1991.

Lesbian Loses a Ruling on Parent's Rights

By KEVIN SACK

Special to The New York Times

ALBANY, May 2 — In the first ruling of its kind by any state's highest court, the New York Court of Appeals decided today that a lesbian cannot seek visiting rights to the child of her former partner.

The ruling was seen as a major setback for gay rights, but also applies to stepparents and others who may have cared for children but did not conceive them.

Two years ago the court broke ground by ruling in a housing case that a homosexual couple could fit the legal definition of a family. But today it declined to expand the definition of parenthood to include what it called "biological strangers."

Because stepparents would also qualify as biological strangers, the significance of the ruling extends far beyond the gay com-

---

Upholding privacy laws, the high court rejected doctors' requests that AIDS testing be made mandatory. Page B6.

---

munity. But Paula L. Ettelbrick, who represented Alison D., the woman seeking visiting rights, said lesbians placed particular significance on the decision because there are, by her organization's estimate, about 10,000 children in the United States being reared by lesbians who conceived through donor insemination.

Fairly Major Setback

"It's a fairly major setback for the gay and lesbian rights movement because it says that society does not recognize our relationships," said Ms. Ettelbrick, the legal director of the Lambda Legal Defense and Education Fund in New York City, a gay-rights group.

In its 6-to-1 decision, the court wrote that state law restricts visiting rights to parents and other blood relatives of children, like siblings and grandparents. Although the Legislature has never explicitly defined the word "parent," the court said it was not the judiciary's role to expand the term beyond its traditional meaning.

"We decline to read the term parent to include categories of nonparents who have developed a relationship with a child or who have had prior relationships with a child's parents and who wish to continue visitation with the child," the court ruled.

If the court had broadened the legal definition of parenthood, the decision would have had a vast impact on the state's

Continued on Page B6

(opposite, top) Lambda Legal staff, board members, cooperating counsel, and donors at our tribute to Pat Logue on March 1, 2018.

(opposite) Congressional Commendation for Pat Logue by Representative Jan Schakowsky, presented by Heather Sawyer.

A TRIBUTE TO PATRICIA M. LOGUE

For many years, Lambda Legal's work to secure rights for LGBTQ+ parents was led by Pat Logue, who opened our Midwest Regional Office in 1993 after serving for five years on our Board. She helped guide our legal program until appointed to the Cook County Circuit Court bench in 2007. She retired from her judicial role in 2019 and died in February 2024 after living with Alzheimer's disease.

"Pat was my mentor. She was a brilliant lawyer, leader, and champion of our boldest, bravest arguments, and she won first-of-its-kind victories all over the country. She was a visionary and she taught that the path to winning in court is introducing LGBT people through stories of people who had been through hell due to discrimination. She challenged judges to see in our clients a version of themselves, and she gave our clients back their dignity. That was part of Pat's genius."
– Camilla Taylor, Deputy Legal Director for Litigation

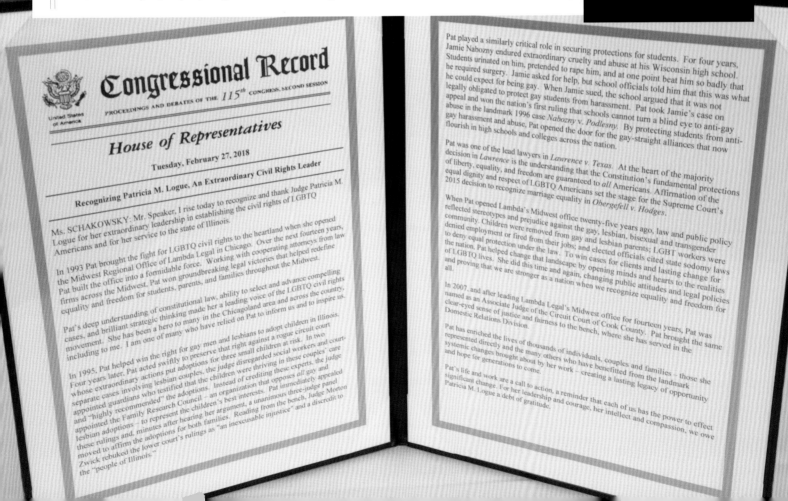

Congressional Record
PROCEEDINGS AND DEBATES OF THE 115th CONGRESS, SECOND SESSION

United States of America

House of Representatives

Tuesday, February 27, 2018

Recognizing Patricia M. Logue, An Extraordinary Civil Rights Leader

Ms. SCHAKOWSKY: Mr. Speaker, I rise today to recognize and thank Judge Patricia M. Logue for her extraordinary leadership in establishing the civil rights of LGBTQ Americans and for her service to the state of Illinois.

In 1993 Pat brought the fight for LGBTQ civil rights to the heartland when she opened the Midwest Regional Office of Lambda Legal in Chicago. Over the next fourteen years, Pat built the office into a formidable force. Working with cooperating attorneys from law firms across the Midwest, Pat won groundbreaking legal victories that helped redefine equality and freedom for students, parents, and families throughout the Midwest.

Pat's deep understanding of constitutional law, ability to select and advance compelling cases, and brilliant strategic thinking made her a leading voice of the LGBTQ civil rights movement. She has been a hero to many in the Chicagoland area and across the country, including to me. I am one of many who have relied on Pat to inform us and to inspire us.

In 1995, Pat helped win the right for gay men and lesbians to adopt children in Illinois. Four years later, Pat acted swiftly to preserve that right against a rogue circuit court whose extraordinary actions put adoptions for three small children at risk. In two separate cases involving lesbian couples, the judge disregarded social workers and court-appointed guardians who testified that the children were thriving in these couples' care and "highly recommended" the adoptions. Instead of crediting these experts, the judge appointed the Family Research Council – an organization that opposes all gay and lesbian adoptions – to represent the children's best interests. Pat immediately appealed these rulings and, minutes after hearing her argument, a unanimous three-judge panel moved to affirm the adoptions for both families. Reading from the bench, Judge Morton Zwick rebuked the lower court's rulings as "an inexcusable injustice" and a discredit to the "people of Illinois."

Pat played a similarly critical role in securing protections for students. For four years, Jamie Nabozny endured extraordinary cruelty and abuse at his Wisconsin high school. Students urinated on him, pretended to rape him, and at one point beat him so badly that he required surgery. Jamie asked for help, but school officials told him that this was what he could expect for being gay. When Jamie sued, the school argued that it was not legally obligated to protect gay students from harassment. Pat took Jamie's case on appeal and won the nation's first ruling that schools cannot turn a blind eye to anti-gay abuse in the landmark 1996 case Nabozny v. Podlesny. By protecting students from anti-gay harassment and abuse, Pat opened the door for the gay-straight alliances that now flourish in high schools and colleges across the nation.

Pat was one of the lead lawyers in Lawrence v. Texas. At the heart of the majority decision in Lawrence is the understanding that the Constitution's fundamental protections of liberty, equality, and freedom are guaranteed to all Americans. Affirmation of the equal dignity and respect of LGBTQ Americans set the stage for the Supreme Court's 2015 decision to recognize marriage equality in Obergefell v. Hodges.

When Pat opened Lambda's Midwest office twenty-five years ago, law and public policy reflected stereotypes and prejudice against the gay, lesbian, bisexual and transgender community. Children were removed from gay and lesbian parents; LGBT workers were denied employment or fired from their jobs; and elected officials cited state sodomy laws to deny equal protection under the law. To win cases for clients and lasting change for the nation, Pat helped change that landscape by opening minds and hearts to the realities of LGBTQ lives. She did this time and again, changing public attitudes and legal policies and proving that we are stronger as a nation when we recognize equality and freedom for all.

In 2007, and after leading Lambda Legal's Midwest office for fourteen years, Pat was named as an Associate Judge of the Circuit Court of Cook County. Pat brought the same clear-eyed sense of justice and fairness to the bench, where she has served in the Domestic Relations Division.

Pat has enriched the lives of thousands of individuals, couples and families – those she represented directly and the many others who have benefitted from the landmark systemic changes brought about by her work – creating a lasting legacy of opportunity and hope for generations to come.

Pat's life and work are a call to action, a reminder that each of us has the power to effect significant change. For her leadership and courage, her intellect and compassion, we owe Patricia M. Logue a debt of gratitude.

Matter of Dana
(1993-1995)

Decisions like *Alison D.* made clear that Lambda Legal and our Roundtable colleagues would need to get creative and test various legal theories to persuade judges to broaden definitions of parenthood to include lesbian, gay, and bisexual parents. In *Matter of Dana*, for example, we argued that New York should adopt the principle of *second-parent adoption*, which would give unmarried adults the ability to adopt their partner's biological children and therefore provide additional financial, legal, and emotional security to those children. Our clients were Gail Messina and Patty Irwin, life partners who were jointly raising the child that Patty had carried in pregnancy. The New York Court of Appeals agreed with us, making New York the third state in the nation to fully embrace second-parent adoptions after Massachusetts and Vermont.[34] Over the next two decades, the principle of second-parent adoption spread to nearly a dozen states. The advent of broad domestic partner rights and then marriage equality have made second-parent adoptions less crucial than they once were, but for a while they were the primary way for same-sex couples to ensure that both parents had legal connections to their children.

Finstuen v. Crutcher
(2004-2007)

Over the next decade, many states began recognizing adoptions by same-sex couples. But not every state was as willing. In 2004, Oklahoma passed the "Adoption Invalidation Law," which nullified adoption judgments issued by courts outside Oklahoma if they involved same-sex couples. In the context of second-parent adoptions, this law would strip non-biological parents of their parental rights. But in cases when same-sex couples jointly adopted a child, the law would make those children legal orphans in Oklahoma.

"The Adoption Invalidation Law was reckless. It jeopardized the safety and well-being of children and undermined parents' rights. Same-sex couples who adopt are entitled to have their relationships with their children secure and respected in every state of this country."

—KEN UPTON, OUR LEAD ATTORNEY ON *FINSTUEN*

New York's Highest Court Rules Unmarried Couples Can Adopt
Decision Cites the Changes in American Families

(left, top) *The New York Times* headline from November 3, 1995

(left) Lambda Legal clients Gail Messina and Patty Irwin

126

We challenged the law in federal court on behalf of three families.[35] Heather Finstuen and Anne Magro were the parents of twin girls who were carried by Anne and adopted by Heather. They lived in New Jersey at the time, but later moved to Oklahoma. A second lesbian family also lived in Oklahoma. They had adopted their Oklahoma-born daughter when they were living in California. Ed Swaya and Greg Hempel lived in Seattle, but their adopted daughter had been born in Oklahoma. They wanted to bring their daughter to meet her birth mother, but worried that the law might cause their roles as her parents to be disregarded in an emergency.

We argued that the law denied these parents equal protection and due process of law, and violated the constitutional requirement that states respect—give "full faith and credit" to—judgments issued by courts of other states. The district court agreed and ordered Oklahoma officials not to enforce it. The state appealed to the Tenth Circuit which, in 2007, rejected the state's defense and effectively struck down the law. That ruling sent reassurance nationwide to same-sex couples raising children who had feared that copycat laws in other states would cause this harsh new form of attack on their families to spread.

PEOPLE TO KNOW

MOMS | Anne Magro and Heather Finstuen

OK in Oklahoma

After Anne Magro and Heather Finstuen moved to Oklahoma from New Jersey with twin daughters, the state passed a law prohibiting recognition of adoptions by gays and lesbians from other states. Backed by Lambda Legal, the couple of 15 years fought the law in court. In May they won.

4 / July 18, 2006

advocate.com

THE ADVOCATE

What was your reaction when you first heard about the law?
Magro: I was angry and sad. I remember thinking that if I died, Heather should put the kids in the car and get out of the state as quickly as possible.

Did the girls understand what was happening?
Magro: We decided to talk to the kids about what was going on. They were just 5 at the time, but they understood it was a challenge to their right to have Heather as a parent. We were in the car listening to the 2004 Republican National Convention on NPR when Bush was talking about protecting traditional families. Our daughter Kate started bawling—really sobbing—for a good 20–30 minutes. When I finally got her to calm down, she said, "If he wins, are they gonna take Mommy away from us?"

Why stay and fight? Why not just leave Oklahoma?
Finstuen: I had just started law school, and Anne was midway though getting tenure [at the University of Oklahoma]. In a very real sense, we didn't have the luxury of saying, "OK, I'm leaving." But also, with all the antigay legislation around the country, going to another state seemed like a temporary solution at best. Once you start running, you never stop.
Magro: We had to fight. If you don't, you're complicit in your own oppression. And we were in a unique position: We're out to everybody, we have the support of our friends and families, and we didn't have to worry about losing our jobs.

Did the community embrace you?
Magro: Norman [where we live] is dominated by the university, so it's more liberal than most of the state. Our neighbors, the kids' teachers—it's never been an issue. I'm a Girl Scout leader, I'm the soccer coach. A student said to me, "I was raised to believe that what you're doing is wrong, but I don't see how anyone can meet your family and not respect who you are."

How did you react when the law was struck down?
Magro: Heather and I had a little champagne. The girls were dancing around the living room, singing, "Mommy is our mommy!" We're relieved, but we're also mindful this is just the first step. There are two more levels of court this could potentially be appealed in, so it could be years before we get a final decision.
Finstuen: It changed everything—even the way I looked at the kids. Even with the appeals, I felt like, OK, now nothing can come between us. —*Interviewed by Dan Avery*

"I worry about being allowed to care for my children. What would happen if Anne died tomorrow—would Oklahoma take our girls away from me? Anne and I decided to raise children together. We are a family. That means protecting them as much as we can. Oklahoma should not be putting my children at risk."

—HEATHER FINSTUEN

(left) Ed Swaya and Greg Hempel with their daughter.

(above) Heather Finstuen (L), Ann Magro, and their daughters were featured in *The Advocate* on July 18, 2006.

Brooke S.B. v. Elizabeth A.C.C. (2015-2016)

As for the precedent established in *Alison D.*? It took fifteen years but we got it overturned in 2016. The case, *Brooke S.B. v. Elizabeth A.C.C.*, had a fact pattern similar to *Alison D.*: a biological parent (Elizabeth) using her privileged legal status to deny the parenthood of her ex-partner (Brooke), despite clear evidence that the women jointly decided to have a child and jointly raised the child for several years. We argued that the precedent set by *Alison D.* did not account for the many ways that people make families and was not in the best interest of children, who risked having their relationship with one parent disrupted at the whim of the other. This time, the New York Court of Appeals agreed with us, ruling that when couples are in a committed relationship and agree to bring a child into the world and raise the child together, *both* parents should be recognized as such if the relationship ends.

New York's Highest Court Expands Definition of Parenthood

By Alan Feuer
Aug. 30, 2016

Expanding the definition of what it means to be a parent, especially for same-sex couples, the New York State Court of Appeals ruled on Tuesday that a caretaker who is not related to, or the adoptive guardian of, a child could still be permitted to ask for custody and visitation rights.

The ruling emerged from a dispute between a gay couple from Chautauqua County, known in court papers only as Brooke S.B. and Elizabeth A. C.C.

Susan L. Sommer, Brooke's lawyer and the national director of constitution litigation at Lambda Legal, called the decision a "landmark in New York" a said it brought the state "into line with the mainstream in the United State recognizing that children frequently have a second parent not related to th by blood, adoption or marriage."

Ms. Sommer added, "The state's highest court is recognizing the diversit New York families and reversing a bitter precedent that has kept childre from their parents."

Brooke and Elizabeth began their relationship in 2006 and announced t engagement the following year, even though same-sex marriage was n permitted in New York at the time and they did not have the resources travel to a state where it was allowed.

"We have seen a trail of tears in New York involving these types of situations. Until now, the courts' hands were tied. This allows a far more humane New York."

–SUSAN SOMMER, OUR ATTORNEY FOR BROOKE B.

"My son has two mothers, and he deserves the right to both of his parents. I'm here trying to make good on my promise to love and care for him for the rest of my life. I want to make sure that our son knows that I love and support him forever."

–BROOKE B.

(above) *The New York Times,* August 30, 2016

(opposite) Susan with Brooke at the New York State Court of Appeals on June 2, 2016.

PROTECTING ADULT PARTNER RELATIONSHIPS

The AIDS epidemic drove home the legal vulnerability of same-sex partnerships. Unlike straight married couples, same-sex couples had no automatic authority to provide health insurance for each other, to make medical and end-of-life decisions for each other, and to inherit from each other. Prior to marriage equality, there were two main workarounds for this problem: legal documents and domestic partnerships.

Langbehn v. Jackson Memorial Hospital (2008-2011)

Legal documents such as healthcare proxies and visitation directives offer some measure of protection to unmarried couples who want to authorize each other to make medical and legal decisions in emergency situations. But as our client Janice Langbehn discovered, these documents do not always work. When she, her life partner Lisa Pond, and three of their four children were getting ready to depart on a family cruise in 2008, Lisa suffered a brain aneurysm and was rushed to nearby Jackson Memorial Hospital in Miami. Even though Janice held Lisa's durable healthcare power of attorney, the hospital refused to let Janice see her or consult about treatment. A social worker told her it was because the hospital was in an "anti-gay city and state." Because it was a holiday weekend, the courts were closed, so Janice could not turn to them for assistance. After waiting endlessly, Janice and the children finally got to sit at Lisa's bedside while a priest performed last rites. By then, Lisa had lost consciousness. They never got to say goodbye.

We knew Florida law was stacked against Janice and her children. But the hospital treated the family with such casual and cruel disregard, we felt compelled to at least try to secure a measure of justice for them. Unfortunately, the court ruled that under Florida law the hospital had no duty to honor the couple's paperwork.

But Janice's story did not end there. Our lawsuit brought nationwide attention to the family's tragedy. President Obama saw the news coverage and was appalled. He called Janice to express his sympathies and tell her that he had directed the Health and Human Services Department (HHS) to address hospital visitation and other healthcare issues facing LGBTQ+ families. In November 2010, HHS released new regulations requiring respect not just for healthcare powers of attorney, but for LGBTQ+ patients and their families, in all federally funded hospitals.

"We want to send a message to hospitals. If they don't treat families as families, then they will be held accountable."

—BETH LITTRELL, OUR ATTORNEY FOR THE LANGBEHN FAMILY

(above) Janice and Beth meet with HHS Secretary Kathleen Sebelius in Washington, DC, in June 2010.

(opposite, top) At an LGBT Pride Month event in the White House on June 22, 2010, President Obama greets Janice and her children (L-R): David, Danielle, and Katelyn Langbehn-Pond.

(opposite) Presidential Citizens Medal

In 2011, Janice was awarded the Presidential Citizens Medal "for her efforts to ensure all Americans are treated equally." A military aide read the following citation as President Obama awarded the medal: "Janice Langbehn transformed her own profound loss into a resounding call for compassion and equality. When the woman she loved, Lisa Pond, suddenly suffered a brain aneurysm, Janice and her children were denied the right to stand beside her in her final moments. Determined to spare others from similar injustice, Janice spoke out and helped ensure that same-sex couples can support and comfort each other through some of life's toughest trials. The United States honors Janice Langbehn for advancing America's promise of equality for all."

REGISTERED DOMESTIC PARTNERSHIPS

In 1999, California became the first state in the nation to establish a domestic partnership registry. Its scope was limited, but it allowed registered partners to visit each other in hospitals and allowed state employees to put their registered partners on their health insurance. Life partners Keith Bradkowski and Jeff Collman registered as domestic partners when the option became available, adding that to their healthcare proxies. Then Jeff, who was a flight attendant, died in the 9/11 terrorist attacks, and Keith discovered the limits of his legal protections. American Airlines initially gave a victim compensation payment and Jeff's last paycheck to his parents, not his surviving partner. Under the initial framework of the federal 9/11 Victim Compensation Fund, Keith didn't count as family.

Lambda Legal stepped in to assist Keith and several other people who had lost same-sex partners on 9/11. We convinced American Airlines to change its policy regarding domestic partners, so that Keith received the same compensation that the airline gave to other families of employees on Jeff's flight. We educated the Special Master of the 9/11 Fund about the realities for same-sex couples and ultimately won compensation for Keith. We also helped persuade the New York legislature to give spousal workers' compensation benefits to people whose nonmarital partners had died at work on 9/11. Together with Keith, we helped convince the California legislature to provide more protections to domestic partners facing death or disaster.

Two years later, we pushed to make registered domestic partnerships in California even stronger, drafting a bill (known as "AB 205") for Assemblymember Jackie Goldberg and the Legislative LGBT Caucus. AB 205 expanded registered domestic partnerships to include almost all the rights, benefits, and responsibilities of marriage under California law. Our client Lydia Ramos (see the beginning of this chapter) provided powerful testimony supporting the bill, which passed in 2003 and took effect in 2005.

Despite our strong advocacy for domestic partnership protections, we were well aware of their limits. They gave same-sex couples most, but not all, of the state-level rights of marriage. They were not portable across state lines. They included none of the federal rights of marriage. And, of course, they didn't have the same status as marriage. These differences made domestic partnerships politically palatable to legislators who would not have voted for marriage equality. But at the same time, every additional right or responsibility given to domestic partners undermined some of the rationale for excluding same-sex couples from marriage. We used that in our fight for marriage equality, which we turn to in the next chapter.

"Jeff and I got as close to marriage as we could with our domestic partnership. But it wasn't protection enough, and now I am legally vulnerable in ways I never imagined."

–KEITH BRADKOWSKI

(opposite, left) Keith Bradkowski and Jeff Collman

(opposite, right) Note from Jeff to Keith

(right) Keith remembers Jeff at the Garden of Remembrance, part of the September 11th Memorial in the Boston Public Garden on September 10, 2016.

CHAPTER 6

LOVE UNITES US

WINNING THE FREEDOM TO MARRY

Baehr v. Lewin (1993-1999) and Political Backlash

Marriage equality moved from the margins to the center of American politics between 1993 and 2015. The initial impetus for this change was a case brought by three same-sex couples in Hawai`i seeking the right to marry under the state's constitution. *Baehr v. Lewin* was not a Lambda Legal case at its outset in 1991.[37] At that time, there was no movement consensus that marriage equality was a desired goal. Lambda Legal had helped crystallize the issues via a series of public debates between then-Executive Director Tom Stoddard, arguing for marriage, and then-Legal Director Paula Ettelbrick, arguing against. Tom championed the view that marriage should be a top priority because it would bring comprehensive legal rights and social recognition; Paula countered that LGBTQ+ people should aim to be respected for their differences and create new legal protections rather than seek access to a patriarchy-based, one-size-fits-all model of family. Many people expressed the view that America was nowhere near ready for marriage equality (and, indeed, polling showed that few Americans supported the idea at the time) and that other concerns, such as prohibiting job and housing discrimination, were more immediately important and attainable goals.

But when the Hawai`i Supreme Court ruled in 1993 that barring same-sex couples from marrying arguably violated the equal rights amendment of the state's constitution and required the state to prove that it had adequate reasons for excluding same-sex couples from marriage, everything changed. Then-Lambda Legal attorney Evan Wolfson called the decision "nothing less than a tectonic shift [and] a fundamental realignment of the landscape."[38] Ready or not, the fight for marriage equality was here.

"The issue is not the desirability of marriage, but rather the desirability of the *right* to marry."[39]

−TOM STODDARD

(page 134) After we won them an emergency order, Vernita Gray and Pat Ewert were married by Judge Pat Logue, becoming the first same-sex couple to marry in Illinois. Vernita died shortly thereafter.

"Justice for gay men and lesbians will be achieved only when we are accepted and supported in this society *despite* our differences from the dominant culture and the choices we make regarding our relationships."[40]

−PAULA ETTELBRICK

(opposite) *OUT/LOOK*, Fall 1989

(top) Plaintiffs Genora Dancel and Ninia Baehr

(middle, left) Plaintiffs Joe Melillo and Pat Lagon

(middle, right) Plaintiffs Antoinette Pregil and Tammy Rodrigues

(bottom, right) Evan Wolfson flanked by Genora and Ninia and legendary activists Del Martin and Phyllis Lyon, 1995.

We quickly agreed to become co-counsel for the next phase in the litigation, with Evan taking the lead. He had believed in the transformative power of marriage advocacy for years. Knowing that courtroom wins might well spark political backlash, he launched Lambda Legal's Marriage Project in 1994. The Marriage Project focused on state-by-state advocacy and public education.

And political backlash there was. Until roughly 2010, the mere possibility of marriage equality sparked enormous and generally successful opposition. For example, in the fall of 1996, as Evan Wolfson and Dan Foley, our co-counsel, presented expert trial testimony debunking Hawai`i's excuses for marriage discrimination, Congress reacted to our likelihood of success by passing the Defense of Marriage Act (DOMA). Once Bill Clinton signed it into law, DOMA allowed states to refuse to respect the legal marriages of same-sex couples ("Section 2") and prohibited the federal government from honoring same-sex couples' marriages for any purposes ("Section 3"). Within three years, more than half the states had passed "mini-DOMA" laws specifically barring recognition of same-sex couples' out-of-state marriages.

This backlash hit Hawai`i, too. When the trial court presiding over *Baehr* ruled resoundingly in favor of our clients in December 1996, the Hawai`i legislature invited voters to take away that victory by amending the state constitution. In 1998, voters did just that, effectively ending *Baehr*. Over the next decade, voters in more than two dozen states followed Hawai`i's lead, amending their state constitutions to bar marriage equality.

"There's no question that marriage is not a perfect institution, but it is the institution that both in the law and in society is held up on a pedestal as something respected by the community. If it's reserved only for heterosexuals, gay people will always be, to some extent, second-class citizens."

—RUTH HARLOW, LEGAL DIRECTOR (2000-2003)

(opposite) Text of the federal Defense of Marriage Act bill

(opposite, top left) New Jersey marriage plaintiffs Erica and Tevonda Bradshaw on Lambda Legal's *Impact* magazine, Fall 2011.

(opposite, top right) *Baehr* co-counsel Evan Wolfson and Dan Foley

(opposite, bottom) Approved talking points provided to President Clinton in support of the federal Defense of Marriage Act.

One Hundred Fourth Cong
of the
United States of Ameri

AT THE SECOND SESSION

egun and held at the City of Washington on Wednesday,
the third day of January, one thousand nine hundred and ninety-six

An Act

To define and protect the institution of marriage.

Be it enacted by the Senate and House of Representatives of the United States of America in Congress assembled,

SECTION 1. SHORT TITLE.

This Act may be cited as the "Defense of Marriage Act".

SEC. 2. POWERS RESERVED TO THE STATES.

(a) IN GENERAL.—Chapter 115 of title 28, United States Code, is amended by adding after section 1738B the following:

"§ 1738C. Certain acts, records, and proceedings and the effect thereof

f the United States, or
t to any public act,
ate, territory, posses-
ween persons of the
der the laws of such
or a right or claim

sections at the begin-
tes Code, is amended
n 1738B the following

effect thereof.".

1, United States Code,
ng:

e'

Act of Congress, or of
the various administra-
ates, the word 'marriage'
man and one woman as
refers only to a person
ife.".

THE PRESIDENT HAS SEEN
4/9/96

THE WHITE HOUSE
WASHINGTON

April 8, 1996   96 APR 8 P 7:01

MEMORANDUM FOR THE PRESIDENT

FROM: JACK QUINN
               COUNSEL TO THE PRESIDENT

SUBJECT: GAY MARRIAGE

The White House has received numerous inquiries concerning your position on gay marriage. In addition, The Advocate, a widely-read gay and lesbian newspaper, is planning to publish a story on this issue and would like to include a statement of your position. The deadline for that story is tomorrow -- Tuesday, April 9.

With input from Marsha Scott, we have prepared the attached talking points. George Stephanopoulos has reviewed and approved them.

-- The institutions of traditional marriage and family face tremendous pressures in today's society. We must do everything we can to support and strengthen these institutions. The President has previously said that he does not personally support same-sex marriages.

-- The President is aware that many communities and institutions are considering whether certain basic benefits can be provided outside the context of traditional marriage. The challenge in addressing these issues is to remain sensitive to the traditional values of our communities while preserving the fundamental right to live free from unjustified discrimination.

-- In our country's history we have, for good reason, looked first to state and local governments, as well as the private sector, to consider issues like these involving community values and matters of conscience. The President believes that these issues continue to be best resolved at this level of civil discourse.

<u>Recommendation</u>

That you approve the talking points set forth above.

___✔___   AGREE   _____ DISAGREE   _____ DISCUSS

DEVELOPING A MULTI-PRONGED STRATEGY TO WIN MARRIAGE EQUALITY

These political losses hurt, but Lambda Legal's Marriage Project had been launched in anticipation that the road to marriage equality was likely to be long and bumpy. As we had done to address sodomy laws, we teamed up with an array of LGBTQ+ rights litigators, academics, and activists to develop a two-pronged strategy to win the freedom to marry, notwithstanding the still-limited public support and cycles of political opportunism.

The litigation prong had three stages. In stage one, litigators would bring marriage cases in a handful of states with favorable legal climates. These cases would rely solely on state constitutional claims. Once marriage equality had become the law in several states, we would move to stage two: federal lawsuits attacking DOMA's Section 3 as unconstitutional under the equal protection clause. When stage two was complete, stage three would begin: lawsuits arguing that the U.S. Constitution protected the right of same-sex couples to marry nationwide.

The second prong—advocacy and education—was designed to complement the first prong by bringing broader public attention to the lived experiences of same-sex couples as a way of shifting public attitudes about marriage equality. This work became so important that Evan left Lambda Legal to start a new organization, called Freedom to Marry, in 2003. For the next twelve years, Freedom to Marry, Lambda Legal, and the universe of organized legal and political LGBTQ+ rights groups worked hand in hand to put this unified strategy into action. And make no mistake: winning marriage equality required an unprecedented level of mobilization and cooperation among LGBTQ+ rights organizations—a challenge that was fully embraced.

(above) A meeting of the National Freedom to Marry Coalition with representatives of national and regional movement groups.

(right) New York marriage plaintiffs Curtis Woolbright and Daniel Reyes on Lambda Legal's *UPDATE* magazine, Summer 2004.

"It is time for a peacetime campaign to win the freedom to marry. We cannot win equality by focusing just on one court case or the next legislative battle—or by lurching from crisis to crisis. Rather, like every other successful civil rights movement, we must see our struggle as long-term and must set affirmative goals, marshal sustained strategies and concerted efforts, and enlist new allies and new resources."

—EVAN WOLFSON, FOUNDING MARRIAGE PROJECT DIRECTOR (1994-2001)

(top) Evan Wolfson maps out state support in the campaign to win the freedom to marry for same-sex couples.

(right) Tony Auth cartoon published in *The Philadelphia Inquirer,* March 9, 2004.

BEHIND THE SCENES

"In order to win marriage equality in the courts, we also had to win it in the courts of public opinion. We knew from bitter experiences in Hawai`i and California that voters can take away victories won in court. So, we used every tool we had to educate and engage advocates and allies—press conferences and town meetings, social media campaigns, posters, videos, Pride booths and banners, t-shirts and mugs, and even a fashion show in New Jersey! Early in the campaign, a photographer created a beautiful set of portraits of same-sex couples that we exhibited at conferences and events. We used all these tools to tell our stories and to amplify our common humanity. We talked as much about love as we did about legal rights. And it worked."

—Leslie Gabel-Brett, PhD, Director of Education and Public Affairs (2006-2016)

BUILDING THE CASES

With the strategy set, Lambda Legal and our Roundtable colleagues began the time-consuming process of determining where first to bring marriage cases. We asked lawyers in major law firms and in every state to help us research a number of key areas, including whether the state recognized same-sex co-parents, offered domestic partner benefits, had a strong, independent judiciary, and had a constitution that was resistant to heat-of-the-moment amendments. That research was instrumental to generating a list of good candidates for marriage litigation.

With states chosen, we turned to the process of assembling test cases. The plan was to bring test cases with multiple plaintiffs who demonstrated to courts that same-sex and different-sex relationships were the same in terms of love and commitment, and illuminated the many ways that exclusion from marriage deeply hurt same-sex couples and their families. Here are just a few of the many courageous same-sex couples we represented over the years. We describe them as they were when their cases began.

Jennifer and Dawn BarbouRoske (*Varnum v. Brien*, 2005-2009)

Jennifer and Dawn BarbouRoske and their daughters McKinley and Breeanna were among the plaintiffs who sued for the right to marry in Iowa. Jen and Dawn had been together for nearly sixteen years and had done all they could legally to protect their family: they were registered domestic partners in Iowa City and carried healthcare proxies. They were raising two daughters: Breeanna (four), who they'd jointly adopted through the foster care system and McKinley (eight), who Jen had carried and who was born prematurely. McKinley had been in neonatal intensive care for twenty-four days— days in which Dawn had no legal relationship to her daughter and feared that her parental status would not be recognized by the hospital. She had reason for concern: she had already been kept away from Jen during an ER visit caused by Jen's

heart condition. Dawn pursued a second-parent adoption as soon as possible, which cost thousands of dollars. Dawn and Jen were worried about the practical and dignitary harms of being excluded from marriage, both for themselves and for their daughters. By including McKinley and Breeanna as plaintiffs, together with their parents, we turned the "protect the children" rhetoric used for decades to smear LGBTQ+ people into a powerful argument for marriage equality, detailing the many ways the girls would be better off if their parents were legally married. In 2009, a unanimous Iowa Supreme Court struck down the state's exclusionary marriage law, making Iowa the fourth marriage equality state in the nation—and the first in the Midwest. Notably, the ruling emphasized the interests of children being raised by same-sex parents.

(left) The Iowa Supreme Court listens to oral arguments by Roger Kuhle, an assistant Polk County attorney, in the *Varnum* case, December 9, 2008.

(opposite) *The Des Moines Register*, April 4, 2009

BEHIND THE SCENES

"We made two strategic decisions in *Varnum* that felt risky, but paid off. Our opponents argued that same-sex couples should be barred from marriage because children fare best with different-sex parents. But science said otherwise. First, our experts were prominent child welfare scholars, and we dared the state to take that issue to trial. Second, we included the children of the same-sex couples as plaintiffs themselves. The state's lawyer had to look those children in the eye and claim they were less deserving of the benefits of having married parents. I am especially proud that we made this strategic shift to include the children, and of how compelling their voices were. I will always remember young plaintiff McKinley BarbouRoske, who was just eight when we filed the lawsuit, raising her arms above her head in triumph as she learned of the decision. She had explained bravely and patiently for years why her moms should be allowed to marry. This victory was hers as much as it was anyone's.
—Camilla Taylor, our lead attorney on *Varnum*

The Des Moines Register

SATURDAY, APRIL 4, 2009 | DESMOINESREGISTER.COM | THE NEWSPAPER IOWA DEPENDS UPON | 75¢ | METRO EDITION

IOWA GAYS HAVE A RIGHT TO MARRY, JUSTICES RULE

Unanimous decision cites fairness; law can't be reversed before 2012

Gay couples who sued for the right to marry in Iowa learn of their victory Friday. From left are Trish and Kate Varnum, and Jason Morgan and Chuck Swaggerty

BEHIND THE SCENES

The night before decision day, our team and the clients were all gathered at the Hotel Fort Des Moines. Over the four years of the case, we'd asked a lot from the client couples, and I had another big request: I wanted them to hear the Iowa Supreme Court's decision for the first time at the press conference—in front of A LOT of cameras. I knew it was important that Iowa—and the nation—see and understand how much the freedom to marry meant to same-sex couples. Everyone agreed, and so the next morning they waited in a sequestered room without their phones. As they filed into the packed press conference, the feeling in the room was electric. Camilla walked to the front of the room and said, "We won! And not only that . . . it's unanimous." The room erupted, and the front page of the *The Des Moines Register* and the *Associated Press* image will live forever as expressions of our victory.
—Lisa Hardaway, our media lead on *Varnum*

George Martinez and Fred McQuire Martinez
(*Majors v. Jeanes*, 2014)

George and Fred were two of the plaintiffs in our case that brought marriage equality to Arizona in 2014. A committed couple for forty-five years, the two men were facing George's imminent death from pancreatic cancer. They had traveled to California to marry, but Arizona did not recognize their marriage. George very much wanted Fred to be listed as his husband on his death certificate so Fred could collect additional Social Security benefits as George's surviving spouse. And both men wanted to be sure Fred's right to be at George's bedside would not be questioned. George passed away while *Majors* was in progress, and we filed emergency papers asking the federal judge hearing the case to order Arizona to provide a death certificate that accurately listed Fred as George's surviving spouse. The judge did so, writing that the right to marry confers "a dignity and status of immense import," and that Fred would likely face "irreparable emotional harm by being denied this dignity and status" as he grieved George's death. One month later, the judge struck down Arizona's marriage ban as unconstitutional. And much later, thanks to the Social Security survivor litigation described below, Fred received a lump sum benefits payment as George's surviving husband that enabled him to pay for new teeth and a more secure home.

BEHIND THE SCENES

"It meant so much to George to participate in the case to have his marriage to his beloved husband Fred recognized. It was important for him that Fred could receive benefits as his survivor after he passed so Fred could keep their house. That's why he kept fighting despite being very ill. But even though we won, the Social Security law was a second problem. And Fred did lose their home before we could win that second fight. He was part of the class recognized in *Ely*. And eventually, he did receive benefits as George's spouse. The payment meant he got a safer apartment. But what made him happiest was getting new teeth and finally being able to eat his favorite candy again. Milky Way bars. I'll never forget it. I was very honored to represent and help them."
—Carmina Ocampo, one of our attorneys on *Majors*

(pages 144-145) McKinley BarbouRoske, 11, of Iowa City (at left), reacts upon hearing the Iowa Supreme Court has approved marriage equality in *Varnum v. Brien*. Her sister Bre, six, sits between her mothers Dawn and Jean BarbouRoske, April 3, 2009.

(opposite) Photos from the wedding of Fred McQuire Martinez and George Martinez, July 19, 2014.

Cindy Meneghin and Maureen Kilian (*Lewis v. Harris*, 2002-2006 and *Garden State Equality v. Dow*, 2011-2014)

Cindy and Maureen had been a committed couple for twenty-seven years the first time they sued for the right to marry in New Jersey (*Lewis v. Harris*). At that time their son Josh was nine and their daughter Sarah was seven. Cindy's health concerns had made the two women keenly aware of their family's vulnerability. When Cindy came down with meningitis and required emergency care, hospital staff blocked Maureen from being with her, only relenting when they learned that Maureen held Cindy's power of attorney. But every time there was a shift change, Maureen's right to be by Cindy's side was challenged again.

The New Jersey Supreme Court's 2006 decision in *Lewis* held that same-sex couples were entitled to all the state-level benefits of marriage, but left it to the legislature to decide whether to establish marriage equality or create a quasi-parallel institution—civil unions. The legislature opted for civil unions, and Cindy and Maureen entered one, hoping it would protect their family. But they discovered that civil unions did not fully live up to their promise. Hardly anyone understood what it was. And so, when

Cindy once again found herself facing a healthcare emergency, hospital staff didn't understand that Maureen had the legal right to stay with Cindy. One nurse kept repeating, "But [civil unions are] not marriage, right?"

The entire family felt defeated and disheartened when the legislature opted for civil unions and disturbed by legislators who described same-sex relationships as less valuable than different-sex relationships. At one point, Josh wrote to the governor asking, "Why won't you let my parents get married?" That's why Cindy and Maureen were all in when Lambda Legal filed a new marriage equality lawsuit (*Garden State Equality v. Dow*). Sarah, then sixteen, also joined the suit although Josh could not because, at eighteen, he was a legal adult and so not "in the care of" his parents.

Cindy and Maureen always said that they hoped to get married before their children did. In 2013, thanks to *Garden State Equality* and their own persistence, they finally got their wish.

SEEKING SOCIETY'S EMBRACE
Gay couples sue New Jersey for the right to marry

Maureen Kilian and Cindy Meneghin with their children, Josh and Sarah, picking berries in their back yard in Butler. "We're as worthy of marriage as everyone else." Kilian says. "Isn't 28 years together enough to prove that?"

CHRIS PEDOTA/STAFF PHOTOGRAPHER

By RUTH PADAWER
STAFF WRITER

Parish administrator Maureen Kilian regularly enters the names of newly married couples into the church's big, green registry and then sends copies of the crisp licenses to the town clerk.

To the couples on the receiving end, the license itself is just a piece of paper, likely to end up

in a dusty safe-deposit box, forgotten. To Maureen Kilian, it is a piece of gold, in some ways more valuable than the wedding ring she has worn for 28 years.

"Every day those marriage certificates pass through my hands," Kilian says. "I can't help but think, 'Someday that sh-

■ Same-sex couples have **little legal support** if one dies without a will. The inheritance laws won't help. **Business**

have my own.'"

Last month, Kilian and her longtime partner, Cindy Meneghin, joined six other gay couples to sue the state of New Jersey for the right to marry – a right no state in the nation yet grants. They argue that the

right to privacy by not allowing them to marry the person of their choosing, and that it's denying them equal protection by barring them from the same tax, insurance, and death benefits that married couples receive.

Their case – like one in Massachusetts – is part of a growing movement to change the rights

(opposite) (L-R): Maureen Kilian, Josh Kilian-Meneghin, Cindy Meneghin, and Sarah Kilian-Meneghin

(left) Article about the *Lewis* litigation profiling the Kilian-Meneghin family, *The Record*, July 21, 2002.

149

Christopher Inniss and Shelton Stroman
(*Inniss v. Aderhold*, 2014-2015)

Chris and Shelton were the lead plaintiffs in the case that brought marriage equality to Georgia in 2015. They had been a committed couple for thirteen years and were raising their nine-year-old adopted son, Jonathan. Chris and Shelton wanted the legal protections of marriage, but their main concern was Jonathan, who desperately wanted his parents to be married and struggled to understand why they weren't.

This was exacerbated by the confusion their family faced every time they saw a new doctor or had to fill out family-related forms. At one point Shelton attempted to change his last name to match Chris and Jonathan as a way of giving his son some comfort and clarifying the family relationship to outsiders, but he was berated by a judge in open court for seeking to share his last name with another man and trying to "defeat" the court.

Being a plaintiff in impact litigation usually involves some costs: loss of privacy, the responsibility of representing many others and, too-often, harassment. Chris and Shelton began receiving death threats in the mail because of their courageous stance. Undeterred, they collected those threats into a binder to remind themselves and their son that "we have to be willing to stand up if we want to change things."

(above left and opposite)
Christopher Inniss and Shelton
Stroman with son Jonathan.

GOING TO COURT

The three-stage strategy proved remarkably prescient. By the end of 2009, Lambda Legal and our colleagues in other organizations had won cases that led to the implementation of civil unions in two states—Vermont (1999) and New Jersey (2005)—and marriage equality in four—Massachusetts (2003), California (2008), Connecticut (2008), and Iowa (2009).[41] There was political backlash in every instance, but only in California did opponents succeed in overriding courtroom wins, with the passage of Proposition 8.[42]

With stage one accomplished, our network of LGBTQ+ rights litigators began bringing federal challenges to Section 3 of DOMA (stage two). By 2012, there were five marriage cases awaiting possible Supreme Court review. (You read about one of those challenges—*Golinski v. OPM*— in Chapter 5). Four of those cases were brought by litigators with deep roots in the struggle for marriage equality. A fifth case—*Hollingsworth v. Perry*—was an independent federal challenge to the constitutionality of Proposition 8. The Supreme Court chose to review *United States v. Windsor*, and in 2013, it struck down Section 3 as a naked attempt to "impose inequality" and "demean those persons who are in a lawful same-sex marriage."

Advocacy and public education efforts were also reaping rewards. In 2009, Vermont became the first state in the nation to enact marriage equality through legislation, followed quickly by Maine and New Hampshire (although Maine voters repealed the state's new marriage law). By the time the Supreme Court decided *Windsor*, seven more states had enacted marriage equality through legislation while several additional states had passed civil union laws.[43]

Windsor signaled the end of stage two and the start of stage three of litigation: arguing that the U.S. Constitution protected the right of same-sex couples to marry. This phase proceeded with astonishing speed. Within twenty months of *Windsor*, litigators had won marriage equality in twenty-two states and the Supreme Court had agreed to hear a consolidated set of marriage cases from four states, including our case *Henry v. Hodges*, under the name *Obergefell v. Hodges*. On June 26, 2015—exactly two years after *Windsor* and nineteen years after *Romer v. Evans*, the Supreme Court ruled that same-sex couples have the constitutional right to marry. In a fitting note, the majority opinion was written by Anthony Kennedy, the same justice who had authored the majority opinions in *Windsor* and *Romer* (and *Lawrence*!).

(left) Supporters of the freedom to marry celebrate the *Obergefell* victory outside the Stonewall Tavern in New York City on June 26, 2015.

(opposite, clockwise from top left) *Burlington Free Press*; *The Economist*, January 6, 1996; *Politico.com*, February 22, 2012; *The New Yorker*, June 13, 1994; *USA Today*, June 27, 2015; *Newsweek*, July 7, 2003

Gay couples join hands with history

In towns across Vermont, men now they're ready to test new

By Adam Lisberg
and Nancy Remsen
Free Press Staff Writers

For the first time in American history, gay and lesbian couples became full partners in the eyes of the law Saturday — breathing life into Vermont's novel legal concept of civil unions, and setting the stage for a new struggle to recognize them in other states.

Starting a minute after midnight, same-sex couples walked into municipal offices across Vermont, filled out paperwork, paid a fee and walked out with civil union licenses — the gay and lesbian equivalent of marriage licenses. Some prepared to cer-

The Economist

JANUARY 6TH - 12TH 1996

TORY TIGHTROPES — pages 20, 23 and 30
RUSSIA'S NEXT PRESIDENT — page 31
CHINA AND HONG KONG — pages 19 and 49
THE SAUDI SUCCESSION — page 18

Let them wed

Australia A$6.90 Germany DM7.90 Ireland IR£2.20 Japan ¥850
France FFr26 Hong Kong HK$35 Italy Lire7,500 Switzerland SFr7.70

POLITICO

Under the Radar
Josh Gerstein on the Courts, Transparency, & More

Another court finds Defense of Marriage Act unconstitutional

By JOSH GERSTEIN
02/22/2012

Another federal judge has found unconstitutional a key part of the Defense of Marriage Act, the federal law that forbids providing federal government benefits to same-sex spouses.

U.S. District Court Judge Jeffrey White, who sits in San Francisco and was appointed to the bench by President George W. Bush, issued the ruling Wednesday ...ernoon in a case involving federal judicial law clerk Karen Golinski's request for ...efits for her female spouse. White said the stated goals of DOMA, passed in ...6 and signed by President Bill Clinton, could not pass muster under a so-...led heightened scrutiny test or even a lower "rational basis" threshhold.

...he imposition of subjective moral beliefs of a majority upon a minority cannot ...ovide a justification for the legislation. The obligation of the Court is 'to define the ...erty of all, not to mandate our own moral code,'" White wrote. "Tradition alone, ...owever, cannot form an adequate justification for a law....The 'ancient lineage' of a ...assification does not render it legitimate....Instead, the government must have an ...terest separate and apart from the fact of tradition itself."

...White's 43-page decision is similar to a ruling from a federal judge in Massachusetts ...n 2010, who also struck down an aspect of DOMA.

...n White's ruling, he also gave an unusual back of the hand to the Chief Judge of the ...th Circuit, Alex Kozinski, who ruled at an earlier administrative stage of the ...ispute that federal personnel managers had authority to cover Golinski's spouse as ...a nonspousal member of her family. White called that reasoning "unpersuasive."

...The case is one of those that lawyers hired by Congress defended after President ...Barack Obama and the Justice Department declined to do so, stating that they ...believed the statute to be unconstitutional.

THE HUNT FOR SADDAM • SNOOP DOGG UNPLUGGED

Newsweek

Is Gay Marriage Next?

Behind the Supreme Court's Privacy Ruling

The Fights Ahead— From Adoption To the Military

Partners Lauren Leslie and

USA TODAY
06.27.15

A GANNETT COMPANY

MARRIAGE FOR ALL

Supreme Court gives same-sex couples equal rights nationwide

Richard Wolf and Brad Heath
USA TODAY

FOR THE MAJORITY

WASHINGTON The Supreme Court legalized same-sex marriage across the United States Friday in a closely divided ruling that will stand as a milestone in its 226-year history.

The justices ruled 5-4 that states cannot deny gay men and lesbians the same marriage rights enjoyed for thousands of years by opposite-sex couples.

"They ask for equal dignity in the eyes of the law," Justice Anthony Kennedy said in his 28-page ruling. "The Constitution grants them that right."

Within hours, county clerks were issuing marriage licenses from Michigan to Texas. "I cannot imagine forcing them to wait a moment longer," said Ingham (Mich.) County Clerk Barb Byrum.

Kennedy announced the decision to a hushed courtroom; his colleagues watched stone-faced. As the sweep of his decision became clear, some in the audience embraced and cried.

"The past alone does not rule the present. The nature of injustice is that we do not always see it in our own time," Kennedy said.

In a show of the court's dis-...

"Same-sex couples seek in marriage the same legal treatment as opposite-sex couples, and it would disparage their choices and diminish their personhood to deny them this right."

Justice Anthony Kennedy

IN DISSENT

"A system of government that makes the people subordinate to a committee of nine unelected lawyers...

FIRST TAKE

Kennedy's opinion opens door

Brad Heath
and Richard Wolf
USA TODAY

WASHINGTON Justice Anthony Kennedy cracked the door to same-sex marriage more than a decade ago. Friday, he finally flung it open.

The Supreme Court's decision legalizing gay marriages nationwide came on the 12th anniversary of another of his opinions, striking down state laws against same-sex relations. That, Kennedy said Friday, was not enough.

"Outlaw to outcast may be a step forward, but it does not achieve the full promise of liberty," he said.

The decision was a logical next step for Kennedy, an often-conservative voice on the...

June 13, 1994   Price $2.50

THE NEW YORKER

"Under the Constitution, same-sex couples seek in marriage the same legal treatment as opposite-sex couples, and it would disparage their choices and diminish their personhood to deny them this right."

–U.S. SUPREME COURT JUSTICE ANTHONY KENNEDY, *OBERGEFELL V. HODGES*

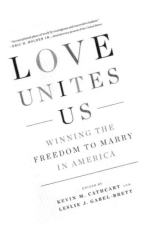

BEHIND THE SCENES

"I remember sitting in the Supreme Court when the *Obergefell* decision was announced. So much work from so many people, so many of them at Lambda, had gone into that moment, and as Justice Kennedy spoke, the scope of the victory reduced me to tears. Newspapers reported that you could hear sobs in the courtroom; some of them were mine!"

—Kevin Cathcart, Executive Director (1992-2016)

(opposite, top left) Front pages of *The Boston Globe* and *The Des Moines Register*, June 27, 2015

(opposite, bottom) The Obama White House is lit in rainbow colors to celebrate the U.S. Supreme Court's ruling requiring marriage equality, June 26, 2015.

(above, top) Lead plaintiff Jim Obergefell speaks outside the Supreme Court after the historic victory on Friday, June 26, 2015.

(above, left) A definitive collection of essays by Lambda Legal staff and many partners directly involved in the advocacy and organizing work to win the freedom to marry, published in 2016.

FACES OF MARRIAGE EQUALITY

See p. 287 for the names of these marriage plaintiffs.

FIGHTING FOR EQUALITY IN MARRIAGE

The existence of marriage equality has made it easier for LGBTQ+ couples to protect their families, but equal access *to* marriage does not always mean equal treatment *within* marriage. In recent years, Lambda Legal has focused on two problem areas: ensuring that children born to married same-sex couples receive accurate birth certificates and that widowed LGBTQ+ spouses are able to access spousal survivor benefits from the Social Security Administration.

THE PARENTAGE PRESUMPTION

Torres v. Seemeyer (2015-2016)

When a woman married to a man gives birth, the birth certificate lists both spouses as parents, whether or not the husband is genetically related to his newborn child. That's because birth certificates document the legal relationship between parents and children, not the biological relationship. But when a same-sex spouse gives birth, not all states automatically treat the other spouse as a parent. That's what happened to Chelsea and Jessamy Torres. When Chelsea gave birth to A. T. in 2015, she and Jessamy filled out the application for a birth certificate at the hospital, indicating that they were married and that they were both A. T.'s parents. But when the Wisconsin Department of Health Services

(DHS) issued the birth certificate, only Chelsea's name was on it. The DHS had essentially erased Jessamy from her own child's family, something that Jessamy said felt like getting "punched right in the stomach." We sued in federal court on their behalf, where our case was heard by the same judge who had earlier struck down Wisconsin's discriminatory marriage law.[44] She agreed with us that the DHS was unconstitutionally discriminating against same-sex married couples, and ordered it to produce an accurate birth certificate for A. T. as well as to take steps to identify and correct any other birth certificates it had already issued to the children of married same-sex couples.

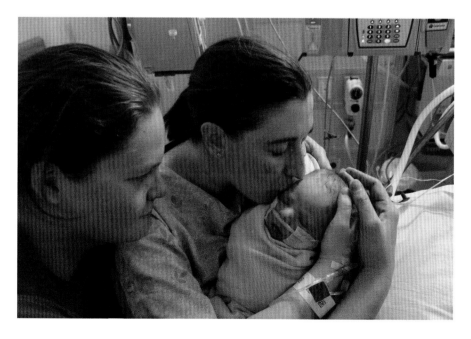

(opposite) Jessamy and Chelsea Torres

(below) *Star Tribune,* September 17, 2016

Both moms win names on birth certificate

Court ruling ends "long road" for same-sex parents in Wisconsin.

By MARY LYNN SMITH
marylynn.smith@startribune.com

When their son was born 1½ years ago, Jessamy and Chelsea Torres shared the joy of being first-time parents. But the

"We are tremendously relieved that the court recognized what we always knew: that our daughter was a U.S. citizen. And we are proud we taught our little girl to stand up for what's right even before she could crawl. No child should be denied her rights because her parents are LGBT."

—ROEE AND ADIEL KIVITI

Kiviti v. Pompeo (2019-2020) and *Mize and Gregg v. Pompeo* (2019-2020)

The spousal parentage presumption applies to citizenship as well as birth certificates. Children born abroad to married American citizens are automatically U.S. citizens. But during the Trump administration, the State Department treated a child born abroad to a married same-sex couple as an "out-of-wedlock" birth, even when both parents were listed on the child's birth certificate. In order to obtain citizenship for their child, at least one parent needed to show a biological relationship to their child *and* have lived in the United States for at least five years prior to their child's birth. This policy wreaked havoc on Adiel and Roee Kiviti's family. The two men, both naturalized U.S. citizens, married in California and in 2019 welcomed the birth of their daughter, Kessem, who was born via surrogacy in Canada. Both men were listed as her parents on her birth certificate. But the State Department refused to treat Kessem as a U.S. citizen, because she was only biologically related to Adiel, and Adiel was one year shy of the five-year residency requirement. The Kivitis had to bring Kessem home on a tourist visa, which was only good for three months. Faced

with the prospect of keeping Kessem in the United States illegally or travelling back and forth to Canada several times a year, the Kivitis decided to sue the State Department.

Derek Mize and Jonathan Gregg faced the same barrier when their English-born daughter, Simone, was refused citizenship and only allowed into the United States on a tourist visa. Together with Immigration Equality, we filed two lawsuits, one on behalf of the Kivitis, and one on behalf of the Mize-Greggs. We argued that the State Department's policy unlawfully discriminated against children because their parents were same-sex couples, contrary to the plain language of the Immigration and Naturalization Act. The judges in both cases determined that we were right and that the children of married U.S. citizens are also citizens, whether or not they are biologically linked to both parents. Kessem and Simone were both granted U.S. citizenship and in 2020 the State Department ended its appeal in both cases and changed its policy.

Derek Mize and Jonathan Gregg with their newborn daughter.

SURVIVOR BENEFITS

In re Robina Asti (2013–2014)

Lambda Legal has also worked to ensure that widowed LGBTQ+ spouses like Robina Asti are able to access spousal survivor benefits through the Social Security Administration (SSA). Robina, a transgender World War II veteran and pilot, married her husband Norwood Patton in 2004 after a long courtship. When Norwood passed away in 2012, at the age of ninety-seven, Robina applied for spousal survivor benefits. She was denied because the SSA determined that she was "legally male" at the time of her marriage, even though almost all her government-issued identity documents marked her as a woman—including her passport, driver's license, pilot's license, and Social Security card. The SSA, though, had relied on Robina's birth certificate from 1921, which listed her as male. From 1921!

We appealed that decision in 2013, arguing that Robina was legally a woman when she married Norwood, as shown by her many identity documents. On Valentine's Day in 2014 (a detail that Robina appreciated), the SSA deposited all the money Robina was owed into her bank account and announced that it was updating its spousal survivor benefits policy to reflect the lived experiences of transgender spouses.

Former Lambda Legal Transgender Rights Project Director Dru Levasseur with Robina Asti marching in New York City's Pride parade.

BEHIND THE SCENES

"She came into our office to speak, and I remember looking at a room of 40 people and seeing the young trans people in the room sobbing. And I understood their tears because ... they haven't had that experience from maybe their families, that acceptance and that hope. And Robina gave that hope to all of us."[45]

–Dru Levasseur, counsel for Robina Asti

> "I was so insulted that the Social Security Administration refused to recognize me as a woman and treated my marriage to Norwood in such a disrespectful way. I have lived a very private life, but the SSA forced me to speak out."
>
> **–ROBINA ASTI**

To raise awareness about Robina's story, Lambda Legal produced *Flying Solo: A Transgender Widow Fights Discrimination*, a short film that played at LGBTQ+ film festivals in 2015 to rave reviews. Robina spent the last years of her life as an outspoken activist for transgender rights. She died peacefully in 2021, just a month shy of her one-hundredth birthday. Her death was covered widely by the media.

(opposite, inset) Snapshot from Robina's collection

Thornton v. Saul (2018-2021) and *Ely v. Saul* (2018-2021)

Robina Asti was not the only LGBTQ+ person confronting discriminatory treatment from the SSA. In *Thornton v. Saul*, we represented Helen Thornton, who had been together with her life partner Margery ("Margie") Brown for nearly three decades before Margie died in 2006. Helen applied for spousal survivor benefits the year she turned sixty—which is when most people become eligible for them—but was rejected because she and Margie were never legally married. But they couldn't have married! And in *Ely v. Saul*, we represented Michael Ely, whose husband, James "Spider" Taylor, died just six months after the couple married—three months shy of the legal threshold to be eligible

for survivor benefits. But Michael and Spider had married as soon as it became legal in their home state of Arizona! In both cases, the presiding judges recognized that unconstitutional marriage laws had prevented our clients from meeting the SSA's requirements. Both judges also certified our cases as class actions, meaning that they included all same-sex couples sharing similar circumstances. In November 2021, the SSA discontinued its appeal of both cases and opened spousal survivor benefits to same-sex couples who can show that they would have married, or married earlier, had the laws allowed it.

(above) Michael and his husband Spider in their final photo together before Spider's death.

(above, inset) Helen and Margie

"I wanted Social Security to see that here was a lesbian couple that was together for twenty-seven years, and here are the consequences of not having equal rights under the law."

—HELEN THORNTON

BEHIND THE SCENES

"The whole purpose of Social Security survivor benefits is to care for those who lose their romantic and economic partners, a huge financial hardship. We suspected there were thousands of people in these long-term relationships who never bothered to apply, because they thought it was futile."[46]

—Karen Loewy, one of our attorneys on *Thornton* and *Ely*

THE FIGHT FOR MARRIAGE EQUALITY IN THREE ACTS

This chart shows the three big waves of law-making concerning marriage equality from 1993 to 2015, while the maps below show the freedom to marry movement gaining ground over time.

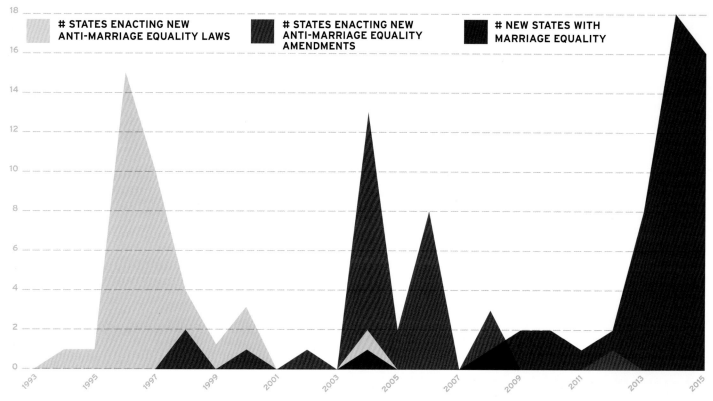

STATES ENACTING NEW
ANTI-MARRIAGE EQUALITY LAWS

STATES ENACTING NEW
ANTI-MARRIAGE EQUALITY
AMENDMENTS

NEW STATES WITH
MARRIAGE EQUALITY

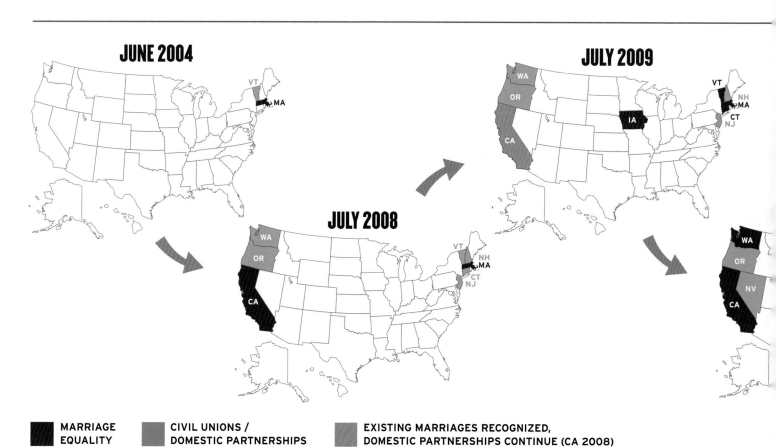

JUNE 2004

JULY 2008

JULY 2009

MARRIAGE
EQUALITY

CIVIL UNIONS /
DOMESTIC PARTNERSHIPS

EXISTING MARRIAGES RECOGNIZED,
DOMESTIC PARTNERSHIPS CONTINUE (CA 2008)

The **first wave** of lawmaking occurred primarily from **1996 to 2000** and was sparked by the 1993 **Hawai`i** Supreme Court decision in *Baehr* and the passage of the federal **Defense of Marriage Act (DOMA)** in 1996. In this wave, dozens of states adopted new laws to deny in-state legal recognition to same-sex couples' out-of-state marriages and otherwise to restrict marriage only to different-sex couples. No state allowed same-sex couples to marry during this time, although **Vermont** enacted civil unions in response to a 1999 decision of the Vermont Supreme Court (*Baker v. State of Vermont*).

The **second wave** took place primarily from **2004 to 2008**. In this wave, dozens of states amended their constitutions to enshrine exclusionary marriage restrictions. This was a gut punch to all those fighting for the freedom to marry, including those litigating in state courts making state constitutional claims. This wave was sparked by the 2003 **Massachusetts** Supreme Judicial Court ruling in *Goodridge v. Department of Public Health,* which held that same-sex couples had the right to marry under the state's constitution, overruling existing state laws that limited marriage to different-sex couples.*

The **third wave** began in **2008**, on the tail of the second wave. In this final wave, states began to join Massachusetts in implementing marriage equality, a process that accelerated sharply after the U.S. Supreme Court struck down part of DOMA in **2013's** *Windsor* **case**. Court cases were the biggest driver of this change, although some states, like **New York**, adopted marriage equality legislatively and others, like **Washington**, adopted marriage equality through the popular vote. In 2015, our victory in *Obergefell* finished the process.

Goodridge was litigated by our New England-based movement ally GLAD, then called Gay and Lesbian Advocates and Defenders and now known as GLBTQ Legal Advocates & Defenders.

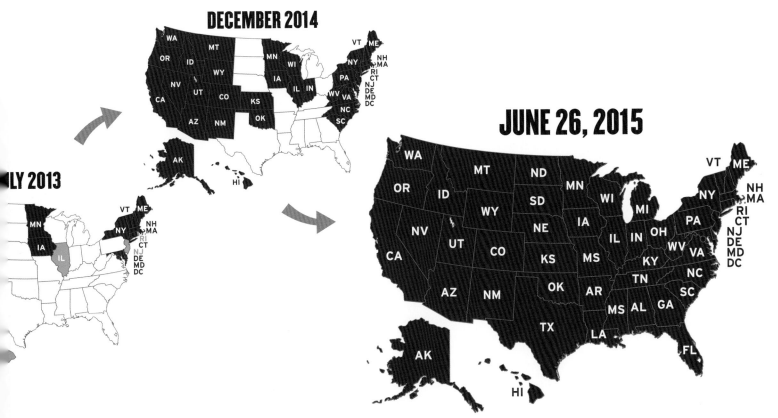

JULY 2013

DECEMBER 2014

JUNE 26, 2015

STUDENT LIFE

MAKING SCHOOLS SAFE AND WELCOMING FOR LGBTQ+ YOUTH

Many LGBTQ+ youth face bullying, exclusion, and discrimination in school. This treatment impacts their education and damages their psychological, emotional, and physical well-being. To make things worse, attendance at school is mandatory until a student turns sixteen or older, and many students cannot transfer schools or switch to home schooling if they find themselves in a hostile school climate. Nor should they have to.

For the past thirty years, Lambda Legal has prioritized making schools welcoming for LGBTQ+ youth and the LGBTQ+ faculty who serve as symbols of possibility. Except for one early case involving college students, we held off on sustained involvement during the 1970s and 1980s due to the false but effective narrative that LGBTQ+ adults were dangerous to children, a theme played on by Florida beauty queen Anita Bryant in the '70s and which has made an ugly reappearance in the 2020s courtesy of Florida governor Ron DeSantis, Fox News, and a reactionary movement intent on using discomfort with our movement's gains for social and political purposes. We were not alone—LGBTQ+ rights groups in the '70s and '80s generally avoided youth work.

In the mid '90s, we had made enough progress as a movement that Lambda Legal decided the time had come to confront the pervasive abuse heaped on young people who identified as LGBTQ+ or were perceived to be. We prepared materials about the law and served as an informational resource for youth, parents, schools, and movement partners that support pro-LGBTQ+ educators and provide training—work that continues today, thanks to our Help Desk. And, of course, Lambda Legal continues to advocate in courts and policy arenas. Here is a view into that work. Note: recent efforts to censor classroom discussion of sexuality and gender identity are covered in Chapter 10.

(opposite) Will Larkins, 17, co-founded his school's Queer Student Union saying, "No one's going to help us, clearly, so we've got to help each other." (See *Cousins v. Orange County School Board* in Chapter 10.)

(page 168) Izzy Smith and Alexander Fitzgerald, both 18, are co-presidents of their high school's Gender and Sexuality Alliance (GSA). They spoke to the Portland, Maine school board about protecting transgender students, 2017.

ADVOCATING FOR STUDENT ORGANIZATIONS

Gay Students Organization v. Bonner (1974)

When lesbian and gay student groups began emerging on college campuses in the Stonewall era, campus administrators often opposed them. Lambda Legal's second case probed whether the University of New Hampshire (UNH) could place restrictions on the newly-formed Gay Students Organization (GSO) that differed from the restrictions placed on other student groups. The New Hampshire Civil Liberties Union represented the students, and Lambda Legal filed its very first friend-of-the-court brief, educating the First Circuit Court of Appeals about homosexuality and arguing that UNH's restrictions violated the students' rights of free speech and association. The First Circuit agreed, establishing the widely cited precedent that public universities cannot discriminate against LGBTQ+ student groups.

This Is at UNH!

Union Leader
3|17

NOTE: We consider this both a disgusting and unpleasant picture but we also believe it our duty to inform our New Hampshire readers of what is taking place at our state university. This photo shows the general scene at UNH Friday night as the homosexual Gay Students Organization hosted a "dance" in the Memorial Union Building. More than 200 persons attended as males danced with males, females with females, all to the tune of a lesbian band.

(Photo by Bob Murray)

(opposite, left) Ad for a dance to be hosted by the University of Washington's Gay Students Association. 1974.

(opposite, right) "Boot Out the Pansies," an editorial published by the Manchester, New Hampshire, *Union Leader* on May 20, 1973.

(above) Photo of a dance hosted by the University of New Hampshire's Gay Student Organization, as published in the *Union Leader* on March 17, 1973.

Colín v. Orange County Unified School District (1999-2000)

LGBTQ+ student organizations in middle and high schools took much longer to appear. Beginning in Massachusetts in the late '80s, students and faculty began creating clubs called Gay-Straight Alliances (GSA), and over the next decade GSAs flourished in schools across the country. But not everywhere.

In 1999, Anthony Colín and Heather Zetin petitioned to create a GSA at El Modena High School in Orange, California. Their application received unusual scrutiny, including a public forum hosted by the school board at which board members cited the Bible as grounds for saying "no." Anthony's principal told him the club's name was inappropriate and suggested the "Tolerance Club," the "Acceptance Club," or the "Alliance" instead. After repeated delays, the school board unanimously denied the GSA's application, announcing it would only reconsider if the group changed its name and agreed to limits on speech not required of other clubs.

Lambda Legal partnered with People for the American Way to sue the district on behalf of Anthony and Heather, with full support from their parents. Our suit argued that the district's actions violated students' speech and association rights as well the 1984 Equal Access Act, a federal law saying that once a school allows student clubs that aren't related to the curriculum, it must treat all such clubs equally.

The federal judge heard testimony from the students, including Anthony's explanation that he had decided to form the club after college student Matthew Shepard was brutally murdered for being gay earlier that year in Laramie, Wyoming. After the court issued a preliminary order finding that the students were likely to win at trial, the school district settled, agreeing to recognize the GSA and treat it like any other club. *Colín* marked the first time a federal court ordered a school district to allow a GSA. It's since been cited to support the formation of GSAs around the country.

(left) Sacramento Country Day School's GSA

(above) Anthony Colín with supporters at an Orange Unified School District board meeting on December 7, 1999.

The Advocate
gay & lesbian news magazine
April 11, 2000 | www.advocate.com

David Geffen
The book he doesn't want you to read

GAY TEENS FIGHT BACK

Anthony Colin leads a new generation of high school activists out of the closet

Plus! Gay battles in your school district

DID WE BUNGLE
THE GAY MARRIAGE
FIGHT IN CALIFORNIA?

THE LARAMIE PROJECT

WHY *POPULAR*
IS SO POPULAR

$3.95 USA • $4.95 CAN • £2.95 UK

"I want us to talk about the experiences that gay, lesbian, and bisexual kids go through in their everyday lives such as harassment, coming out of the closet or telling people that they are gay: the fear and the emotions such as self-hatred or denial that a lot of kids go through and the harassment they get and how to deal with that."[47]

–HEATHER ZETIN

"The Board Members may be uncomfortable about students discussing sexual orientation and how all students need to accept each other, whether gay or straight....[However,] defendants cannot censor the students' speech to avoid discussions on campus that cause them discomfort or represent an unpopular viewpoint."

–U.S. DISTRICT JUDGE DAVID O. CARTER, *COLÍN*

STOPPING ANTI-LGBTQ+ ABUSE IN SCHOOLS

Nabozny v. Podlesny (1995-1996)

When Lambda Legal added youth issues to our portfolio, the first case we litigated was *Nabozny v. Podlesny*: the first legal challenge to pervasive and violent anti-LGBTQ+ bullying in public schools. Jamie Nabozny had been subjected to relentless harassment and violence from his fellow students because of his sexual orientation while attending middle and high school in Ashland, Wisconsin. Students spat and urinated on him, pretended to rape him during class, and kicked him so many times in the stomach that he required surgery. Officials in both schools knew about the horrific bullying but took no disciplinary action, telling Jamie he should expect it if he was "going to be so openly gay." Although Jamie's parents tried to protect him, they were stymied at every turn.

Jamie filed a federal lawsuit against the school district and school officials in 1995, arguing that their failure to try to protect him violated his constitutional rights to equal protection and due process. The trial court dismissed his case, however, saying that a public school can't be held liable for

the actions of students. Lambda Legal stepped in to handle the appeal to the Seventh Circuit and in 1996 Jamie prevailed. Public school officials, the court said, can be held liable for failing to act to prevent known anti-LGBTQ+ bullying; Jamie had the right to sue. At the trial, a jury found that school officials had intentionally left Jamie to fend for himself because of his gender and sexual orientation. Before the jury decided how much compensation Jamie was owed for that discrimination, the school district settled the case for nearly $1 million.

The horrific abuse Jamie endured, and the hefty price tag for the school's complicity, brought nationwide attention to the harassment faced by LGBTQ+ students and the potential liability of responsible adults. School officials around the country began contacting Lambda Legal to learn how they could take preventive action, and sexual harassment prevention programs began expanding to educate teachers, staff, and students about the harms of anti-LGBTQ+ harassment.

A TRIBUTE TO DAVID S. BUCKEL

David Buckel joined Lambda Legal in 1995 and launched our initiative to address anti-LGBTQ+ school bullying. He researched and developed the legal theories we deployed in *Nabozny* and other cases, which transformed the law and school officials' understanding of their duties to their students. He later served as our Marriage Project director. David left Lambda Legal in 2008 and dedicated himself to environmentalism. On April 14, 2018, at sixty years of age and inspired by a Buddhist practice of personal sacrifice, he ended his life as a protest against our society's inaction on fossil fuel consumption.

"David's thoughtful and engaging advocacy broke through many stubborn misconceptions and showed it was possible and necessary for our movement to speak up for bullied, ostracized LGBT young people. . . . He had this faith in the goodness of other people, and believed we could win a marriage case, even in the heartland. . . . He had the idea that people would be moved by seeing families who were left unprotected . . . and wanted to introduce the country to LGBT people."[48]
– Camilla Taylor, Deputy Legal Director for Litigation

(top, right) (L–R) Jamie Nabozny, Pat Logue, David Springer, and David Buckel upon reaching the settlement in Jamie's case in November of 1996.

(right) Jamie's case attracted nationwide media coverage.

"[O]ne Texas student later told Jamie that he taped the news articles about Jamie's case inside his locker door so that every morning he could take from it the strength he needed to get through one more day of abuse."[49]

–DAVID BUCKEL, ONE OF OUR ATTORNEYS ON *NABOZNY*

"[C]ountless gay kids have paid a high price for abuse. Now the tables have turned, and it is prejudice that is costly."[50]

–PAT LOGUE, ONE OF OUR ATTORNEYS ON *NABOZNY*

Jamie Nabozny sued his Wisconsin high school after anti-gay harassment by schoolmates escalated to a mock rape and a severe beating.

RITA REED

Henkle v. Gregory (2000-2002)

At first glance, *Henkle v. Gregory* sounds a lot like *Nabozny*. Like Jamie, Derek Henkle suffered severe harassment from other students because of his sexual orientation, including one instance where students lassoed a rope around his neck in the school parking lot and threatened to kill him by dragging him behind their truck. Like Jamie, Derek reported the unrelenting harassment to the officials at his Reno, Nevada high school. As happened with Jamie, the officials did nothing to help.

Here's where the cases diverge. When Derek asked to transfer to another Reno, Nevada, high school, the transfer was approved on the condition that he conceal his sexual orientation. The new school was barely better, and even though Derek restricted what he said, the principal repeatedly told him to "stop acting like a fag." Derek transferred to a third school and again was told to keep his sexuality to himself. But the harassment continued. At one point, Derek was physically attacked and beaten bloody while onlookers shouted anti-LGBTQ+ epithets. School staff witnessing the attack did not intervene. When Derek reported the incident to administrators, they not only declined to punish the attackers but pushed Derek not to report the attack as a hate crime. Instead, they had him take classes at the local community college to get a GED rather than a high school diploma.

Because the administrators at all three of these schools refused to protect Derek, Lambda Legal stepped in and sued the district and the responsible adults. In addition to arguing that the school violated his equal protection rights, we focused on the First Amendment. School officials repeatedly had told Derek that he was the problem: that his speech, clothing, and mannerisms invited harassment and that Derek needed to change. We explained that this violated Derek's right to speak and express his identity without being censored or retaliated against by school officials.

In 2001, the federal judge hearing the case not only agreed, but also allowed Derek to pursue punitive damages against those officials as individuals because their actions had been egregious. In response, the school district agreed to a ground-breaking settlement that included sweeping new policies to protect students from sexual orientation discrimination and a payment of nearly half a million dollars to Derek. These policies became a model for schools seeking to prevent anti-LGBTQ+ discrimination.

"[T]he Supreme Court [has] clearly established that students in public schools have the right to freedom of speech and expression. This is a broad right that would encompass the right of a high school student to express his sexuality."

–U.S. DISTRICT JUDGE ROBERT A. MCQUAID JR., *HENKLE*

"I felt like I didn't belong anywhere... Just me by myself, having to fight a very, very hard battle of just trying to be safe, just trying to go to school and just trying to be out there in the world— have an education, be loving, and just be who I am."[51]

–DEREK HENKLE

Out Safe & Respected: A Guide to LGBTQ Youth in Schools for Educators and Parents (2010)

Stopping Anti-Gay Abuse of Students in Public Schools: A Legal Perspective (1996)

PROTECTING LGBTQ+ TEACHERS

Murray v. Oceanside Unified School District (1999-2000)

Discrimination against LGBTQ+ teachers is not just an issue of workplace fairness. Out teachers offer LGBTQ+ students a sense of belonging and possibility. They serve as advocates and allies for LGBTQ+ students who need support and guidance. They are role models for students who may not have any other LGBTQ+ adults in their lives. And when students see openly LGBTQ+ teachers harassed and driven out, it can reinforce all their worst fears.

That's why we represented Dawn Murray in her lawsuit against the Oceanside Unified School District in California. Dawn, an award-winning biology teacher at Oceanside High School, suffered severe harassment from her co-workers after they learned that she was a lesbian. The trouble began in 1993, when she was denied a promotion to student activities director after a school official said that someone with her "lifestyle . . . shouldn't be that close to the kids." Rumors began to spread, and Dawn became the target of vicious verbal attacks, false rumors, and obscene graffiti outside her classroom. School officials refused to act and later threatened her with retaliation if she pursued her complaints. Undeterred, Dawn went to court, suing the school district for discrimination based on sexual orientation. But the trial court dismissed her suit, ruling that California's law against sexual orientation discrimination didn't cover anti-gay harassment, only discrimination in hiring, firing, and promotion.

Lambda Legal stepped in to handle the appeal and make clear that the law must be understood to prohibit sexual orientation harassment, the same way other statutes had been interpreted to prohibit racial and sexual harassment. In 2000, the California appeals court unanimously agreed and gave Dawn the go-ahead to sue the school district. The district appealed to the California Supreme Court, but the high court refused to dismiss Dawn's case. Faced with the likelihood of losing at trial, the school district settled, paying Dawn $140,000, and agreeing to institute annual sensitivity training about sexual orientation harassment to all its employees. Meanwhile, the published Court of Appeals decision established that such harassment was illegal in California, a decision that protected workers across the state.

"This was the first California appeals court to make clear that harassment of lesbian and gay school employees is wrong, illegal, and cannot be tolerated. Our schools should be teaching respect and not standing by while the reputations of fine teachers are trampled."

—MYRON QUON, OUR ATTORNEY ON *MURRAY*

"I chose to continue to teach throughout this battle because I didn't want the kids to see what harassment can do. I didn't want the district administration to model running teachers out of classrooms and showing them that you can harass and discriminate against someone because they're gay. We're there to teach students. They learn from our actions."[52]

—DAWN MURRAY

YOUTH GROUPS

Boy Scouts of America v. Dale (1992-2000)

Discrimination against LGBTQ+ youth extends beyond schools. When James Dale, an Eagle Scout, lost his position as an assistant scoutmaster in 1990 for being gay, he came to us for help. James had never discussed his sexuality when working with youth, but the Boy Scouts of America (BSA) learned that he was copresident of the Rutgers University Lesbian/Gay Alliance and expelled him. Lambda Legal sued, arguing that a New Jersey law prohibiting discrimination based on sexual orientation in public accommodations made the BSA's actions unlawful. The BSA argued that the law didn't apply, because it was a private group instead of a public accommodation and had a First Amendment right to control its membership. The New Jersey Supreme Court unanimously sided with Lambda Legal, but in 2000 the U.S. Supreme Court reversed, issuing a 5–4 decision that the BSA could exclude gay scoutmasters.

Despite the unfavorable ultimate outcome, *Dale,* and a similar case in California in which we represented Tim Curran,[53] showed the power of litigation to raise awareness and change public opinion. By insisting on their freedom to discriminate, the Boy Scouts showed their true colors. In response, many businesses stopped supporting them, many schools stopped letting Scout troops hold meetings on school grounds, and many police and fire departments ended partnership programs. Facing mounting pressure, the BSA lifted its ban on gay scouts in 2014 and its ban on gay scoutmasters in 2015. In 2017, it announced that transgender boys could become Scouts and participate in boys-only programming.

(left) James Dale and his parents

(right) James receiving the Joshua Huddy Trail Award as Youth Speaker, 1985.

Brandon Teena's Nebraska
Madonna's racy past »

The national gay & lesbian newsmagazine

25 top companies to work for now

the Advocate

October 26, 1999 | www.advocate.com

Be prepared!

How Boy Scout and military values teach gays to fight back when they get kicked out

Including: JAMES DALE on winning his battle with the Scouts and STEVE MAY on his struggle to stay in the military

James Dale

$3.95 USA • $4.95 CAN. • £2.95 UK

Lambda Legal Defense and Education Fund, Inc.

(left) James and former Lambda Legal attorney Evan Wolfson after our victory in the New Jersey Superior Court. August 4, 1999.

CHAPTER 8

SEEKING SHELTER

REDUCING DISCRIMINATION IN HOUSING AND LODGING

A roof over one's head and a feeling of safety can be as essential to well-being as food, clothing, medical care, and love. But many LGBTQ+ people have trouble accessing this basic necessity. Appallingly high numbers of LGBTQ+ youth experience homelessness. Pervasive discrimination in rental housing, public accommodations, and crisis centers denies LGBTQ+ people access to safe and affordable places to live. And on the flip side, pervasive discrimination in adoption and foster care agencies prevents LGBTQ+ adults from providing safe homes to youth in crisis, youth who may be LGBTQ+ themselves. Lambda Legal is especially concerned about residential systems of care: places where LGBTQ+ people are particularly vulnerable to abuse and exclusion by other residents, staff, and institutional policies. This chapter spotlights two facets of Lambda Legal's litigation in this area: our work to affirm that the Fair Housing Act prohibits anti-LGBTQ+ discrimination and our challenge to religiously motivated discrimination in public accommodations and foster care.

San Francisco Pride parade, 2015

THE FAIR HOUSING ACT AND HOUSING DISCRIMINATION

Smith v. Avanti (2016-2017)

In 2015, Rachel and Tonya Smith decided it was time to find a new home for their growing family. They wanted a place with good schools, where the kids could play in the yard and where they would be closer to nature. A duplex in Gold Hill, Colorado, seemed perfect. After touring it with Deepika Avanti, the landlord, Rachel and Tonya told Avanti they were ready to sign a lease. Rachel also mentioned that she is transgender. Hours later Avanti emailed the Smiths, rejecting them because their "uniqueness" would attract attention and be the source of local gossip. She went on to say that it would be "better" for the Smith family if they lived in a "larger town," and noted that a psychic

friend had given her the same advice and had "a transvestite friend herself."

We sued on behalf of the Smiths, arguing that Avanti's refusal to rent to them violated the federal Fair Housing Act of 1968 (FHA). The federal judge hearing the case drew on the precedent we had established in *Hively v. Ivy Tech* (see Chapter 3) to anchor his ruling that discrimination based on sexual orientation and gender identity is a form of illegal sex discrimination under the FHA. *Smith* was the first case to establish that the FHA protects LGBTQ+ people from housing discrimination.

"No one should ever have to go through what we went through, and hopefully this ruling will protect other couples like us who are trying to provide safe homes for their families."[54]

—TONYA SMITH

(left) This is the house at issue.

(opposite) Rachel and Tonya Smith at home with their children.

"It got out, and I thought, oh, here we go again. Gay hate."
—MARSHA WETZEL

Wetzel v. Glen St. Andrew Living Community (2016-2019)

Seniors can be extra vulnerable to abuse. The harassment that Marsha Wetzel endured after losing her partner, Judith Kahn, is a poignant example of her pride and others' prejudice.

Marsha met Judy in 1982 and they had a commitment ceremony the following year. After thirty years together, Judy passed away, and her family evicted Marsha from the home the couple had shared. Marsha eventually found a senior-living apartment to rent at Glen St. Andrew Living Community in Illinois. When she was open about her lesbian identity, other residents made her life hell, calling her hateful slurs and assaulting her repeatedly. One rammed her mobility scooter with his walker so hard he tipped it over, injuring her; the same resident also called her a "fucking dyke." Instead of responding to her pleas for help, staff branded her a liar and retaliated by barring her access to some common facilities, making false accusations against her, and even slapping her across the face.

We sued Glen St. Andrew for violating the FHA by not intervening to help Marsha when it knew about the harassment and by retaliating against her when she complained. The trial court dismissed the case, holding that landlords are only liable under the FHA when they intentionally discriminate against a tenant. Our appeal to the Seventh Circuit brought Marsha a measure of justice. The court determined that discrimination based on sexual orientation and gender identity is a form of illegal sex discrimination under the FHA, citing *Hively v. Ivy Tech*. It then ruled that landlords are liable when they have been notified about tenant-on-tenant harassment and don't take reasonable steps to stop it. The upshot: Marsha got her day in court, and landlords are now on notice that they are required under the FHA to protect their tenants from anti-LGBTQ+ harassment.

"Being trapped with the people who bullied you in high school is terrifying."

–KAREN LOEWY, OUR COUNSEL ON *WETZEL*

"For 15 months, [Wetzel] was bombarded with threats, slurs, derisive comments about her family, . . . physical violence, and spit. The defendants dismiss this litany of abuse as no more than ordinary 'squabbles' and 'bickering' between 'irascible,' 'crotchety senior resident[s].' A jury would be entitled to see the story otherwise. (We confess to having trouble seeing the act of throwing an elderly person out of a motorized scooter as one of the ordinary problems of life in a senior facility.)"

–U.S. DISTRICT JUDGE DIANE WOOD, *WETZEL*

(opposite, inset) Lambda Legal booklet about the rights of LGBTQ+ elders, 2000.

NO ROOM AT THE INN: CHALLENGING RELIGIOUS BIAS IN COMMERCIAL LODGING

Cervelli v. Aloha Bed & Breakfast (2011-2019)

Diane Cervelli and Taeko Bufford decided to visit a close friend and her newborn baby in Hawai`i. Diane searched online to find lodging near their friend's home and came across ads and the website for Aloha Bed & Breakfast. In October 2007, she called the owner, Phyllis Young, to book a room, only to be asked if she and Taeko were a lesbian couple. When Diane answered truthfully, Young responded that as a strong Christian she was uncomfortable accepting the reservation and hung up. After Diane called Taeko in tears, Taeko called Young back and was explicitly told that Young would not rent a room to lesbians for religious reasons.

Taeko and Diane then filed complaints with the Hawai`i Civil Rights Commission (HCRC). When the HCRC interviewed Young, she defended her actions by saying same-sex relationships are "detestable" and "defile our land." She also claimed the state's anti-discrimination law—which explicitly protects LGBTQ+ people—did not apply to her because she lived in the B&B. The HCRC disagreed. In November 2011 it issued a "right to sue" notice authorizing Taeko and Diane to sue in state court.

Diane and Taeko asked for Lambda Legal's help, and we filed a lawsuit on their behalf in December 2011. The HCRC joined our suit to represent Hawai`i's interest in stopping unfair discrimination in public accommodations, and to prevent the damage that would result if businesses could simply ignore laws based on their owners' personal beliefs. Our frequent opponent, the Alliance Defending Freedom (ADF), soon joined the case to represent Young and Aloha B&B, and especially to press religious freedom arguments.

In April 2013, the Hawai`i trial court determined that Young and her business had violated the state's public accommodation law and ordered the B&B to stop discriminating against same-sex couples. ADF appealed. In 2018, the Hawai`i appellate court agreed with the trial court. ADF immediately asked the state's Supreme Court to hear the case, which it declined, and then the U.S. Supreme Court, which also declined. In the end, we won a clear ruling that businesses like B&Bs cannot evade Hawai`i's anti-discrimination law. That's a big victory in a state that depends heavily on tourism.

B&B discriminated against lesbians, appeals court affirms

The Hawaii Kai owner is weighing her options, her lawyer says

By Nelson Daranciang
ndaranciang@staradvertiser.com

The lawyer for a Hawaii Kai bed-and-breakfast business that was found to have discriminated against a lesbian couple says the operator is considering all of her legal options, including pursuing further appeal.

The Intermediate Court of Appeals on Friday upheld a finding by a trial

cause she told the women she is uncomfortable with having lesbians in her house.

Aloha advertises itself as a Christian B&B home that rents up to three rooms at $95 to $110 per night.

Cervelli and Bufford said they first took their complaint to the Hawaii Civil Rights Commission, where Young said she believes homosexuality is

He rejected Aloha's claim that under state housing law, an owner or lessor who resides in the dwelling can refuse to rent to people based on their sex, sexual orientation or marital status.

Nacino found that Aloha B&B is an inn, hotel, motel or other establishment that provides lodging to transient guests and th

ASSOCIATED PRESS / 2011

A Hawaii appeals court has ruled against a Hawaii Kai bed-and-breakfast that denied Taeko Bufford, left, and Diane Cervelli a room because they're gay. The Intermediate Court of Appeals affirmed a lower court's ruling against Aloha Bed & Breakfast, whose owner appealed based on her and her husband's religious views.

"I can't tell you how much it hurt to be
essentially told, 'we don't do business with your
kind.' It still stings to this day. We thought
the days when business owners would say 'we're
open to the public—but not to you' was a thing of
the past."

–TAEKO BUFFORD

(opposite) *Honolulu Star
Advertiser,* February 27, 2018

(above) Taeko Bufford and
Diane Cervelli

FOSTERING PREJUDICE: CHALLENGING RELIGIOUS BIAS IN FOSTER CARE

Lambda Legal's Youth in Out-of-Home Care Project works to improve cultural competence and support for LGBTQ+ children and youth in child welfare and juvenile justice systems nationwide. Those systems often are plagued by underfunding, unresponsive bureaucracy, and many types of entrenched bias. One type of bias we face regularly is anti-LGBTQ+ religious doctrine, in large part because religious charities have a very long history of involvement in caring for children. A complicated relationship has evolved to allow religious organizations to participate in public systems via grants of taxpayer funds. In the past, these funds came with nondiscrimination requirements and bans on using government funds for religious activities. But some religiously affiliated organizations object to the inclusion of LGBTQ+ people in nondiscrimination rules and in recent years they've argued that their constitutional guarantees of religious freedom mean that nondiscrimination rules should not apply to them. (This was the motivation behind *Fulton v. City of Philadelphia*, a 2021 Supreme Court case where Catholic Social Services (CSS) argued it had a right to continue to receive large government contracts to provide social services without having to abide by Philadelphia's non-discrimination rules. While the court declined to grant CSS the broad license it was seeking, it found a way to rule for CSS on facts specific to that case.)

Lambda Legal is fighting back against the argument that social service providers with exclusive government contracts can invoke religion to exempt themselves from obeying the law. The following cases show how we've been challenging religious discrimination in foster care. (For more on our work to confront religious exemption arguments, see Chapter 10.)

(opposite) Lambda Legal clients Fatma Marouf and Bryn Esplin at home with their daughter in Fort Worth, Texas.

(below, left) Letter to the Editor, *Austin American Statesman*, May 27, 2017

(below, middle) Editorial, *Fort Worth Star Telegram*, April 2, 2017

(below, right) *Austin American Statesman*, March 20, 2017

EDITORIALS

Religious liberty bills discriminate, not liberate

THE EDITORIAL BOARD

...gious liberty laws don't give religious freedom — ...ke it away.

...Constitution protects religious freedom. It's a ...mental right that any American can exercise, so ...bills don't do anything but discriminate against a ...ity group — this time the LGBTQ community. ...ne of these laws are necessary, and all of them are ...ging.

...enteen "religious liberty" bills have been filed in ...ear's legislative session, all discriminating against ...GBTQ community in one way or another.

...e most controversial is House Bill 3859. ...ong with three similar bills, it would protect faith- ...d child welfare organizations when they exercise ..."sincerely held religious beliefs." ...hich means this bill protects these organizations ...being sued for not providing abortions or contra- ...ives, or for denying adoptions or foster care place- ...t that somehow go against their religious beliefs, says ...ill author Rep. James Frank, R-Wichita Falls, says ...3859 isn't politically charged, but rather is mean ...p provide quality homes for children in child wel ...vices.

...Organizations like the Texas Catholic Conferenc ...hops are worried about litigation and hesitant ...ntinue in the child welfare system without reli ...erty protections.

...But "sincerely held religious beliefs" is so vag ...could open up some worrisome doors. ...The bill says the "sincerely held religious be ...discriminate against race, rel

YOU SAY LETTERS TO THE E

Children are the real losers under HB 3859

Texas has passed House Bill 3859 – a bill protecting the religious rights for child welfare agencies.

There are many articles discussing the discrimination at hand here, but what most are failing to recognize are the people who are truly going to lose. Are potential adoptive and foster parents going to be affected? Absolutely – but they have options. They can go to another state and adopt through another agency.

The real losers are the children.

TEXAS HOUSE

Foster-care bill would allow faith-based shunning of gays

By Chuck Lindell
clindell@statesman.com

The Texas Legislature opened debate Wednesday on the first of more than a dozen bills that would allow people, businesses or government employees to refuse to provide services based on their religious beliefs.

Supporters say the legislation is essential to protecting the freedom of Texans to practice their religion in ways that do not violate their deeply held beliefs.

Opponents argue that the bills would authorize discrimination under the guise of religious liberty, allowing believers to opt out of laws they don't like in ways that harm others, particularly gay, lesbian and transgender people.

The competing sides clashed Wednesday in the House State Ag...

said the bill was designed to keep faith-based organizations – which account for about 25 percent of child-placement agencies – open and providing a desperately needed service for a vulnerable population.

"It is not a license to discriminate. It is, I believe, a license to participate in the foster care system," Frank said, adding that HB 3859 would allow faith-based groups to continue operating without compromising their religious values.

Opponents said Frank's bill seeks to elevate the requirements of religious groups over the needs of the children they should be serving.

"The primary point seems to be to allow organizations to use religious belief to justify discrimination against LGBT children or famil...

State Rep. Byron Cook, R-Corsicana, chairman of the committee, confronted several opponents, saying Frank's bill was a necessary option.

"These children are coming in from bad situations. We need more folks who are willing to be part of the fostering system, not less," he said.

A second bill that seeks to accommodate religious belief will be heard Thursday by the Senate State Affairs Committee.

Senate Bill 522 by Sen. Brian Birdwell, R-Granbury, would let county clerks opt out of providing marriage licenses to same-sex couples if they have religious objections to gay marriage. Before opting out, the cler...

Marouf v. Becerra (2018-ongoing)

Fatma Marouf and Bryn Esplin knew they wanted children. When they became aware of the enormous need for foster parents to care for unaccompanied refugee children in Texas, they decided to apply. The U.S. Office of Refugee Resettlement (ORR) is responsible for unaccompanied refugee children. It regularly contracts with the U.S. Conference of Catholic Bishops (USCCB) to provide care. USCCB then subcontracts with local organizations around the nation. In Fort Worth, Texas, the subcontractor was Catholic Charities of Fort Worth (CCFW). Fatma and Bryn reached out to CCFW, but during their initial meeting in early 2017, CCFW staff told them they did not "qualify" because foster parents must "mirror the Holy Family." They were shocked, but Fatma rallied and suggested that they foster LGBTQ+ children. The CCFW staff responded that there were no such children among the 700 young refugees needing homes.

Fatma contacted ORR repeatedly to report CCFW's discriminatory behavior and seek a workaround. She never got a meaningful response. So, in 2018, Lambda Legal sued USCCB and the Department of Health and Human Services (HHS), which oversees ORR. The following year, the Trump administration granted special permission for federally funded programs to discriminate based on their religious beliefs. Lambda Legal and our movement partners fought back and, in 2021, the Biden administration withdrew those permissions.

The Biden Administration, however, continues to partner with USCCB, despite knowing that its discriminatory actions reduce the number of available homes for children and send damaging messages to LGBTQ+ children and adults alike. Instead of enforcing federal nondiscrimination rules, HHS is attempting to resolve our case by creating a separate program for LGBTQ+ adults wishing to be foster parents, while allowing USCCB to continue to run the overall system in a discriminatory manner. Our litigation continues as this book goes to print.

The Holy Family of Nazareth, a print in the Popular Graphic Arts series at the Library of Congress, 1883. Artist unknown.

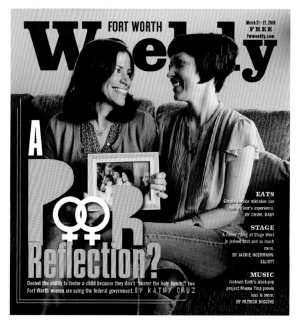

Easter v. HHS (2021-2022)

Kelly Easter's story shows how unpredictable and idiosyncratic religious agencies' doctrines can be, and why they must not be allowed to drive discrimination in public programs. Like Fatma and Bryn, Kelly wanted to provide a home to a refugee child. In 2020, she approached Bethany Christian Services, the subgrantee of USCCB in East Nashville, Tennessee, but was rejected because of her sexual orientation. Like Fatma and Bryn, she reported the foster care agency to ORR with no success. But then Bethany Christian's national leadership announced that it would begin accepting LGBTQ+ families. Kelly tried again, only to be told in the summer of 2021 that she was still ineligible because Bethany was subject to USCCB's rules and USCCB excluded LGBTQ+ people.

Together with Americans United for Separation of Church and State, we sued HHS on Kelly's behalf. In early 2022, however, USCCB stated that there had been a misunderstanding and that single LGBTQ+ adults were not barred from fostering; only married, same-sex couples. Kelly is now officially licensed as a foster parent with Bethany Christian Services, but she does not know whether she will still be permitted to foster children if she becomes partnered. Lambda Legal will be by her side if that day comes.

> "I know that LGBTQ+ people can have thriving families and that they are as important and deserving as any other. . . . [H]ow can the government tell me that my beliefs are wrong while denying vulnerable children the right to caring and stable homes?"

–KELLY EASTER

Rogers v. HHS (2019-ongoing)

While foster care through the Refugee Resettlement Program is run entirely by the federal government, most foster care programs are run by state governments. They, too, contract with religiously affiliated organizations to provide foster care to children in crisis.

Miracle Hill Ministries is South Carolina's largest state-contracted foster care agency for licensing foster care parents in Greenville. When Eden Rogers and Brandy Welch, who were already raising two young children, decided to expand their family through fostering in 2019, they turned to Miracle Hill, which rejected them because they didn't meet the agency's religious criteria, which require prospective foster parents to be evangelical Protestants and "have a lifestyle that is free of sexual sin."

Unknown to Eden and Brandy, South Carolina officials had already determined that Miracle Hill was violating both state and federal nondiscrimination rules. But in 2018, instead of enforcing the law, South Carolina had requested and received HHS permission to distribute federal child welfare funds to agencies that discriminate based on religion and sexual orientation.

Lambda Legal joined with the ACLU to sue HHS and various South Carolina defendants in federal court on Eden and Brandy's behalf. As of June 2023, we have defeated multiple government attempts to get the case dismissed. After the Biden administration withdrew the permission-to-discriminate the Trump administration had earlier granted South Carolina, we dismissed the federal government from the case. We are now exchanging legal arguments with South Carolina and seeking an order that it cannot continue this discrimination.

Our litigation in this area always benefits from the deep knowledge and professional network of our Youth in Out-of-Home Care Project staff. Read more about their accomplishments in Chapter 9.

Nathaniel Cary Greenville News
USA TODAY NETWORK – SOUTH CAROLINA

President Donald Trump's administration, South Carolina Gov. Henry McMaster and the state Department of Social Services face a federal lawsuit filed by a married lesbian couple over the religious exemption granted to Miracle Hill Ministries that allows the organization to exclude prospective foster parents who aren't evangelical Protestant Christians or don't meet the organization's religious policies, including same-sex couples.

Eden Rogers, 33, and Brandy Welch, 40, a Greenville couple who have been married for three years and have two daughters, ages 7 and 10, said their application to foster through Miracle Hill in Greenville was rejected based on their religion and their sexual orientation. They are members of Greenville Unitarian Universalist Church.

"We work hard to raise our own two girls in a loving and stable home," Welch said in a prepared statement. "Faith is a part of our family life, so it is hurtful and insulting to us that Miracle Hill's religious view of what a family must look like deprives foster children of a nurturing, supportive home."

Miracle Hill received about $600,000 last fiscal year from the state Department of Social Services to assist in paying care coordinators after the state

asked the religious nonprofit organization to expand its foster-care program to recruit more foster parents, said Sandy Furnell, Miracle Hill spokeswoman.

In January, South Carolina was granted a religious exemption by the U.S. Department of Health and Human Services to continue its faith-based foster care program. The organization's policy came under scrutiny soon after President Obama implemented a new regulation for recipients of federal funding before he left office that no longer allowed discrimination based on religion.

McMaster had requested an exemption on Miracle Hill's behalf in March 2018.

See FOSTER, Page 3A

Rogers and Welch during a press conference about a lawsuit against HHS and the state of South Carolina for discriminating against same-sex foster parents.

> "There are children waiting for homes who don't have to be waiting. If there's anything I can do to try to make the situation better for the kids . . . then I'm going to do it."
>
> **—EDEN ROGERS**

(left) Eden and Brandy at case launch press conference with Lambda Legal's Currey Cook behind. *The Greenville News*, June 12, 2019.

(opposite) Brandy and Eden with their children.

INTERLUDE.
THE LEGAL HELP DESK:
OUR EYES AND EARS ON
COMMUNITY LEGAL NEEDS

Members of our community have been asking Lambda Legal for information and guidance since Bill Thom installed a separate phone line in his apartment to accept calls in 1973. As Lambda Legal's name recognition grew, so did the requests for help. In recent years, the numbers have fluctuated between 5,000 and 7,000 calls annually. That's a lot of calls.

Those calls concern many subjects. Many are about diverse problems affecting LGBTQ+ people and people living with HIV but that do not clearly involve the discrimination issues that Lambda Legal exists to address. Other callers do need help with discrimination problems. However, Lambda Legal is an impact litigator, not a direct services agency. That means we search carefully for cases that we think might have the potential to achieve changes in the law to benefit many people. Nonetheless, whatever the problem our callers describe, the Help Desk team strives to provide helpful information to people who are often stressed, frustrated, and confused about the legal options available to them.

The Help Desk also serves several other important functions. Calls offer us a constant flow of information about the problems our community members are encountering. We use this information in many ways. It is invaluable for our legislative advocacy and our friend-of-the-court briefs. Calls also serve as an early warning system about when particular forms of discrimination are becoming more or less prominent.

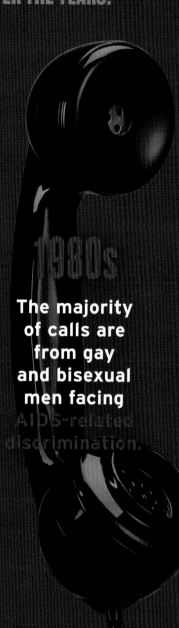

HOW HELP DESK CALLS HAVE CHANGED OVER THE YEARS:

1980s

The majority of calls are from gay and bisexual men facing AIDS-related discrimination.

FROM CALLER TO CLIENT

Knowing what problems are on the horizon helps us to set our priorities to maximize our impact. And every so often, a caller presents issues and facts that we think can help drive significant change for our community. Here are some examples:

Robina Asti
Trans Equality
(See Chapter 6)

Matthew Cusick
HIV Discrimination
(See Chapter 2)

Lydia Ramos
Parenting Rights
(See Chapter 5)

Our Help Desk staffing has changed over the years. For many years we depended on dedicated volunteers, paralegals, and non-attorney Help Desk specialists. With additional resources, we have been able to staff the Desk with four full-time attorneys who have broad knowledge of legal issues of relevance to LGBTQ+ people and skill at responding to people in crisis.

"The hardest part for the Help Desk staff is receiving calls from people who are experiencing difficult and painful legal problems, and having to tell them that we can only offer them information and can't directly represent them. On the other hand, it's so satisfying to see a Help Desk call mature into an actual Lambda Legal case, and the ultimate is to see that case come to a successful ending for the caller."

—STEFAN JOHNSON, HELP DESK ATTORNEY AND DIRECTOR (1998-2022)

1990s

We saw increasing numbers of calls about parental rights, primarily from lesbian mothers seeking to create legal relationships with their children via adoption or maintain custody of their children after a breakup.

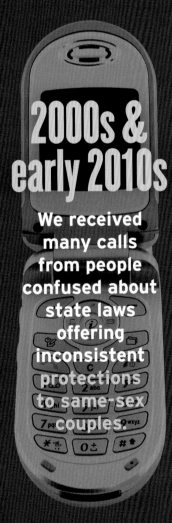

2000s & early 2010s

We received many calls from people confused about state laws offering inconsistent protections to same-sex couples.

2020s

The number of calls related to new state laws cutting off the rights of transgender and nonbinary people has skyrocketed.

LambdaLegal.org/helpdesk
(212) 809-8585

FROM LAMBDA LEGAL'S HELP DESK: OUR EYES AND EARS ON COMMUNITY LEGAL NEEDS

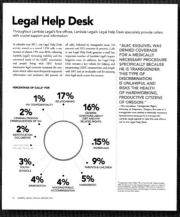

We track data about Help Desk calls on an annual basis, and periodically publish a breakdown of the data by category in order to inform community members and policy makers about the legal issues LGBTQ+ people are facing. We did a deeper dive into the data in 2021 to help guide congressional consideration of federal nondiscrimination legislation.

The resulting publication examined calls made in 2020, a year in which we received 4,468 calls for help. Of those calls, roughly 30% were requests for information and research or about topics that fall outside the kinds of discrimination we address, so our discrimination analysis does not include them.

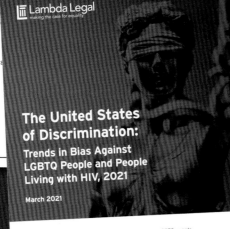

(above) Lambda Legal Annual Report pages detailing annual Help Desk call data from various years.

2020 KEY FINDINGS ON ANTI-LGBTQ+ DISCRIMINATION:

Anti-LGBTQ+ discrimination remains ubiquitous. We received calls from all 50 states, the District of Columbia and Puerto Rico.

Anti-LGBTQ+ discrimination cuts across socioeconomic boundaries. In 2020, callers reported the following income ranges:

33%	33%	32%
< $20K	$20K-$60K	> $60K

2023 HELP DESK DATA

TOP ISSUE AREAS

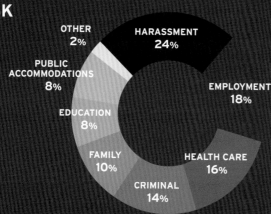

- OTHER 2%
- HARASSMENT 24%
- PUBLIC ACCOMMODATIONS 8%
- EMPLOYMENT 18%
- EDUCATION 8%
- FAMILY 10%
- HEALTH CARE 16%
- CRIMINAL 14%

CALLS BY GENDER

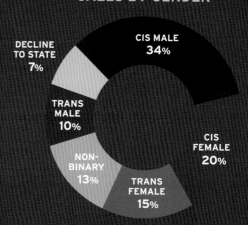

- DECLINE TO STATE 7%
- CIS MALE 34%
- TRANS MALE 10%
- NON-BINARY 13%
- CIS FEMALE 20%
- TRANS FEMALE 15%

202

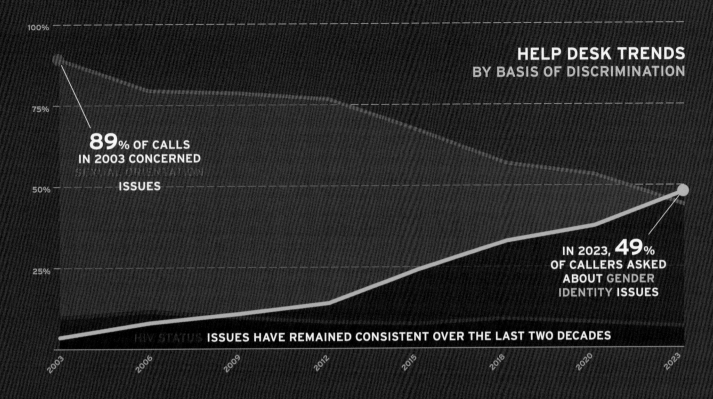

HELP DESK TRENDS
BY BASIS OF DISCRIMINATION

89% OF CALLS IN 2003 CONCERNED SEXUAL ORIENTATION ISSUES

IN 2023, **49**% OF CALLERS ASKED ABOUT GENDER IDENTITY ISSUES

HIV STATUS ISSUES HAVE REMAINED CONSISTENT OVER THE LAST TWO DECADES

100%

75%

50%

25%

2003 · 2006 · 2009 · 2012 · 2015 · 2018 · 2020 · 2023

"The calls for help are a barometer of the climate for our community. Recently, the targeting of trans and nonbinary people has been overt and intense, and our data confirm the scale of the impact we've been sensing from callers. After years of increasing calls about gender identity discrimination, those requests in 2023 actually surpassed sexual orientation help requests. It's a devastating measure of our community's trauma."

–HUONG LAM, LEGAL HELP DESK DIRECTOR

II

117TH CONGRESS
1ST SESSION

S. 393

To prohibit discrimination on the basis of sex, gender identity, and sexual orientation, and for other purposes.

IN THE SENATE OF THE UNITED STATES

FEBRUARY 23, 2021

Mr. BALDWIN, Mr. BOOKER, Mr. BENNET, Mr. CARDIN, Mr. CARPER,

A BILL

To prohibit discrimination on the basis of sex, gender identity, and sexual orientation, and for other purposes.

1   *Be it enacted by the Senate and House of Representa-*
2   *tives of the United States of America in Congress assembled,*
3   **SECTION 1. SHORT TITLE.**
4   This Act may be cited as the "Equality Act".

To prohibit discrimination on the basis of sex, gender identity, and sexual orientation, and for other purposes.

1   *Be it enacted by the Senate and House of Representa-*
2   *tives of the United States of America in Congress assembled,*

Lambda
Legal

The Honorable Richard J. Durbin
The Honorable Chuck Grassley
Members of the Senate Committee on the Judiciary
March 24, 2021, Page 14

A. Anti-LGBTQ Discrimination in the Private Sector

Employment Discrimination

Throughout this period, we consistently received more calls regarding anti-LGBTQ workplace discrimination than any other single issue, with the inquiries totaling just under ,000. These calls included:

- the Arizona psychiatrist fired when his boss learned he is gay, with the boss calling him "a sinner who would compound his sins to his eternal peril" and a "vile sociopath."
- the California woman who is a teacher and transgender, who repeatedly was told to cut her hair and not to wear a skirt, and then had her contract not renewed.
- the gay Georgia man who was working for McKesson and then was fired upon reporting harassment based on his sexual orientation.
- the transgender woman working at a car detail shop in Illinois, who was told she was not allowed to transition socially on the job.
- the New Mexico lesbian who was told by her supervisor that she "should be sucking dick because of Adam and Eve."
- the Omaha, Nebraska resident who was promoted repeatedly until he came out as a transgender man, after which he was passed over nine times.
- the transgender woman hired by the Boys and Girls Club of Greensboro, North Carolina based on her application papers filled out with her legal name (which was still male), for whom the job offer was revoked when her transgender identity was understood.
- the auto insurance agent in Texas who had been steadily climbing within the business until she came out as a transgender women, at which point co-worker harassment began and escalated until she felt driven out.

dition, numerous examples of discrimination in public sector employment are page 25-26 below.

ver, based on our experience with our Legal Help Desk, we can say with t the approximately 5,000 help request figure understates the problem. Over ave learned many reasons why employees choose not to seek legal guidance cluding that many have known that legal remedies are limited in their d many others are afraid to disclose their LGBTQ identity and thus refrain dering legal action.

 more, this issue's resonance goes far beyond numbers. People define e part by the work they do. They spend significant portions of their time in

---

HELPING POLICYMAKERS

Help Desk data has been invaluable in our policy advocacy. This material—both aggregate data and specific examples of real problems reported to us by real people—has been presented to Congress to inform federal legislation, to agencies to show why we need better rules, to allies in states opposing attacks, and to courts in our amicus briefs. The diversity and large numbers make this data set unique and priceless in our policy development and advocacy.

CHAPTER 9

IMPERFECT INSTITUTIONS

MANAGING IN AND REFORMING OUR LEGAL SYSTEMS

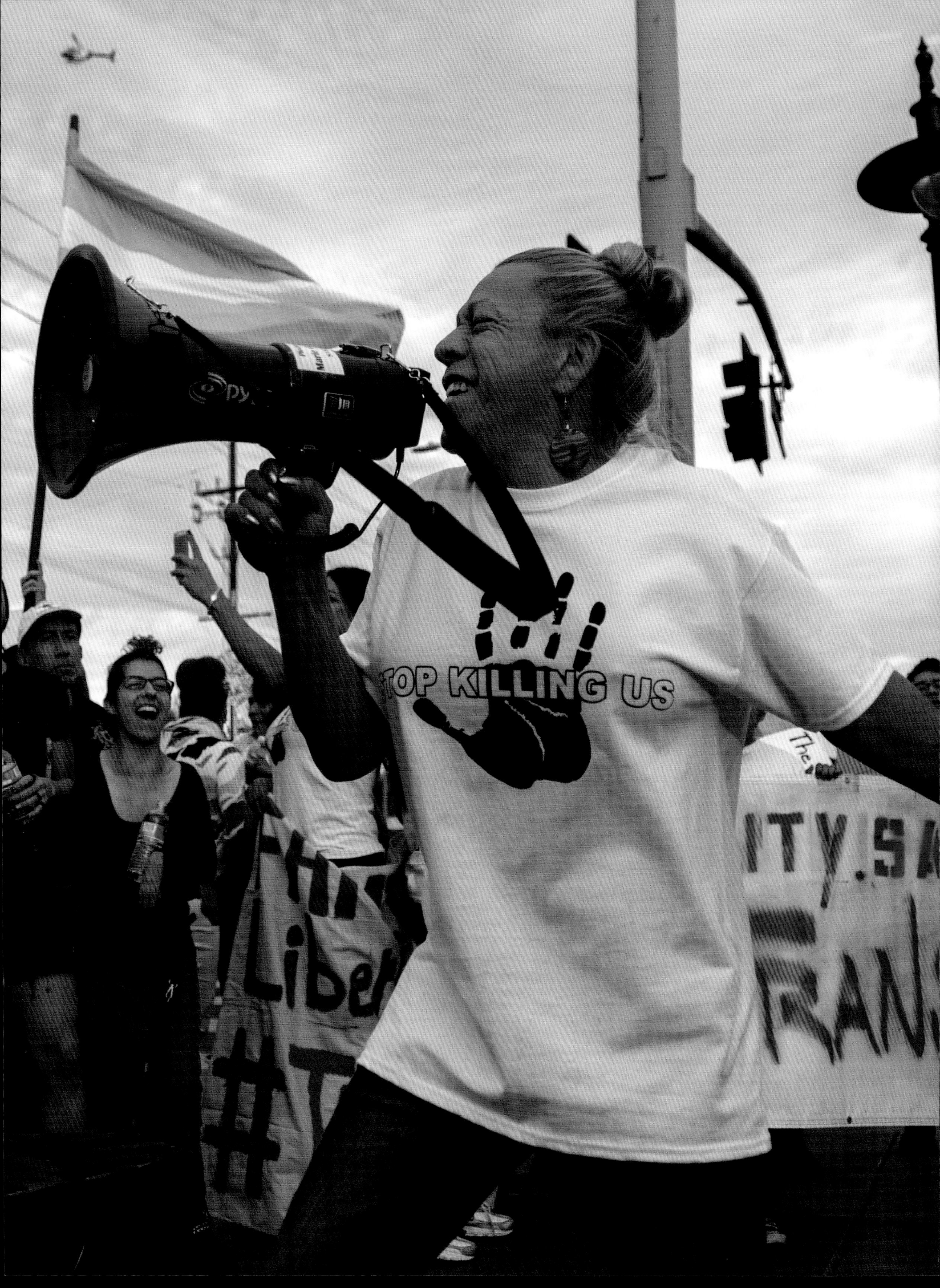
TOP KILLING US

f bigotry and discriminatory laws have burdened LGBTQ+ people and people living with HIV, the burdens are even greater for people living in settings where institutional authorities exert outsized control over their lives—settings like immigration, policing and prisons, child welfare, and courtrooms. Discrimination and bigotry there often take place out of public view, and the challenges are less familiar to outsiders. Lambda Legal has worked extensively to make these challenges visible and to demand accountability from the government.

(opposite) Bamby Salcedo, president and CEO of the TransLatin@ Coalition, speaking at a rally. TransLatin@ Coalition is one of Lambda Legal's clients in *Immigration Equality v. U.S. Department of Homeland Security*.

(page 204) Ola Osaze came to the U.S. as a refugee when he was 15 years old. The organization he directs, Black LGBTQIA+ Migrant Project, was a plaintiff in our lawsuit to stop the Trump administration's anti-asylum rule.

WELCOMING REFUGEES FLEEING ANTI-LGBTQ+ PERSECUTION

American immigration laws have long offered safe haven to people fleeing persecution in their home country based on their political opinions, religion, race, ethnicity, or membership in a "particular social group" (PSG) that is viewed by the home country government as a threat or is condemned socially or culturally in ways that lead to targeted abuse. The definition of PSG has evolved over time but has traditionally been applied to members of groups that share a common characteristic that is so basic to their identity that they can't or shouldn't be expected to change. Former gang members, political activists, and others have qualified. Until the 1990s, LGBTQ+ people did not. Our efforts helped change that.

"Many transgender and gender-nonconforming Latinx people face unimaginable violence, persecution, and torture around the world. Most transgender women who seek refuge from these threats in the United States have nowhere else to go. The survival of so many depends on finding a safe haven in this country."

—BAMBY SALCEDO, PRESIDENT & CEO OF TRANSLATIN@ COALITION, A LAMBDA LEGAL CLIENT

(left) LGBTQ+ refugees seeking asylum due to persecution in Venezuela march in New York City Pride, 2023.

(opposite) Honduran Alexa Amaya, traveling with a group of LGBTQ+ migrants hoping to reach the U.S. border. "I know it will be difficult to win asylum," she said, "but we have to make the attempt," 2018.

EVERY DAY
LESBIANS AND
GAY MEN ARE
FIRED
EVICTED
ARRESTED
DEPORTED.

Lambda
Legal
Defense
and Education
Fund, Inc.

"As persecution of LGBTQ individuals continues abroad, like persecution based on one's ethnic or racial background or religious or political views, the United States must welcome refugees fleeing prejudice-based violence in their homelands as our laws require."

—CARMINA OCAMPO, OUR FORMER IMMIGRANTS' RIGHTS STRATEGIST

Pitcherskaia v. Immigration and Naturalization Service (1993-1998)

Alla Pitcherskaia emigrated from Russia to the United States in 1992. In her home country, government agents had harassed, beaten, and detained her, and organized crime syndicates had persecuted her, because she had self-identified as a lesbian and engaged in LGBTQ+ civil rights advocacy. She believed that if she returned to Russia, she would be put into a "reeducation" center, where electric shock would be used to "cure" her, or worse. In 1993, she requested asylum. The U.S. government denied her request, and then her appeal of that denial within the immigration courts. That's when Lambda Legal stepped in to file a federal appeal. At the time, no federal appeals court had ever considered persecution based on sexual orientation as a basis for political asylum.

In June 1997, we won a breakthrough ruling from the Ninth Circuit. It said that lesbians and gay men who suffer violence in their homelands need not prove malicious intent if their persecutors claim they are helping gay people by inflicting forced psychiatric hospitalization, electroshock therapy, or drugs. The unanimous appellate panel said: "Human rights laws cannot be sidestepped simply by couching torture in benevolent terms such as 'curing' or 'treating' the victim." The ruling opened a new chapter of hope for immigrants like Alla who seek asylum due to sexual orientation-based persecution in their home countries.

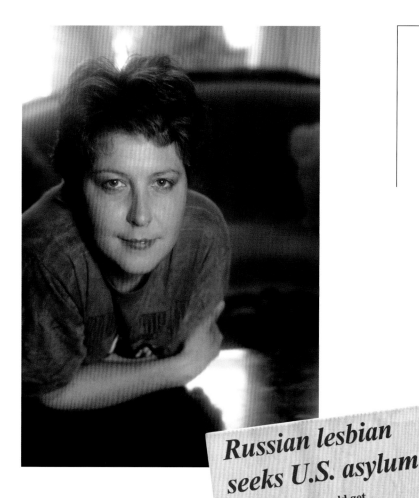

"The court recognized the cruelty and discrimination in government anti-gay persecution, regardless of the excuses that governments may give."

—SUZANNE B. GOLDBERG, OUR ATTORNEY ON *PITCHERSKAIA*

Russian lesbian seeks U.S. asylum
Lawyer says she could get electroshock if returned home

(far left) Alla Pitcherskaia

In re Soto Vega (2002-2007)

In his hometown of Tuxpan, Mexico, Jorge Soto Vega's family and neighbors routinely harassed him because he was gay. Then the police abducted, beat, and sexually assaulted him, using anti-gay slurs and threatening to kill him if they saw him again. Jorge knew he had to get away. He fled to the United States and requested asylum, but his claim was denied. The immigration judge agreed that Jorge had been persecuted because of his sexuality, but also decided that Jorge didn't "look gay." To the judge, that meant Jorge could have hidden his gay identity and avoided the abuse, and that he could do so upon being returned to Mexico. After an immigration appeals court affirmed this decision, Lambda Legal spotted the legal error: our laws do not require people to avoid persecution by hiding. We took on Jorge's case to make that argument to the federal appeals court. We also pointed out that the Mexican police had identified Jorge as gay despite the U.S. immigration judge's perceptions and assumptions. The Ninth Circuit was persuaded and overruled the immigration courts.

That ruling returned the case to the immigration judge to reconsider whether Jorge had reasonable cause to fear persecution if returned to Mexico. This time, the judge applied the rule that no one should have to hide their sexual orientation to be safe and concluded that nowhere in Mexico was safe for Jorge. He was granted asylum in 2007.

The Ninth Circuit decision reinforced the foundation for asylum claims based on anti-gay persecution and made clear that our immigration laws do not require LGBTQ+ people to live in the closet to stay alive.

> "Many of Lambda Legal's victories bring sweeping changes in the law. While this one did not, it was one of my sweetest victories. I will never forget my client hugging me in tears afterwards and asking, 'so does this mean I can now stay in the U.S.?'"

–JON DAVIDSON, OUR LEAD COUNSEL FOR JORGE SOTO VEGA

(above) Jorge Soto Vega

(left) *Los Angeles Times*, January 31, 2007

Gay Mexican immigrant is granted asylum

Reversing an earlier decision, a judge rules that Jorge Soto Vega would be subject to persecution in his homeland.

By TAMI ABDOLLAH
Times Staff Writer

An immigration judge granted a Mexican immigrant asylum, citing his sexual orientation and persecution of gays in...

co since "it would not be obvious that he was homosexual unless he made it obvious himself."

The case was returned to Taylor after the U.S. 9th Circuit Court of Appeals ruled it is the government's responsibility to prove Soto Vega had no "well-founded fear of persecution" in Mexico.

At the hearing Tuesday, the judge agreed that a person should not have to conceal his or her sexual orientation in order to be free from persecution, said Jon W. Davidson, legal director at Lambda Legal, a nonprofit gay-rights group. The U.S. Immigration and Customs Enforce-

Immigration Equality v. U.S. Department of Homeland Security (2020-ongoing)

In the final weeks of 2020, the Trump administration issued a new rule severely limiting access to asylum. At the time there were more than 70 countries in the world where it was a crime, or extremely unsafe, to be LGBTQ+ or HIV-positive, including places where sodomy is punishable by death. Under the new restrictions, refugees would have to apply for asylum in the first country they entered on their way to the U.S., whether or not that country was safe for them. Spending more than two weeks in any nation while in transit to the U.S. would also bar refugees from receiving asylum. The new rule would have made it virtually impossible for LGBTQ+ people, those living with HIV, and others to secure asylum in the U.S., contrary to longstanding American law. That's why we called it the "Death to Asylum" rule. We joined with our partners at Immigration Equality and others to challenge it, filing our case in federal court within days of the rule's release in December 2020. In January 2021, just before the rule was to take effect, the court blocked the rule in its entirety. The case remains pending while the Biden administration develops a replacement rule.

"This rule was among the Trump administration's relentless efforts to close our doors to migrants, including refugees escaping persecution. It was rooted in xenophobia and cruelty, and also was an attempt to force an overhaul of our entire asylum system, in defiance of the law. Lives were at stake, so we were hugely relieved when the court put the policy on hold."

—OMAR GONZALEZ-PAGAN, OUR LEAD ATTORNEY ON *IMMIGRATION EQUALITY*

"These rules from the Trump
administration were obviously aimed
at eradicating asylum for migrants
who are Black, LGBTQIA+, and/or
women. They would have created a
level of chaos that would further
endanger people whose lives and
safety are already so precarious."

—OLA OSAZE, DIRECTOR OF PLAINTIFF BLACK
LGBTQIA+ MIGRANT PROJECT

Arizona v. United States (2012)

Our immigration work doesn't end at the border. It also has included challenging anti-immigrant laws that affect people living in the United States, including citizens and lawful permanent residents, who are assumed by hostile law enforcement to lack legal status based on perceptions of their appearance. We know that LGBTQ+ and HIV-positive people of color, no matter what their citizenship or immigration status, are at heightened risk of abuse, that anti-immigrant sentiment comes in cycles, and that LGBTQ+ immigrants and refugees are among our most marginalized community members. We oppose these biases and seek to prevent abuses of power by American law enforcement by partnering with community leaders and advocates who challenge discrimination based on perceptions of others' identities and national origins.

That's why we joined the litigation against Arizona's notorious 2010 anti-immigrant law, SB 1070. Among other things, the law required state and local police to ask anyone seen as suspicious to produce documents showing lawful presence in the United States. It quickly came to be known as the "Papers, please" law, and as a tool for police harassment of people based on racial and ethnic stereotypes. We joined leading civil rights groups in asking the U.S. Supreme Court to block SB 1070 because it would lead to the abuse of people lawfully in the United States, interfere with the rights of asylum seekers and crime victims (who might fear going to the police), and otherwise violate federal law. In 2012, the Court struck down most of the law and made clear that any abusive police practices could be subject to future litigation.

"Undocumented LGBT immigrants are among the most invisible of the invisible. Many inhabit a double closet, afraid of disclosing their sexual orientation and/or gender identity and afraid of disclosing that they are undocumented."

—FRANCISCO DUEÑAS, OUR FORMER PROYECTO IGUALDAD DIRECTOR

(opposite, top) Protestors at the "We Are All Arizona" March in New York City, protesting SB 1070, July 29, 2010.

(opposite, bottom) Demonstrators protesting in front of the Immigration and Customs Enforcement (ICE) offices in Phoenix, June 25, 2012.

"The LGBT community knows all too well how easily people who are perceived to 'look different' or 'act different' can be singled out for harassment and persecution."

–IVÁN ESPINOZA-MADRIGAL, OUR ATTORNEY ON *ARIZONA V. UNITED STATES*

CHALLENGING INJUSTICE IN THE CRIMINAL LEGAL SYSTEM

We are a community inspired by the stories of Stonewall, Compton's Cafeteria, and many other protests against police misconduct. Our history teaches us that the criminal legal system has been used again and again to surveil, criminalize, and harass LGBTQ+ people and people living with HIV. Lambda Legal has a proud history of pushing back against abuses of carceral authority. We know that when biases—including anti-LGBTQ+ biases—infect decisions about how police power is exercised, those with little or no ability to object can pay an unconscionable price. In Chapter 1, we discussed our challenge to police misconduct in the form of police harassment (*Calhoun v. Pennington*) and callous indifference (*Brandon v. Richardson*). We touched on our efforts to end unconscionable solitary confinement practices (*Roe v. Precythe*) in Chapter 2. Here we open a window into additional facets of this work, including our efforts to stem police violence and to ensure that inmates receive appropriate medical care.

REINING IN ANTI-LGBTQ+ BRUTALITY BY POLICE AND PRISON GUARDS

Mackler v. City of Los Angeles (1992-1997)

On September 29, 1991, California Governor Pete Wilson vetoed a bill to outlaw sexual orientation discrimination in employment. The veto infuriated LGBTQ+ community members because Wilson had campaigned on his support for such a law. At that time, the Los Angeles Police Department (LAPD) was nationally notorious for its racist and homophobic tactics.

Peter Mackler encountered that bigotry firsthand when he joined the L.A. protest. It was peaceful until LAPD officers decided to forcibly clear the area. Officer David Peck was among them. He prodded Peter repeatedly in the back, prompting Peter to turn around and ask for Peck's badge number. Peck responded by smashing Peter in the face with his baton, which knocked him to the ground and broke his glasses. Two other officers grabbed Peter by the hands and feet, threw him out of the way, and left him bleeding.

Peter sued the LAPD, arguing that Officer Peck reacted with violence because of Peter's sexuality and politics, and because he tried to get Peck's badge number or name. Lambda Legal joined the ACLU of Southern California in representing him. It took five years of legal wrangling to get access to internal police records and video recordings of the demonstration. Once we finally obtained them, the city blinked, settling on the courthouse steps. It agreed to pay Peter $87,000 and to clarify its policy that LAPD officers must give their name or badge number when asked and must not retaliate.

> "I saw the venom in Officer Peck's face. He did that because I was gay and was wearing a gay rights sweatshirt and had asked for his badge number."[61]
>
> —PETER MACKLER

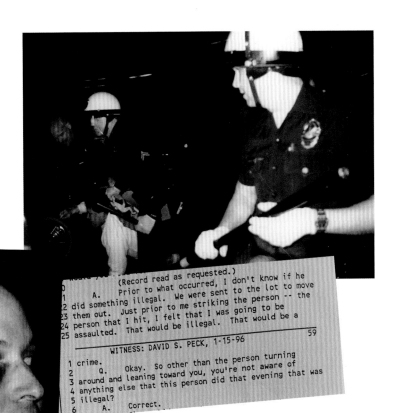

(left) Peter's face after being assaulted.

(top) Peter being forcibly hauled away by LAPD officers.

(above) Transcript of David Peck's deposition. Lambda Legal attorney Jon Davidson is asking the question.

(far left) Our client, Jessica Hicklin, on the day of her release from prison.

217

Hamm v. City of New York (2015-2018)

Like Peter, Thomas Hamm's only "crime" was being a gay man coming face-to-face with bullies with a badge. He was visiting his long-term partner, P.F. at a men's prison facility on Rikers Island in New York City. New York Department of Correction (DOC) rules expressly allow inmates and visitors to "kiss, embrace, and hold hands," as others around them were doing. But when P.F. greeted Thomas with a hug and a kiss, corrections officers ordered them to separate. The two men then sat down and quietly held hands until the officers called them "faggots," ordered them to stop, and abruptly ended the visit. As Thomas prepared to leave, the officers taunted him and then brutally beat him while he begged them to stop. Afterwards, he was taken by ambulance to a local hospital where he was diagnosed with facial fractures and head trauma and held overnight. Officers shackled him to his bed. He was then brought back to Rikers, where he was banned from the facility for 180 days and falsely charged with having assaulted the officers! No mention was made of Thomas's injuries or the implausibility of the 5'6" visitor posing a threat to the multiple, much larger officers who beat him.

We saw this as a particularly important case because abuse of LGBTQ+ people held in carceral facilities remains a pervasive problem and it often is impossible for the victims to get redress. Our federal lawsuit argued that the officers had violated the U.S. Constitution, the New York Constitution, and the state's human rights law. Three years later, in 2018, we secured a settlement which included $280,000 in monetary damages, a public affirmation of DOC's nondiscrimination policy, and training for Rikers officers on that policy.

"I went to visit my partner but ended up being assaulted in the visitors' room by corrections officers because I'm gay. They beat me severely. I'll carry the physical scars from the facial fractures forever, but the larger scars of anti-gay violence are what I hope to begin to heal with this settlement."

–THOMAS HAMM

"No one—not an inmate or a visitor—forfeits the right to safety when passing through the gates of a jail or prison."

–OMAR GONZALEZ-PAGAN, ONE OF OUR ATTORNEYS ON *HAMM*

(above) Thomas with his partner, P.F.

PRISON DENIALS OF NECESSARY MEDICAL CARE

Fields v. Smith (2006-2012)

Wisconsin opened a new era of discrimination in 2005 when it passed the Inmate Sex Change Prevention Act, a first-in-the-nation law requiring its Department of Corrections to stop providing gender-affirming medical care to transgender inmates. The law barred access to both hormone therapy and medically necessary surgery for everyone held in state custody who had been diagnosed with gender dysphoria.

Lambda Legal joined with the ACLU and the ACLU of Wisconsin to challenge the law on behalf of three transgender women who lost access to their hormone treatment when the law took effect. When a person is held in government custody, the government must provide access to medically necessary care. In *Fields v. Smith*,[55] we argued that gender dysphoria is a serious medical need and that failure to appropriately treat it violated the Eighth Amendment's prohibition on cruel and unusual punishment as well as the Fourteenth Amendment's guarantee of equal protection of the law.

The federal district court agreed, striking down the law as unconstitutional under both amendments. Wisconsin appealed, but the Seventh Circuit unanimously upheld the district court's decision. The state then sought review from the U.S. Supreme Court, which declined to hear the case, thereby cementing our victory.

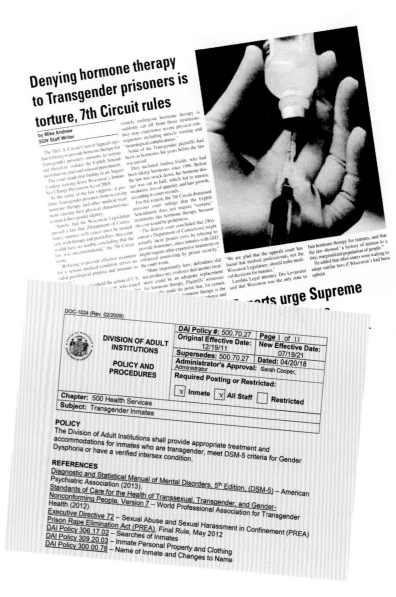

> "Surely, had the Wisconsin Legislature passed a law that DOC inmates with cancer must be treated only with therapy and pain killers, this court would have no trouble concluding that the law was unconstitutional. Refusing to provide effective treatment for a serious medical condition serves no valid penological purpose and amounts to torture."

–U.S. DISTRICT JUDGE JOAN B. GOTTSCHALL, SITTING BY DESIGNATION[62] ON *FIELDS*

(above) *Seattle Gay News,* August 12, 2011

Hicklin v. Precythe (2016-2018)

Jessica Hicklin is a transgender woman who was convicted of first-degree murder when she was just 16 years old. She had been suffering from paranoia due to methamphetamine addiction and shot a friend after a drug deal went bad. She was sentenced to life without the possibility of parole.

Twenty-one years later, she was incarcerated in the Potosi Correctional Center, a men's prison in Missouri. Although she had struggled with gender dysphoria since childhood, she had only learned as an adult about transgender people. She sought medical care and was formally diagnosed by multiple mental health providers employed by the Missouri Department of Corrections (MDOC). They recommended hormone therapy, permanent hair removal, and access to gender-affirming canteen items. But these recommendations were denied because MDOC followed a then-common "freeze-frame" policy that barred access to medically necessary treatment for transgender people in custody who had not been receiving that treatment before incarceration.

We filed a lawsuit on Jessica's behalf, arguing that MDOC's refusal to provide medically necessary care was cruel and unusual punishment in violation of the Eighth Amendment.[56] The federal district court agreed with us, concluding that the freeze-frame policy was unconstitutional and ordering MDOC to discontinue it.

As for Jessica? Her sentence was reviewed due to unrelated Supreme Court decisions restricting the circumstances under which juveniles can be sentenced to life imprisonment without the possibility of parole.[57] And because she had used her years in prison impressively, her parole application had strong support. Among other things, she had taught herself software coding and co-founded Unlocked Labs, which trains incarcerated people in technical fields so they can get well-paying jobs upon release. Jessica was released in 2022 at the age of 42, and has continued to expand Unlocked Labs, which is considered a model program.

"I had no references for what it meant to be trans. Like, there was nobody around. I didn't know any trans folks. I'd never seen an image of one."[63]

–JESSICA HICKLIN

(opposite) Jessica at Unlocked Labs, which she co-founded.

"The decision was such a welcome relief. Forcing Jessica to go for so many years without medically necessary treatment was cruel and the source of a lot of pain and anguish for her."

—DEMOYA GORDON, ONE OF OUR ATTORNEYS ON *HICKLIN*

BEHIND THE SCENES

"One of my proudest moments was after representing Jessica Hicklin and winning one of the first court decisions that denying hormone therapy to someone who was not receiving it before incarceration is a violation of the Eighth Amendment. When Ms. Hicklin walked out of prison as a free woman after 26 years in custody, it was an unbelievable, memorable moment."
–Richard Saenz, one of our attorneys on *Hicklin*

PROTECTED AND SERVED?

In 2012, Lambda Legal published *Protected and Served?*, a first-of-its-kind study of government misconduct by police, prisons, school security, and courts in the United States against LGBTQ+ people and people living with HIV. Drawing on the results of a community survey, the report detailed shocking levels of abuse, especially for people of color and transgender people. Since that survey, awareness of the ways that the criminal legal system harms Black, Indigenous, and other people of color (BIPOC), LGBTQ+ people, and others who experience marginalization has grown significantly, and LGBTQ+ people and organizations have been at the forefront of the push to address this systemic violence against marginalized people in this country.

In 2022, we launched the second *Protected & Served?* community survey, in partnership with Black and Pink National.[58] Despite a decade of advocacy and publicized police reforms, the results were grim. About a quarter of the respondents reported having directly experienced police misconduct in the past five years, including verbal, physical, and sexual assault. These rates jumped for BIPOC, HIV-positive, and trans people, as well as for noncitizens and sex workers. More than 80% of respondents who had been incarcerated at some point during the past five years reported having been verbally assaulted by prison staff and over half reported sexual harassment. Nearly two-thirds of people who had been held in custody and were on medication, including hormone therapy and HIV medication, reported having missed it for two weeks or more. Respondents with marginalized identities consistently reported experiencing higher levels of misconduct. Unsurprisingly, those who had had face-to-face encounters with police often reported being less trusting of law enforcement as a result. Finally, as in 2012, the survey found pervasive racial bias and anti-LGBTQ+ treatment by court personnel, bigotry that has no place in a system that purports to mete out justice.

We know facts and data are essential when we challenge abusive misconduct by government against our communities and demand accountability. The results and targeted recommendations of *Protected & Served?* were designed to contribute to ongoing conversations about abolition and reform, two important movements seeking to end systemic oppression of marginalized communities in the name of "the law."

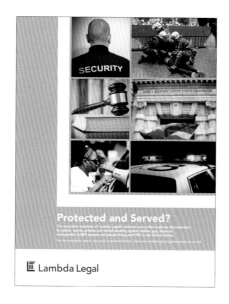

Protected and Served?

The executive summary of Lambda Legal's national survey that explores discrimination by police, courts, prisons and related security against lesbian, gay, bisexual, transgender (LGBT) people and people living with HIV in the United States.

For the complete report, visit and recommendations, visit www.lambdalegal.org/protected-and-served

Ⅲ Lambda Legal

BEHIND THE SCENES

"Protected and Served? has been a vital resource for understanding the experiences of our communities as we interact with the criminal legal system—and has been used to advocate for policy reforms and in litigation. It is urgent and imperative that we address the root causes and devastating consequences of the obscene levels of abuse, discrimination, and misconduct reported throughout the criminal legal system—and hold those responsible accountable."

—Richard Saenz, Senior Attorney and project manager for the 2023 edition of *Protected & Served?*

PROTECTED
&SERVED?
A community survey of LGBTQ+
people and people living with HIV

Negative Experiences in Court

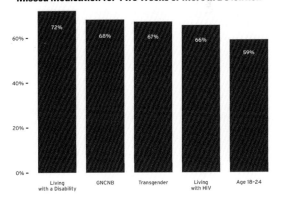

- 55% Used the Wrong Name or Pronoun (of TGNCNB)
- 30% Inappropriately Revealed Transgender Status (of Trans)
- 25% Inappropriately Revealed HIV Status (of Those Living with HIV)
- 17% Inappropriately Revealed Sexual Orientation (of LGBQ+)

Abuse Experiences in Prison

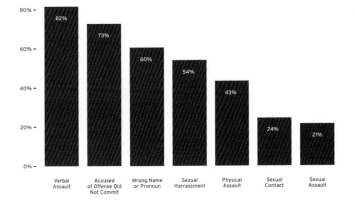

- 82% Verbal Assault
- 73% Accused of Offense Did Not Commit
- 60% Wrong Name or Pronoun
- 54% Sexual Harrassment
- 43% Physical Assault
- 24% Sexual Contact
- 21% Sexual Assault

Missed Medication for Two Weeks or More in Detention

- 72% Living with a Disability
- 68% GNCNB
- 67% Transgender
- 66% Living with HIV
- 59% Age 18-24

Police Behavior in Most Recent Face-to-Face Contact

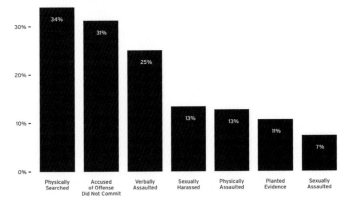

- 34% Physically Searched
- 31% Accused of Offense Did Not Commit
- 25% Verbally Assaulted
- 13% Sexually Harassed
- 13% Physically Assaulted
- 11% Planted Evidence
- 7% Sexually Assaulted

Transgender and GNCNB Participants Have Lower Levels of Trust in Local Police

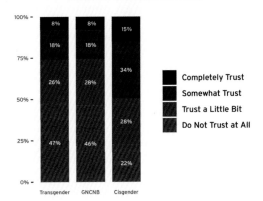

	Transgender	GNCNB	Cisgender
Completely Trust	8%	8%	15%
Somewhat Trust	18%	18%	34%
Trust a Little Bit	26%	28%	28%
Do Not Trust at All	47%	46%	22%

SECURING SAFETY, RESPECT, AND SUPPORT FOR LGBTQ+ YOUTH IN OUT-OF-HOME CARE

Lambda has advocated for LGBTQ+ youth in foster care, juvenile justice systems, and systems of care for unhoused children and young adults for more than twenty years. We have pushed governments to adopt non-discrimination policies and to enforce them. We have provided support through our Legal Help Desk. We have published resources for young people who are experiencing discrimination or who have questions about their rights. Here are some examples of this advocacy.

(below) Youth rally for safe and fair housing in San Francisco's Castro district, August 10, 2010.

Lesbian, gay, bisexual, transgender and questioning youth in foster care, juvenile justice systems and homeless shelters have rights:

- to feel safe
- to be free from discrimination because they are LGBTQ or living with HIV
- to have people accept them for who they are
- to have adults stick up for them

If you or someone you know needs help, call toll free:
1-866-LGBTeen
1-866-542-8336

Lambda Legal
making the case for equality

CWLA
CHILD WELFARE LEAGUE OF AMERICA

THE FOSTER CARE PROJECT

We began our dedicated work in this area in early 2000 by launching an initiative to address the needs of youth in child welfare systems. We started by focusing on the massive foster care systems maintained in every state and later expanded to juvenile justice systems and other institutions of out-of-home care for youth. Because LGBTQ+ young people are significantly overrepresented in these systems, and LGBTQ+ youth of color are especially so, we have called for systems that:

- ensure placement of LGBTQ+ youth in supportive homes free of verbal, physical and sexual abuse

- recognize and respect LGBTQ+ identity rather than treating expressions of such identities as a behavioral problem or moral failing to be corrected

- provide appropriate medical care, including HIV-prevention, safer-sex and reproductive health information, and gender-affirming medical care for youth experiencing severe gender dysphoria

> "Life in foster care is difficult for all young people, but for LGBT youth, that stress is compounded by anti-gay bias that increases risk for homelessness, HIV infection, substance abuse and suicide."
>
> **—COLLEEN SULLIVAN, OUR INAUGURAL FOSTER CARE PROJECT DIRECTOR**

(below, left) Rallying for safe and affordable housing in San Francisco, August 10, 2010.

(below, right) A young homeless person begging with his dog, 2005.

ASSESSING THE PROBLEM

Social work professionals have historically shied away from working with LGBTQ+ youth because of personal biases as well as the career-crushing stigma of working with this population. This has resulted in a lack of basic research. So we joined with a coalition of youth advocates and conducted a first-of-its-kind, fourteen-state survey, with the findings published in a groundbreaking report titled *Youth in the Margins* (2001).

The survey confirmed that LGBTQ+ youth in foster care systems were subjected to elevated rates of harassment and violence, not just by their peers and foster parents, but by child welfare professionals charged to care for and protect them. The report recommended crucial remedial measures for foster care systems to implement. Because no state foster care agencies had nondiscrimination policies to protect

LGBTQ+ young people and to require cultural competence training of staff, the report also recommended specific, systemwide reforms for states to adopt to prevent anti-gay abuse and to begin supporting LGBTQ+ youth in professionally sound ways. The report stressed that nondiscrimination polices must apply not just to government agencies, but also to the many private agencies that contract to care for children for whom the government is responsible. And the policies must protect not just children in care, but also adults who wish to serve as foster parents and child welfare staff who care for them.

In the more than two decades since the report, we have made priorities of its core findings and driven profound change by publishing model policies and best practices, conducting trainings, and advocating in courts and policymaking bodies. Along the way, our Foster Care Project became the Youth in Out-of-Home Care (YOHC) Project, reflecting the project's embrace of young people in juvenile justice and runaway and homeless youth systems as well as foster care.

CALLING FOR SAFE HAVENS FOR LGBTQ+ YOUTH

Fifteen years after *Youth in the Margins*, we partnered with Children's Rights and the Center for the Study of Social Policy on another trailblazing report. *Safe Havens: Closing the Gap Between Recommended Practice and Reality for Transgender and Gender-Expansive Youth in Out-of-Home Care* delivered the first fifty-state analysis of the lack of explicit, state-level laws and policies to protect transgender, gender-expansive and gender non-conforming (TGNC) youth in our country's child welfare systems. It examined the additional burdens for TGNC young people in systems routinely segregated by sex or perceived gender, creating elevated risks of bullying and both physical and sexual assault when youth are placed in facilities inconsistent with their gender identity. The report offered detailed law and policy reforms, together with authoritative legal support. It was a breakthrough resource for social work professionals, and quickly became a popular training and advocacy tool.

Safe Havens became our strategic roadmap for proactive reform advocacy, giving the YOHC Project the ability to identify states that appeared to be ripe for change. In 2019, for example, we selected New Mexico and followed an approach that has worked well in several states—reaching out to state and local leaders and forming a work group to engage with the state's child welfare leadership. The work group developed the state's first nondiscrimination rules to protect LGBTQ+ youth in care, which now bar discrimination, prohibit attempts to "change" a young person's identity, and ensure that trans youth can be placed consistently with their identity. Four years later, New Mexico took another critical step. The state's Human Rights Act was expanded with model protections that our team helped to craft, and which now bar discrimination by government agencies and government contractors, including those with responsibility for children and adolescents in state care.

Safe Havens continues to have the impact we hoped it would. An expanded, second edition will be published in 2024.

ADVOCACY FOR YOUNG PEOPLE

In re Soul (2014)

Some of our cases make plain the overlaps between our work to improve the law and our focus on protecting vulnerable populations. One example brought together our asylum advocacy and our YOHC Project. Soul knew he was gay growing up in Mali and Senegal. He came to the United States for college both for a better education and for safety. But that safety was threatened when he came out to his parents, who cut him off completely. Soul was terrified because he knew he could not stay in school without their financial support and would probably be sent back to Senegal, which criminalizes people for being LGBTQ+.

In desperation, Soul reached out to a childhood friend who helped him make his way to our YOHC Project. There he found help to obtain his legal permanent resident status or "green card" through a federal process called Special Juvenile Immigrant Status (SJIS). The process grants SIJS status to people under 21 if a juvenile court finds them abused, neglected, or abandoned by one or both parents, and determines that being sent back to their home country would not be in their best interest. Obtaining his green card allowed Soul to thrive. He joined the U.S. Army, received a scholarship, and studied computer science. He was able to work legally as a computer programmer and to plan for future studies and a successful life.

"I knew I was part of the LGBTQ community. But in Senegal and other countries in West Africa, it's not something you talk about. You have no rights; you can be jailed and even killed. I came to the U.S. to attend college. That way, I could be safe. Yet, when I came out to my father, he cut me off completely. I had no way to pay my rent or stay in school. I was afraid I was going to be homeless. I was all by myself and felt abandoned."

—SOUL

THE TRUMP ADMINISTRATION ATTACKS LGBTQ+ YOUNG PEOPLE

Facing Foster Care in Alaska v. HHS (2021-2022)

The Department of Health & Human Services issues approximately $500 billion in federal grants annually to private agencies that provide crucial services, including foster care and other services for out-of-home youth. Under President Obama, HHS banned anti-LGBTQ+ discrimination in all HHS-funded programs. But in the waning days of the Trump Administration, HHS issued a new rule that stripped out Obama-era protections and permitted private agencies providing HHS-funded services to discriminate against LGBTQ+ people.

Together with our co-counsel at Democracy Forward, we immediately challenged this rule change on behalf of four organizations, including Facing Foster Care in Alaska, an organization of current and former foster youth dedicated to improving the foster care system. We argued that the new rule violated numerous federal laws by leaving some of the most vulnerable members of our society exposed to unlawful discrimination based on sex, sexual orientation, and/or gender identity in a wide array of grant-funded programs, including services for youth and seniors experiencing homelessness and HIV-prevention programs. (For specific examples of such discrimination in the context of foster care, see Chapter 8.) In February 2021, the federal judge hearing the case agreed and blocked implementation of the new rule. The Biden administration subsequently withdrew the rule and, in July 2023, proposed an improved replacement.

Proposed HHS rule would roll back LGBTQ protections in adoption, foster care

There is no federal agency within this administration that has incited more widespread harm to LGBTQ people than HHS, the agency charged by Congress with enhancing the health and well-being of everyone in the United States. Instead of advancing the health and well-being of all Americans however, HHS has done all it can do to undermine and subvert the health and well-being of LGBTQ people and people living with HIV, and this rulemaking is one more example.

"This Trump-era rule threatened some of the most vulnerable members of our society, including LGBTQ+ children, seniors, and people with low income, who depend on federally funded programs to meet their basic needs. The people these HHS-funded programs are supposed to help should be able to expect that they can receive care without being harmed."

—CURREY COOK, YOUTH IN OUT-OF-HOME CARE PROJECT DIRECTOR

ADDRESSING BIAS IN OUR COURTS

In 2009, the Iowa Supreme Court ruled unanimously that the state's constitution gave same-sex couples the right to marry. Many were surprised that a Midwest state would be so early to adopt marriage equality. We weren't. We chose to file *Varnum v. Brien* (see Chapter 6) because we knew that Iowa had a constitution that embraced individual liberties and equal rights and we knew that the Iowa Supreme Court had a history of taking those rights seriously. But shortly after *Varnum* was decided, religious conservatives targeted the three justices with upcoming retention elections[64] for defeat. All three lost. Three more justices lost in the next retention election.

Events in Iowa drove home the importance of our Fair Courts Project, first established in 2005. Part of the Project's task is to educate people about the importance of judicial impartiality and to speak out against the politicization of the courts, a mission that has become even more crucial in recent years. It also works to reduce bias among judges, courtroom personnel and juries and to promote diversity on the bench. Here's a look into some of that work.

GEAR UP!
A Fair Courts Toolkit for
Everyday Advocates

Lambda Legal
making the case for equality

(opposite) Headline: *Politico,*
November 1, 2019. Text: excerpt
of our comment critiquing the
proposed rule, December 19, 2019.

(above) People angry over
Varnum cheer the defeat of three
Iowa Supreme Court justices in
the November 2, 2010 election.

JUSTICE OUT OF BALANCE

In 2016, the Fair Courts Projects published *Justice Out of Balance, How the Election of Judges and the Stunning Lack of Diversity on State Courts Threaten LGBT Rights*, the result of a study of state court cases involving LGBTQ+ claims from 2003 to 2015.

The study showed that many judges who are chosen by partisan election are less supportive of LGBTQ+ rights claims than judges chosen by other methods. Looking deeper, we saw that this pattern was especially pronounced in more conservative states. In other words, judges selected in partisan elections were more likely to behave like politicians: to make decisions based more on getting re-elected than on what the law requires. As a result, the vital role of the judiciary in protecting individual rights from the tyranny of the majority is weakened.

Donald Trump's election only accelerated the role of political ideology in judicial decision-making. When he took office in January 2017, he tapped the extremely conservative Federalist Society (FedSoc) and Heritage Foundation to suggest nominees for federal judgeships. The Republican-controlled Senate was quick to confirm even the most outrageous choices, including four judges rated "not-qualified" by the American Bar Association.[65]

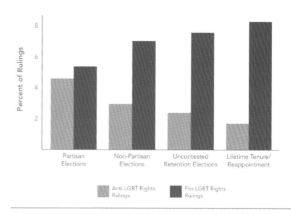

State High Court Rulings on LGBT Issues across Judicial Selection Methods

BEHIND THE SCENES

"Ninety percent of appellate court judges face some kind of election. Here's the problem: judges are not politicians. Unlike legislative and executive officials, judges by design should decide individual cases without taking popular opinion into account. Each day, thousands of elected judges...make decisions that could cost them their jobs if the law requires a ruling that is unpopular enough to anger a majority of voters or inspire special interest attacks. If judges can't safeguard the rights of vulnerable minorities without fear of retaliation, our constitutional right to due process becomes extremely vulnerable."
–*Justice Out of Balance*

RACIAL DIVERSITY OF JUDGES APPOINTED BY OBAMA, TRUMP, AND BIDEN (THROUGH 2023)

Other
Two or More Races
Native American
Asian American
Latino/a
Black
White

Data for this chart come from the Federal Judicial Center and the American Constitution Society.

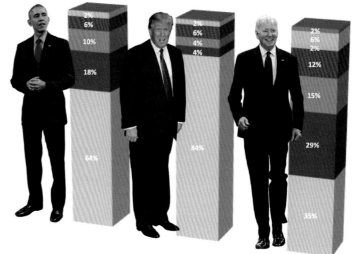

Stephen Clark
FEDERAL DISTRICT COURT

Argued that the holding in *Obergefell* would be a slippery slope and that one of the "next evolutions of same-sex marriage is polygamy."

Kyle Duncan
FIFTH CIRCUIT

• Questioned the legitimacy of the Supreme Court after ruling for marriage equality in *Obergefell*.

• Retained by the Gloucester County School Board to defend its policy singling out transgender students by requiring them to use separate "alternative, private" facilities.

Matthew Kacsmaryk
FEDERAL DISTRICT COURT

• Argued that the State's interest in defending against sexual orientation-based discrimination was not enough of a reason to justify burdens on a wedding cake baker's "constitutionally protected religious freedom."

• Authored an article that denigrates as "problematic" the very idea of gender identity.

David Porter
THIRD CIRCUIT

Sat on the board of an anti-LGBT think thank that advocated for "conversion therapy", and argued against marriage equality and protections for transgender people.

In 2018, the Fair Courts Project published a report assessing the horrific records of these appointees. *Trump's Judicial Assault on LGBT Rights: Bias and Bigotry are the New Norms after Two Years of Trump Nominees* revealed that more than one-third of Trump's Circuit Court appointees had a demonstrated history of anti-LGBTQ+ bias.

Incredibly, things got even worse. By the end of Trump's term in office, he had appointed nearly a third of the nation's appellate judges and almost 40% of his picks had a history of hostility toward LGBTQ+ people.[66] Three of those appointments were to the U.S. Supreme Court—Neil Gorsuch, Brett Kavanaugh, and Amy Coney Barrett—replacing the 5–4 majority that had approved marriage equality with a 6–3 majority aligned the other way. Activists determined to expand religious exemptions and to erase abortion rights, gun restrictions, environmental safeguards, and other regulations, developed ambitious test cases to bring to the Court.

BEHIND THE SCENES

"It felt surreal as a Black woman lawyer to be present at the confirmation hearing of then-Judge Ketanji Brown Jackson during her colloquy with Senator Cory Booker on the significance of a Black woman sitting on the highest court in the land. I pray the overwhelming pride, joy, and hope I felt in that moment will be shared soon with my TGNCNB colleagues when we have a hearing for the first transgender or nonbinary federal judge."
–Kristine Kippins, Deputy Legal Director for Policy

THE JOINT STATEMENT OF LAMBDA LEGAL, GLBTQ LEGAL ADVOCATES & DEFENDERS, THE NATIONAL CENTER FOR LESBIAN RIGHTS, AND THE TRANSGENDER LAW CENTER

The undersigned national LGBTQ+ legal advocacy organizations litigate in our Nation's federal courts, including the United States Supreme Court. We believe the time is long past due to recommit to the essential protections of liberty and equality and the right to vote for all Americans and for generations to come. The Supreme Court has lost the public's confidence in its integrity and has eroded its own legitimacy. To regain a measure of balance and restore confidence in the Court and the rule of law, we call for the following as minimal essential steps:

Lift the filibuster at least to allow Senate consideration of Supreme Court reform and voting rights restoration.

Pass the Judiciary Act of 2021 to expand the number of seats on the Court to equal the number of circuits in the federal judiciary.

Pass the For the People Act of 2021; the John R. Lewis Voting Rights Advancement Act of 2021; and the Washington, D.C. Admission Act.

Adopt an enforceable ethics code for the Supreme Court.

July 1, 2022

Results came swiftly. By the close of its 2022–2023 term, the Supreme Court had eliminated abortion rights, struck down a New York gun safety law, and required taxpayers to fund an ultra-conservative religious school. It also continued its pattern of expanding the religious and speech rights of individuals and businesses to discriminate against LGBTQ+ people.[67] (See Chapter 10 for more on the misuse of religious and free speech rights to discriminate.) The Court said repeatedly that it was applying familiar principles of constitutional law. But the applications were anything but familiar and the freedom-to-discriminate results became all too predictable. Forceful dissenting opinions called out the cherry-picking of history, disingenuous reasoning, and calamitous impacts the American public should expect. We knew we had to sound the alarm, so in 2022 we joined with our movement colleagues at GLAD, NCLR and the Transgender Law Center to call for Supreme Court reform.

The 2020 election gave Joe Biden the presidency and Democrats the Senate. They set out to restore balance to the federal courts and to diversify the demographic and professional backgrounds of judicial appointees—goals our Fair Courts Project had been stressing for twenty years. But there is a lot of ground to make up and the Supreme Court, especially, is likely to skew rightward for quite some time.

JUDGES WHO SHOULDN'T BE

One of the ways we address judicial bias is by filing formal complaints with judicial ethics boards/commissions. These complaints usually prompt an investigation, sometimes result in penalties, and often shine a light that educates court personnel and the public about unacceptable conduct. Here are three examples.

Mississippi Commission on Judicial Performance v. Wilkerson (2002-2004)

In 2002, we filed a judicial conduct complaint with the Mississippi Commission on Judicial Performance against Connie Glenn Wilkerson, a judge in George County. The judge had sent a letter to his local newspaper responding to California's new protections for domestic partners (a law we helped to craft). Said Wilkerson: "I know that GOD in Heaven is not pleased with this. . . In my opinion, gays and lesbians should be put in some type of mental institute instead of having a law like this passed for them." He later doubled down on live radio.

(top) *Seattle Gay News,* April 12, 2002

(middle) Headline from WLOX, the largest TV station in Mississippi, April 10, 2002.

(bottom) *Clarion Ledger,* December 21, 2002

The Commission concluded that Wilkerson's conduct violated the Mississippi Code of Judicial Conduct and the state constitutional rule against prejudicial conduct by judges. It recommended sanctions. Judge Wilkerson appealed to the Mississippi Supreme Court, which frustratingly ruled that his statements were made in his private capacity and were protected by the First Amendment. It dismissed our complaint.

These issues remain front and center for our judicial bias work. Twenty years after the Mississippi Supreme Court dismissed our complaint against Judge Wilkerson, we still contend with First Amendment defenses to ignorant and overtly bigoted statements from judicial officers. The good news is that the resulting public discussion helps more people understand how inappropriate such comments are, and how they impede public confidence in the impartiality and fairness of those speakers when they don their judicial robes.

Lambda Legal files ethics complaint against Mississippi judge

Lambda and Equality Mississippi denounce judge's suggestion that Gay men and Lesbians be put in mental institutions

ATLANTA - Lambda Legal has strongly denounced a letter to a newspaper by a Mississippi judge suggesting that Gays and Lesbians be institutionalized and agreed to represent Equality Mississippi, a statewide civil rights group, in an ethics complaint against the judge.

"The letter is a clear statement of prejudice against Gays and Lesbians that calls into serious questi[on]... decide cases fair[ly]... Greg Nevins, sta[ff]... Legal's Southern...

The *George C*... published a letter...

Judge Wilkerson was referring to a recent Associated Press article about the ability of Gay and Lesbian survivors to sue for the wrongful death of their partners. "I got sick on my stomach as I read the news story?," Judge Wilkerson wrote. The judge also invoked the Bible and Romans 1:32, which suggests that those who break God's law "are worthy of death."

duct specifically calls on judges to avoid "expressions of bias or prejudice," including demeaning remarks based on "sexual orientation."

The judge's remarks come on the heels of an opinion by Alabama Supreme Court Chief Justice Roy Moore in which he called Gay people "abhorrent," "immoral," "detestable," "an inherent evil," and "inhe[rent]...

even judicial opinions may not violate ethics requirements.

"We are extremely concerned about the rash of anti-Gay statements from judges who are duty-bound to give a fair hearing to all," said Hector Vargas, regional director of Lambda Legal's Southern Regional Office. "These kinds of statements make Gays and Lesbians feel that the justice sys[tem]...

Judge's Remarks About Homosexuals Drawing Fire From Gay Rights Groups

Judicial reprimand suggested

By Sherri Williams
swilliams@clarionledger.com

GEORGE COUNTY paper in Lucedale.
In the letter, Wilkerson expressed his opinion

The commission said Wilkerson's statements violated the judicial canon

lo-based American Family Association Center for Law and Policy and Wilker-

and all judges on issues of all sorts."
Lambda Legal filed an

233

Alabama Supreme Court Chief Justice Roy Moore (2002)

In 2002, we filed an ethics complaint with the Alabama Judicial Inquiry Commission (JIC) calling for an investigation of the Chief Justice of the Alabama Supreme Court, Roy Moore, a man who eventually earned the distinction of being removed from the bench *twice* for judicial misconduct. Our complaint concerned the concurrence he wrote in a child custody case. The full court had largely ignored the mother's sexual orientation when deciding the case, but Moore's concurrence was fixated on it. Homosexuality, he wrote, was "an inherent evil" that was "abhorrent, immoral, detestable, a crime against nature, and a violation of the laws of nature and of nature's God." As evidence, he cited "direct revelation found in the Holy Scripture."[59]

We argued that Moore's conduct violated ethical standards requiring Alabama judges to be impartial and to promote public confidence in the judiciary. Amazingly, the JIC disagreed, finding no evidence of "ill will" in Moore's actions. A year later, however, Moore was removed from the bench for defying a federal court order to remove a massive stone monument of the Ten Commandments that Moore personally designed and had installed in the rotunda of the Supreme Court building.

But that was not the end of Roy Moore. Supreme Court justices in Alabama are determined by partisan elections. In 2012, Moore ran for Chief Justice a second time and won. But he again ran afoul of judicial ethics, this time over his hyper-fixation on homosexuality. When, a few months before *Obergefell*, a federal judge struck down Alabama's discriminatory marriage laws and ordered the state to implement marriage equality, Chief Justice Moore claimed that the state's probate judges were not bound by the decision and ordered them to deny same-sex couples marriage licenses. Six months after *Obergefell* was decided, Moore repeated his order. His defiance of the U.S. Supreme Court resulted in his removal from the bench for an unprecedented second time.[60]

(right) *CNN* broadcast, February 12, 2015

NOW THEREFORE, IT IS ORDERED AND DIRECTED THAT:

To ensure the orderly administration of justice within the State of Alabama, to alleviate a situation adversely affecting the administration of justice within the State, and to harmonize the administration of justice between the Alabama judicial branch and the federal courts in Alabama:

Effective immediately, no Probate Judge of the State of Alabama nor any agent or employee of any Alabama Probate Judge shall issue or recognize a marriage license that is inconsistent with Article 1, Section 36.03, of the Alabama Constitution or § 30-1-19, Ala. Code 1975.

Should any Probate Judge of this state fail to follow the Constitution and statutes of Alabama as stated, it would be the responsibility of the Chief Executive Officer of the State of Alabama, Governor Robert Bentley, in whom the Constitution vests "the supreme executive power of this state," Art. V, § 113, Ala. Const. 1901, to ensure the execution of the law. "The Governor shall take care that the laws be faithfully executed." Art. V, § 120, Ala. Const. 1901. "'If the governor's "supreme executive power" means anything, it means that when the governor makes a determination that the laws are not being faithfully executed, he can act using the legal means that are at his disposal.'" Tyson v. Jones, 60 So. 3d 831, 850 (Ala. 2010) (quoting Riley v. Cornerstone, 57 So. 3d 704, 733 (Ala. 2010)). DONE on this 8th day of February, 2015.

Roy Moore

Roy S. Moore
Chief Justice

Roy Moore, Alabama Chief Justice, Suspended Over Gay Marriage Order

"Chief Justice Moore's statements make it abundantly clear that he is incapable of giving any lesbian or gay person in Alabama their fair day in court."

—HECTOR VARGAS, FORMER SOUTHERN REGIONAL DIRECTOR

(top) Shortly after a federal ruling that struck down Alabama's marriage equality ban in 2015, Judge Moore ordered probate judges to refuse to issue marriage licenses to same-sex couples.

(above) *The New York Times* headline, September 30, 2016

235

> Judge W. Mitchell Nance refused to hear adoption cases involving LGB families based on his "convictions."

▼ NATIONAL NEWS

Anti-LGBTQ KY Judge Mitchell Nance resig[n]

Advocacy groups filed ethics complaint in May for refusing adoptions to same-sex coup[les]

"LGBTQ people who seek to provide adoptive homes for children who need them, and all other LGBTQ Kentuckians, now have clarity that anti-LGBT bias from the bench will not be tolerated in their state."

LOUISVILLE, KY – [On Wednesday, October 25] Kentucky Family Court Judge W. Mitchell Nance notified Governor Matthew G. Bevin and the Commonwealth of Kentucky Judicial Conduct Commission of his resignation. In May, Lambda Legal, the American Civil Liberties Union, the ACLU of Kentucky, Kentucky's Fairness Campaign, and University of Louisville Law Professor Sam Marcosson filed a complaint against Judge Nance for violating Kentucky's Code of Judicial Conduct by recusing himself from any adoption proceedings involving lesbian, gay, and bisexual people.

"Judge Nance must have seen the writing on the wall," said Chris Hartman, Director of the Fairness Campaign. "He had proven he could not deliver the basic impartiality required by his office when it came to LGBTQ people and their families. Judge Nance's only possible pathways forward at that point were resignation or removal from office – either is a victory for social justice and LGBTQ civil rights."

"All citizens of Kentucky have the right to fair treatment before the judiciary," said Currey Cook, Counsel and Youth in Out-of-Home Care Project Director at Lambda Legal. "LGBTQ people who seek to provide adoptive homes for children who need them, and all other LGBT Kentuckians, now have clarity that anti-LGBT bias from the bench will not be tolerated in their state."

"Judges, more than anyone else, have a responsibility to follow the law," said University of Louisville Law Professor Sam Marcosson. "By making it clear that he could not, or would not do that, Judge

Nance demonstrated that he simply had no place on the bench. Kentucky's justice system, and all who come before it, are better off in light of his resignation."

On April 27, 2017, Kentucky Family Court Judge W. Mitchell Nance of the 43rd Judicial Circuit Court filed an order that would require attorneys to notify the court if the adoption matter being filed involved same-sex couples or lesbian, gay, or bisex-

ual individuals, so that he could disqualify and recuse himself. Judge Nance cited his personal conviction as the reason for the order. He said that "under no circumstance would '… the best interest of the child … be promoted by the adoption …' by a practicing homosexual."

In the complaint filed in May, Lambda Legal, the American Civil Liberties Union, ACLU of Kentucky, the Fairness

Campaign, and University [of Louisville] Law Professor Sam M[arcosson alleged] that Judge Nance's orde[r violated a] letter to the Chief Jus[tice and a] local rule that would all[ow to disqualify] himself for an entire class[... based] solely on their sexual or[ientation ...] Kentucky's Code of Jud[icial Conduct in] two ways: eroding public c[onfidence in the] judiciary and failing to [perform his] duties impartially and di[ligently. Judge] Nance could not be fair an[d impartial or] rule in the best interests o[f the child if] he declares an explicit bia[s against ...] parents. Judge Nance's or[der demon-] strated a prejudice based o[n an orien-] tation that places a proced[ural burden on] LGB parents that is not on [other individu-] als. Because it was clear tha[t he could not] be fair and impartial whe[n it came to] lesbian, gay, and bisexual pe[ople, advo-] cacy groups urged in the c[omplaint that] Judge Nance be removed fro[m office.]

Lambda Legal is a nati[onal organiza-] tion committed to achieving [full recogni-] tion of the civil rights of lesbi[ans, gays,] bisexuals, transgender peopl[e and every-] one living with HIV through [litiga-] tion, education and public pol[icy work.]

Founded in 1991, th[e Fairness] Campaign is Kentucky's b[roadest-based] community effort dedicated to [fairness] for lesbian gay, bisexual, and [transgender] people. Its primary goal is con[tinuing to pass] civil rights legislation prohibi[ting discrim-] ination on the basis of sexual [orientation] and gender identity, and to [combat] systemic racism.

Courtesy of Lambda L[egal and] Kentucky's Fairness Campaign

Mitchell Nance – Photo courtesy of Glasgow Daily Times

Kentucky Family Court Judge Mitchell Nance (2017)

In April of 2017, Kentucky Family Court Judge W. Mitchell Nance filed an order directing attorneys bringing adoption cases to his court to notify him in advance when a case involved a same-sex couple or lesbian, gay, or bisexual would-be parent, so he could recuse himself. Judge Nance explained that he was doing so based on his personal belief that "under no circumstance would '… the best interest of the child…be promoted by the adoption…' by a practicing homosexual."

Together with the ACLU, ACLU of KY, and Fairness Campaign (Kentucky's state-wide LGBTQ advocacy group), we promptly filed a judicial ethics complaint against Judge Nance. We explained that his plan to refuse to hear cases presented by an entire class of litigants based on his factually erroneous belief that parenting ability is a function of sexual orientation would violate Kentucky's Code of Judicial Conduct both by eroding public confidence in the judiciary and by his failure to perform judicial duties impartially and diligently. That October, as the state's judicial conduct commission was doing its investigation, Nance resigned from the bench and retired.

(above, left) *The Advocate*, October 26, 2017

(above, right) *Seattle Gay News*, October 27, 2017

> "Lambda Legal cannot and will not stand by while this judge ignores the best interests of children in favor of stereotypes that have been thoroughly debunked by social science research."
>
> **–CURREY COOK, YOUTH IN OUT-OF-HOME CARE PROJECT DIRECTOR**

TRAINING JUDGES AND OTHER LEGAL PROFESSIONALS

We don't just go after bad judges, we help to train good ones. In 2018, the Fair Courts Project published a training curriculum for judges, attorneys, and other legal professionals. Entitled *Moving Beyond Bias: How to Ensure Access to Justice for LGBT People*, it explains how systemic biases and discrimination impede access to justice in the courts for LGBTQ+ people and people living with HIV, and that this is especially true for transgender people, people of color and others with multiple marginalized identities. It stresses that information about the lives of LGBTQ+ people greatly reduces such biases and offers specific suggestions for better meeting the needs of LGBTQ+ people in the legal system.

BEST PRACTICES
Address Explicit Bias and Disrespect

- Immediately respond to jokes or disrespectful comments about an individual's actual or perceived sexual orientation, gender identity or expression or HIV status.

- If this happens during a court hearing, attorneys should respond promptly so inappropriate comments, and the pers them, can be addressed immediately. was made on the record, the response reference to the response should also

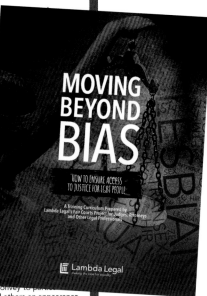

Ethical Considerations

Comment on Rule 2.3
- [1] A judge who manifests bias or prejudice in fairness of the proceeding and brings the judi

- [2] Examples of manifestations of bias or prej limited to epithets; slurs; demeaning nicknam attempted humor based upon stereotypes; t or hostile acts; suggestions of connections b nationality and crime; and **irrelevant referen characteristics.**
Even facial expressions and body language can convey to lawyers in the proceeding, jurors, the media, and others an appearance of bias or prejudice.
A judge must avoid conduct that may reasonably be perceived as prejudiced or biased. [Emphasis added]

BEST PRACTICES
Name changes

- Judges should respect individuals, including their desire to change their names to correspond with their gender identity.

- Frequently, judges deny name changes for transgender individuals for reasons that do not comport with statute.

"When I do trainings for judges, they see a transgender attorney— someone who, like them, attended law school and went to work in the legal field. Most of the time, they see my humanity. They hear what I mean when I say trans people are often having a horrible time in court, and they have the power to remedy it. Not only do I reach the judges in the room, but likely these judges pass information on to others. Not every transgender person is afforded that understanding and respect, and our educational and training work is essential."

—ETHAN RICE, FAIR COURTS PROJECT SENIOR ATTORNEY

trust ~~politicians~~
parents

CHAPTER 10

NEWS FROM THE FRONTLINES

DEFENDING AGAINST ANTI-LGBTQ+ ATTACKS

The past several years have seen an unprecedented deluge of bills, laws and policies targeting LGBTQ+ people—and it's only getting worse. Roughly 500 bills targeting LGBTQ+ people were introduced across forty-six state legislatures in the first half of 2023. By June 30, more than seventy had been signed into law across twenty-two states. The great majority of these laws (and bills) attack trans and nonbinary people, especially youth, commonly through prohibitions on gender-affirming healthcare, school sports participation, and bathroom use. Some bills mimic Florida's "Don't Say Gay or Trans" law or Tennessee's targeting of drag performances, while others require educators to out students to their parents. The Movement Advancement Project, which tracks LGBTQ+ policies, calls the current political environment "a war against LGBTQ+ people in America and their very right and ability to openly exist."[68]

This is infuriating but not entirely surprising. Lambda Legal's fifty years of advocacy have taught us that advances in LGBTQ+ rights and visibility often spark intense opposition by political opportunists who deliberately foment fear and knee-jerk reactions. We work to defang and defuse this opposition in many ways: through lawsuits, expert testimony, media interviews, behind-the-scenes work, how-to guides, and coordination with allies.

Our ability to do this work is shaped by many forces we can't control. Our opposition is extremely well funded. The rise of social media and attacks on major news sources have driven people into information—and misinformation—silos. The Trump administration not only advanced many anti-LGBTQ+ policies but installed many openly anti-LGBTQ+ people into positions of power, including lifetime appointments as federal judges. Trump appointees to the Supreme Court have tipped its balance to the extreme right, undermining decades-old legal principles—like the right of privacy— that have been central to eliminating sodomy laws and winning the freedom

to marry. Many of Trump's would-be successors compete to demonstrate their bona fides by pushing increasingly vicious anti-LGBTQ+ policies.

The road ahead will not be easy. But it has never been easy. It wasn't easy when anti-LGBTQ+ activists used ballot-box campaigns to overturn LGBTQ+ rights laws. It wasn't easy when states passed scores of laws and constitutional amendments to prevent marriage equality. LGBTQ+ people prevailed then and will again. And Lambda Legal will continue to fight back and, in so doing, drive positive change.

Here's a sampling of our efforts to defend against the current chapter of anti-LGBTQ+ attacks. We focus here on three inter-related phenomena: religious carve outs to antidiscrimination laws, censorship of LGBTQ+ people, issues, and culture, and measures that target transgender and nonbinary youth.

(above) Protest at the Supreme Court during the *Masterpiece Cakeshop* oral arguments, December 5, 2017.

(page 238) Vidalia Anne Gentry speaks against Tennessee legislation to ban drag performances, February 14, 2023.

RELIGIOUS RIGHTS AS WEAPONS

When do religious beliefs excuse violating the law? The United States is currently in a period of heightened deference to free exercise of religion claims, and opponents of LGBTQ+ rights are exploiting this. In the past decade, twenty-one states have passed religious exemption laws which variously allow religiously affiliated groups, healthcare workers, and even private businesses to refuse to serve someone if doing so goes against their religious convictions. In state after state, the bills' sponsors have made it plain that these laws are designed to facilitate harm to LGBTQ+ people. Unfortunately, the U.S. Supreme Court has been a vigorous leader in expanding religious rights to discriminate and it's likely to continue in the near future.

Here's a sense of what we're up against and how we're fighting back.

WHEN RELIGIOUS LIBERTY, FREE SPEECH, AND ANTI-DISCRIMINATION LAWS CLASH

Lambda Legal has a lot of experience litigating cases that balance religious freedom against LGBTQ+ equality and inclusion. In *Benitez*, for instance, we won a 2008 California Supreme Court ruling that religious beliefs don't exempt doctors from following the state's civil rights law (see Chapter 4). And in *Cervelli* we won a ruling that a bed and breakfast owner in Hawai`i had to follow the state's LGBTQ+ inclusive public accommodations law (see Chapter 8).

(left) A protester awaits the *Burwell v. Hobby Lobby Stores* decision outside the U.S. Supreme Court, June 2014. The decision allowed a for-profit company to discriminate against its employees for religious reasons.

(opposite) Protesters outside a Hobby Lobby store in Madison, Wisconsin, following the U.S. Supreme Court's *Hobby Lobby* decision.

The Christian Right legal industry, though, has been working overtime trying to forge new case law that would allow religious and free speech exceptions to civil rights laws, and it's been finding a sympathetic ear in the U.S. Supreme Court. One example is *Masterpiece Cakeshop v. Colorado Civil Rights Commission* (2018), a case brought by the Alliance Defending Freedom (ADF) on behalf of a bakery owner who, citing his religious views, refused to make a wedding cake for a gay male couple, even though Colorado's civil rights law bans sexual orientation discrimination. We filed a friend-of-the-court brief in the Supreme Court filled with examples of the diverse harms of anti-LGBTQ+ discrimination, often with religious beliefs given as the reason, which Justice Sotomayor drew from during oral arguments.

To our relief, the case was decided on facts specific to how the Colorado's enforcement agency had handled the case and did not give the bakery owner and his ADF lawyers the broad license to discriminate they were seeking. Several justices wrote separately, though, to say that the business owner was entitled to refuse same-sex couples, notwithstanding Colorado's law.

Although the Christian Right did not get all it wanted in *Masterpiece Cakeshop*, it has dozens of cases in the pipeline. One is *Klein v. Oregon Bureau of Labor and Industry*, another bakery case, this one brought by First Liberty on behalf of owners Aaron and Melissa Klein. In 2013, Aaron Klein refused to provide a wedding cake to our clients Rachel and Laurel

Bowman-Cryer, citing the biblical text calling same-sex relationships "an abomination." Rachel and Laurel filed a complaint with the Oregon Bureau of Labor & Industry (BOLI), because Oregon law outlaws business discrimination against LGBTQ+ people. Klein responded by posting the complaint on Facebook

and going on a right-wing talk show to claim victimhood. As a result, Rachel and Laurel were inundated with vicious online targeting, stalking, and death threats. The harassment got so bad that they changed jobs, refused all media interviews, and largely stopped socializing. Klein, in contrast, made himself a poster child, advocating for religious exemptions and touring with presidential candidate Ted Cruz in 2015.

While Rachel and Laurel were coping with a tsunami of hate, they were also winning their case. The Kleins lost at every step in Oregon's courts. The U.S. Supreme Court, however, sent the case back to the Oregon courts to be reconsidered in light of its ruling in *Masterpiece Cakeshop*.

Meanwhile ADF continued to press dozens of cases challenging LGBTQ+ civil rights protections. In June 2023, the Supreme Court handed down a decision in *303 Creative v. Elenis*. It involved a Christian website designer (Lorie Smith) who wanted to expand into designing wedding websites, but only for heterosexual couples, contrary to Colorado law. To our dismay, if not surprise, the six conservative members of the Court decided Smith's free speech rights trump Colorado's anti-discrimination law, because she intends to blend her messages about marriage with her customers' stories.

In 2022, after losing again in the Oregon courts, the Kleins once again asked the U.S. Supreme Court to review their case. On the same day it handed down *303 Creative*, the Court reversed the Oregon courts (again), this time directing that the case be reviewed in light of *303 Creative*. The safe bet is that the Roberts Court will hear more of these anti-LGBTQ+ challenges going forward.

(above) Aaron and Melissa Klein with their attorney from First Liberty Institute of Plano, Texas, Michael Berry.

"Today, the Court, for the first time in its history, grants a business open to the public a constitutional right to refuse to serve members of a protected class. . . .[T]he immediate, symbolic effect of the decision is to mark gays and lesbians for second-class status."

—U.S. SUPREME COURT JUSTICE SONIA SOTOMAYOR, *303 CREATIVE* (DISSENTING)

(above) Rachel, front, and Laurel
Bowman-Cryer

"To be called an 'abomination' because of
who you are and who you love, and now always
to be afraid that the next store we go
into will reject us with the same contempt
and discrimination—that's the legacy of our
treatment by the Kleins."

–RACHEL BOWMAN-CRYER

RELIGIOUS EXEMPTION MEASURES

Another way the Christian Right works to tip the scales in its favor is by pushing legislators to pass religious exemption laws, which authorize discrimination on the basis of religious belief under various circumstances. Our opposition has taken many forms. Ideally, we work to stop laws before they can take effect. That's what happened with proposed laws in Arizona (2014) and Georgia (2016). We worked with local activists and attorneys to research and publicize the likely consequences of both bills, and engaged with civic and business leaders to educate them about how dangerous the bills were. Ultimately, the Republican governors of both states vetoed the bills.

Similarly, we were able to block multiple rule changes by the Trump administration before they could be implemented. For example, our 2019 lawsuit *County of Santa Clara v. HHS* challenged a new HHS rule cutting federal funding to hospitals unless they allowed healthcare workers to deny treatment on the basis of personal religious or moral beliefs. The administration called it the "conscience rule." But the name we gave it—the "denial of care rule"—was more accurate. After a hearing, the federal trial court granted us a permanent injunction, calling the Trump rule "saturated with error" and preventing it from going into effect. In early 2023, the Biden administration proposed a replacement rule, in line with our advocacy.

We haven't always been able to stop religious exemption measures from becoming law, however, sometimes we get a second bite at the apple. In 2015, we advocated strongly against a religious exemption bill in Indiana with broad implications, including giving private businesses the right to discriminate based on religious belief. The law passed, but growing awareness of the anti-LGBTQ+ bias behind it fueled a firestorm of opposition. The new law was seen as so egregious and hostile to LGBTQ+ people that the *Indianapolis Star* made the extraordinary decision to publish an editorial whose all-caps title, "FIX THIS NOW," took up much of the front page.[69] We worked intensely with civic and business leaders to keep pressure on then-Governor Mike Pence and the statehouse, and a few weeks later they blinked, amending the law to specify that it did not allow discrimination on the basis of sexual orientation, gender identity, race, gender, and other personal characteristics.

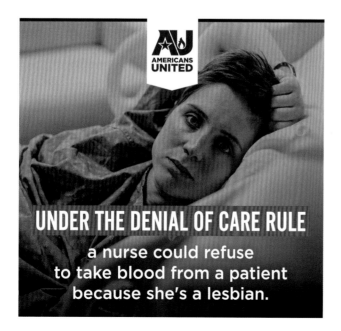

(left) Ad from Americans United, one of our co-counsel in *County of Santa Clara v. HHS.*

(above) *The Indianapolis Star,* March 31, 2015

"There's nothing godly about writing discrimination into the law."[70]

–SIMONE BELL, FORMER SOUTHERN REGIONAL DIRECTOR

"[T]argeting LGBT people and saying that if you don't like them, you don't have to deal with them, is dangerous and harmful."[71]

–BETH LITTRELL, ONE OF OUR ATTORNEYS ON *BARBER*

Sometimes early victories are undone by later court decisions, as happened in *Barber v. Bryant. Barber* challenged a breathtakingly broad 2016 Mississippi law (HB 1523) authorizing individuals, government employees, businesses, and religious institutions to discriminate against LGBTQ+ people based on a religious belief that only male-female couples can marry; that sex should only happen in a different-sex marriage; and/or that a person's sex is immutable and determined at birth.

The Mississippi Center for Justice challenged HB 1523, arguing that by giving preferential treatment to some religious beliefs, the law violated the constitutional guarantee of religious neutrality and that by blatantly allowing discrimination against LGBTQ+ people, it violated the constitutional right of equal protection. The federal trial court agreed and blocked the law from taking effect.

When Mississippi appealed to the Fifth Circuit Court of Appeals, we joined the case. However, in 2017 the appeals court allowed HB 1523 to take effect and refused even to consider our arguments, ruling that our clients couldn't challenge the law because they had not (yet!) been directly harmed. Because HB 1523 went farther than any other religious exemption law—establishing special rights for those with a particular set of beliefs—we asked the Supreme Court to review the case, only to be denied again, bringing *Barber v. Bryant* to an end. We remain vigilant, knowing that this kind of law invites discrimination.

(left) Protestors in Mississippi marching against HB 1523, May 1, 2016.

CENSORSHIP

Lambda Legal is no stranger to government efforts to censor what children learn about sexual orientation and gender identity in school. We now refer to them as "Don't Say Gay or Trans" laws. We used to call them "No Promo Homo" laws. No matter what their name, these laws are harmful. A 2018 GLSEN report found that the school climates in states with such laws were much more hostile to LGBTQ+ students.[72] Students were more likely to be exposed to homophobic remarks and negative representations of LGBTQ+ people, and were less likely to have access to supportive resources, such as faculty allies, GSAs, library materials inclusive of LGBTQ+ people, and relevant school health services. We made it a priority to challenge No Promo Homo laws and we're doing the same with Don't Say Gay or Trans laws. And when the Trump administration tried to muzzle workplace discussions of race, gender, and sexuality, we had something to say about that as well.

"NO PROMO HOMO" LAWS

In the late '80s and early '90s, many states passed laws that prevented educators from portraying homosexuality in a positive light or required them to portray it negatively. This was partly about heterosexual panic over HIV and partly a reaction to the increased visibility of lesbian, gay, and bisexual people. Arizona's 1991 law, for example, prohibited any instruction about HIV and AIDS that "promotes a homosexual lifestyle" or "portrays homosexuality as a positive alternative lifestyle" or "suggests that some methods of sex are safe methods of homosexual sex."[73] Similarly, South Carolina's 1988 law prohibited any health education discussing "homosexual relationships except in the context of instruction concerning sexually transmitted diseases."[74] Most No Promo Homo laws from that time have been repealed, but some remain on the books. Lambda Legal has partnered with the NCLR to take them down. That Arizona law? Within two weeks of our challenging it in 2019, the state repealed it.[75] And two weeks after we challenged South Carolina's law in 2020, the state entered into a binding agreement that it was unconstitutional and would no longer be enforced.[76]

(left) Florida Governor Ron DeSantis displays the signed Parental Rights in Education Act—the "Don't Say Gay or Trans" law—flanked by elementary school students, March 28, 2022.

(opposite) Demonstrators at the Florida State Capitol, March 7, 2022.

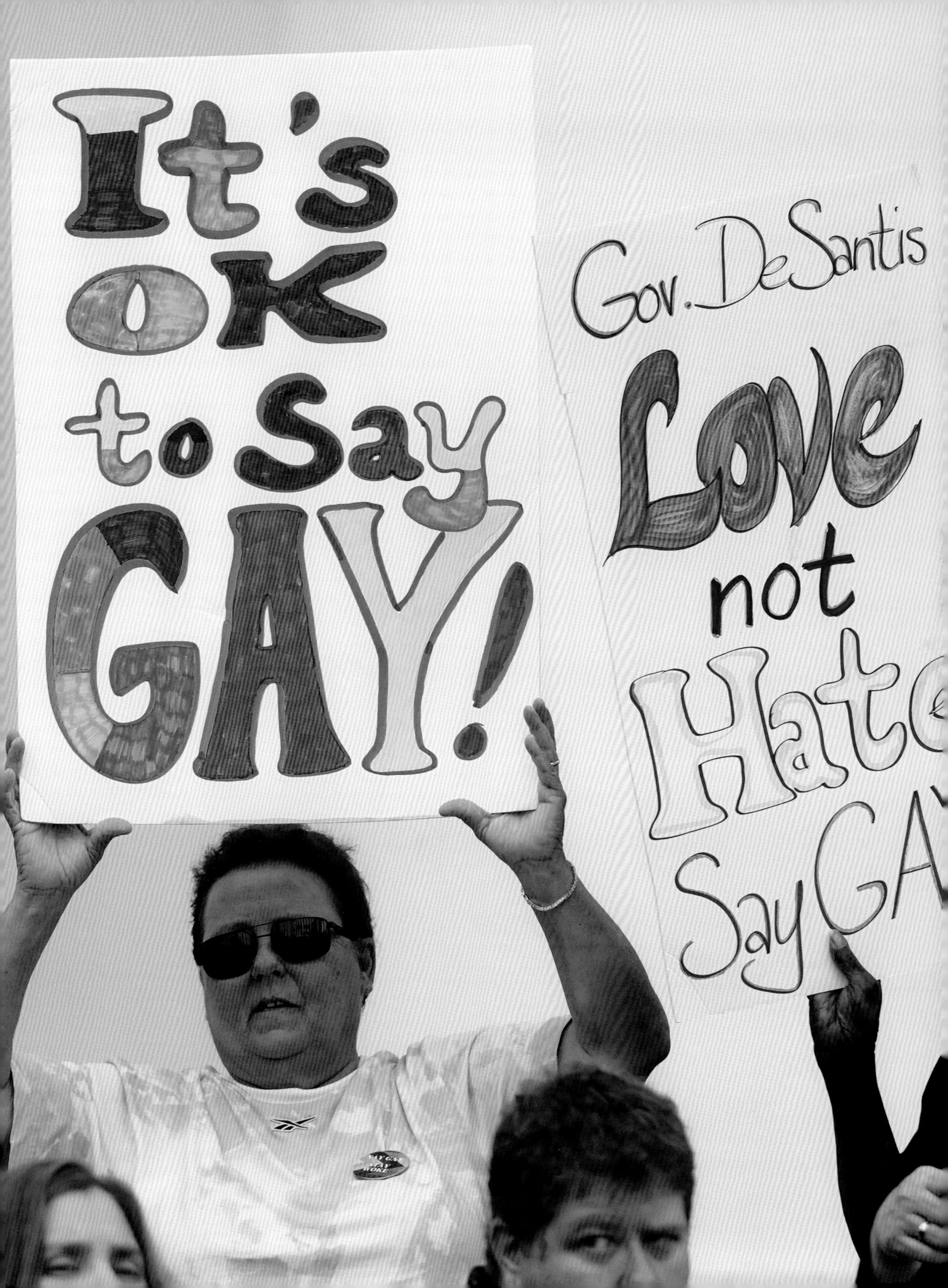
It's OK to Say GAY!
Gov. DeSantis
Love
not
Hat
Say GA

TRUMP'S "ANTI-WOKE" EXECUTIVE ORDER 13950

Santa Cruz Lesbian and Gay Community Center v. Trump (2020-2021)

Government efforts to censor speech are not just remnants of a discriminatory past. They've been making a comeback, driven heavily by White Nationalist backlash against efforts to engage critically with the history of race and racism in the United States. Scholars trace the start of this new trend to Executive Order 13950, issued by President Trump in September 2020 following a summer of street protests against police brutality and systemic anti-Black racism inspired by the murder of George Floyd by Minneapolis police in May of that year. Trump's order, titled "Combating Race and Sex Stereotyping," prohibited government contractors from providing what it called "divisive, anti-American propaganda training sessions" that engaged in "race and sex scapegoating." It also prohibited recipients of federal grants (like universities) from using those funds to acknowledge the existence of structural racism and sexism in the United States. The order caused the cancellation of hundreds of events, trainings, and research projects across the nation.

We challenged Trump's executive order on behalf of six community organizations who serve LGBTQ+ and HIV-positive people and provide diversity, equity, and inclusion trainings for local agencies, healthcare providers, and businesses. We argued that the order blatantly violated free speech rights and asked a federal judge to block its enforcement while we contested it in court. The judge agreed that the order was likely unconstitutional and issued a nationwide injunction, calling the Trump Administration's argument that our clients were engaged in scapegoating "an insult to their work of addressing discrimination and injustice towards historically underserved communities."

The injunction was issued in the final days of the Trump Administration. Then, on President Biden's first day in office, he not only revoked Trump's order, but mandated that federal agencies take measures to ensure the "fair, just, and impartial treatment of . . . underserved communities that have been denied such treatment," specifically including "lesbian, gay, bisexual, transgender, and queer (LGBTQ+) persons."

(left) Pickle reads to children during Drag Queen Story Hour in West Hollywood on February 24, 2018.

(opposite, inset) President Donald Trump displays his signature after signing an executive order.

(opposite) Text of President Trump's September 22, 2020 Executive Order 13950

(pages 252-253) Marchers carry a giant Trans Pride flag during the fourth annual Queer Liberation March in New York City, June 26, 2022.

"This injunction was critically important for our clients—organizations and individuals on the front line combatting COVID-19, HIV/AIDS, and the violence perpetrated against Black and Brown people by law enforcement. Judge Freeman saw this ban for what it is: An effort to quash the truth and sweep under the rug an honest and long overdue reckoning with structural racism and sexism in our society."

– AVATARA SMITH-CARRINGTON, ONE OF OUR ATTORNEYS ON
SANTA CRUZ LESBIAN AND GAY COMMUNITY CENTER

60683

Federal Register
Vol. 85, No. 188
Monday, September 28, 2020

Presidential Documents

Executive Order 13950 of September 22, 2020

Combating Race and Sex Stereotyping

Title 3—

The President

By the authority vested in me as President by the Constitution and the laws of the United States of America, including the Federal Property and Administrative Services Act, 40 U.S.C. 101 *et seq.*, and in order to promote economy and efficiency in Federal contracting, to promote unity in the Federal workforce, and to combat offensive and anti-American race and ~~sex~~ scapegoating, it is hereby ordered as follows:

...d of Gettysburg to the bus boycott ...tgomery marches, heroic Americans ...sure that their children would grow ...ressed in the Declaration of Independ- ...elf-evident, that all men are created ...rent equality of every individual that ...risk their lives, their fortunes, and ...Nation, unique among the countries ...incoln understood that this belief is ...hearts of patriotic and liberty-loving" ...ry of origin. It is the belief that inspired ...th Massachusetts Infantry Regiment to ...cost in the Civil War. And it is what ...Jr., to dream that his children would ...color of their skin but by the content

...ce of our forebears, America has made ...ation of our national creed, particularly ...d his dream with the country.

...re pushing a different vision of America ...based on collective social and political ...erent and equal dignity of every person ...s rooted in the pernicious and false belief ...racist and sexist country; that some people, ...e or sex, are oppressors; and that racial ...mportant than our common status as human

...beings and Americans.

This destructive ideology is grounded in misrepresentations of our country's history and its role in the world. Although presented as new and revolutionary, they resurrect the discredited notions of the nineteenth century's apologists for slavery who, like President Lincoln's rival Stephen A. Douglas, ...d that our government "was made on the white basis" "by white ...men." Our Founding documents rejected these ...ly defeated on the blood-

"DON'T SAY GAY OR TRANS" LAWS

On March 28, 2022, Florida Governor Ron DeSantis signed HB 1557 into law. More commonly known as "Don't Say Gay or Trans," the law prohibits teaching about sexual orientation and gender identity in grades K–3 and requires any such teaching in grades 4–12 be done in an age and developmentally appropriate manner. It also arguably requires educators to out their LGBTQ+ students to their parents. And it deputizes parents to enforce the law themselves, by suing school boards for damages and court costs.

HB 1557 inspired a slew of imitators. By summer 2023, Alabama, Arkansas, Indiana, Iowa, Kentucky and North Carolina had adopted their own Don't Say Gay or Trans laws, while Florida's Board of Education adopted a rule forbidding instruction about LGBTQ+ people in all grades. Several other states had bills still in play as this book went to press, and more are expected in 2024.

Cousins v. School Board of Orange County, Florida (2022-ongoing)

Lambda Legal has moved aggressively to counter these laws. Working with the Southern Poverty Law Center and Southern Legal Counsel, we are challenging Florida's Don't Say Gay or Trans law on behalf of two families and one high schooler. Jen and Matt Cousins want their children, including their nonbinary seventh grader, to feel safe and supported in school, and to be able to describe their family accurately and openly. David Dinan and Vik Gongidi want the same for their children. Will Larkins, a nonbinary student and the co-founder and president of their school's Queer Student Union, was questioned by school officials for giving a presentation on Stonewall and has both witnessed and experienced an increase in anti-LGBTQ+ bullying. Will also worries about the future of groups like the Queer Student Union.

In asking for an order to block enforcement of the law, we argue that it is intended to silence, shame, and erase LGBTQ+ students and families and that its broad and vague language is designed to make teachers, school counselors, and students afraid of accidentally breaking it. If a second grader wants to talk about her gay parents in class, can teachers permit it? What if someone wants to give a presentation about Stonewall, like Will did?

Do school libraries have to remove every book containing LGBTQ+ characters or references to sexuality and gender identity? If a student is bullied because they are LGBTQ+, what can schools do? To add even more pressure, the law's vigilante enforcement mechanism, combined with its vagueness, invites parents who don't want schools to acknowledge that LGBTQ+ people exist to sue, giving school boards a strong incentive to silence students, parents, and teachers.

The law has already harmed our clients and the broader community. School boards have instructed teachers to review books that acknowledge LGBTQ+ people and families, and to eliminate supports that are vital to the development, education, and mental health of LGBTQ+ students. Teachers are being advised to take down pride flags and other supportive messages. Anti-LGBTQ+ bullying is on the rise. We know how quickly conditions can devolve to the dangerous abusiveness we challenged successfully in cases like *Nabozny* and *Henkle* decades ago (discussed in Chapter 7). We will not let that happen without a serious fight. In fact, as this book goes to press, we are preparing to challenge Iowa's copycat Don't Say Gay or Trans law.

(clockwise from top) Will Larkins at home with family; David Dinan and Vik Gongidi with their children; and the Cousins family.

"This discriminatory law puts students at risk and sends a message of shame and stigma that has no place in schools. Many older folks know firsthand what it feels like to be shamed and shoved back into the closet. We need everyone to share their perspective and give hope to the younger generation."

–KELL OLSON, OUR LEAD ATTORNEY ON *COUSINS*

ANTI-TRANS ATTACKS

Transgender and nonbinary people—especially youth— have been the primary target of anti-LGBTQ+ legislation in recent years. Here's a look into our work to beat back anti-trans legislation in four areas: bathrooms, sports, identity documents, and healthcare.

"BATHROOM BANS"

Fearmongering over bathrooms has been a powerful tactic to generate opposition to trans equality. The Christian Right has worked to foment these "penis panics" with false claims that trans women threaten cisgender women and girls and demands for laws restricting people to bathrooms that match the gender markers on their birth certificates.

Carcaño v. Cooper (2016-2019)

In 2016, North Carolina passed a law (HB 2) requiring people to use public bathrooms aligned with their sex designated at birth. Lambda Legal and the ACLU immediately challenged it in federal court. Our litigation gave human faces and names to the harms caused by the law. It also helped to drive a national campaign to oppose HB 2, a campaign that included corporate leaders, entertainers, and sports stars, and that made the state legislature backpedal in 2017. A new law (HB 142) repealed the bathroom provisions while also barring schools and government agencies from regulating access to bathrooms. This meant a ban on both inclusive and exclusionary bathroom policies, leaving transgender and nonbinary people in limbo. We amended our lawsuit to include the revised law and in 2019, over the objections of the state legislature, we secured a consent decree that prohibited North Carolina from using HB 142 to police the bathroom choices of its citizens.

Other states learned at least a temporary lesson from North Carolina's experience. It took until 2021 before another state (Tennessee) enacted a bathroom ban. Frustratingly, Tennessee's ban didn't generate wide opposition, and several additional states have followed suit. Lambda Legal is committed to fighting this new wave of bigoted laws. As this book goes to press, we have two cases in progress: one in Idaho and the other (with the ACLU) in Oklahoma.[77]

(right) Protest on April 2, 2016, in downtown Asheville, North Carolina, against state law HB 2.

(opposite, top) Joaquín Carcaño, lead plaintiff in our challenge to HB 2, was the coordinator of a University of North Carolina at Chapel Hill project providing medical education and services to the Latinx community.

(opposite, bottom right) Protester against HB 2.

"Bathrooms have always been a vulnerable space for transgender people."

–SIMONE BELL, FORMER SOUTHERN REGIONAL DIRECTOR

Adams v. The School Board of St. Johns County, Florida (2017-2023)

Of course, bathroom bans don't only happen via state law. Trans and nonbinary students encounter them all too frequently in school. Drew Adams can attest to that. When he started high school as a freshman, he used the boys' restroom without incident. But after someone complained, Drew was told the boys' rooms were off limits and he could either use girls' bathrooms or one of the far-off single-stall restrooms. Drew felt humiliated by having to walk halfway across the school to use a special bathroom. And as an honors student, he also felt stressed by the distance; he could not use those bathrooms without missing class time. As a result, he began restricting his fluids and trying to hold his bladder. It was a constant reminder that his school didn't recognize him as a real boy. Drew's mother tried to intercede with his school, with no success.

We sued the St. John's County school board on Drew's behalf in 2017, arguing that the board's policy unconstitutionally demeans and humiliates transgender and nonbinary students by treating them differently from their cisgender peers and by making it much more difficult for them, and them alone, to manage their bathroom needs during the school day. We also argued that it discriminates on the basis of sex, in violation of both the U.S. Constitution and Title IX.

After a three-day trial, the federal judge ruled that Drew had to be allowed to use the boys' bathroom, with his seventy-page decision fully adopting our reasoning. The school board then appealed to the Eleventh Circuit. In 2020, the three-judge panel that heard the case also agreed with us, saying that public schools "may not harm transgender students by establishing arbitrary, separate rules for their bathroom use."

Undeterred, the school board asked all eleven judges on the 11th Circuit to review the panel's decision. This time, the decision went the other way. By a 7–4 majority, the court ruled that schools are allowed to segregate bathrooms by sex assigned at birth. With that callous dismissal of the trial court's findings, Drew was done. Six years into this odyssey, he had graduated from college, been long enough in the often-harsh public spotlight, and was ready for a quieter life.

"Being able to safely navigate everyday life when you set foot outside your home is not a luxury. It is a basic foundation for being treated and accepted as co-equal members of society, like everyone else."

–TARA BORELLI, OUR LEAD ATTORNEY ON ADAMS

(opposite) Drew Adams

SCHOOL SPORTS BANS

As of June 2023, twenty-two states had passed laws preventing transgender students from playing school sports that align with their gender identity. Similar laws were near passage in additional states. These new laws often have nearly identical language because they're usually based on models shopped to sympathetic lawmakers. It's all part of a calculated campaign by Christian Right activists who see gender diversity as an ideological threat and opposition to transgender rights as a social and political winner: a way to rile up and mobilize supporters.

B.P.J. v. West Virginia Board of Education and L.E. v. Lee (2021-ongoing)

These laws are built on unfounded stereotypes, false scientific claims, and ignorance about transgender people, especially trans girls and women, who are painted as dangerous to cisgender girls and women. Lambda Legal works to disrupt these and other falsehoods by sharing the truths of our clients' lives and the real harms that laws like this cause. In *B.P.J. v. West Virginia Board of Education*, for instance, we represent Becky Pepper-Jackson, a transgender girl from a family of runners who was looking forward to trying out for the girls' cross-country and track teams when she got to middle school. But shortly before she graduated from elementary school in 2021, West Virginia passed a law restricting girls sports to people assigned female at birth. Notably, Becky is the *only* student in the state who is currently openly affected by this law.

In *L.E. v. Lee* we represent Luc Esquivel, a high school student who wants to try out for the boys' golf team but can't because a 2021 Tennessee law bars transgender students from participating on teams matching their gender identity.

In both cases, we and the ACLU are arguing that the bans are solutions in search of a problem. Advocates of the bans in both states have been unable to identify *a single* example of a trans student athlete in their state who has taken opportunities from or injured a cisgender student. These bans aren't about addressing problems in sports—they're about excluding trans students to make them unequal to everyone else. In doing so, they violate the 14th Amendment's Equal Protection Clause as well as Title IX, which bars sex discrimination in schools that receive federal funding.

Although *B.P.J.* and *L.E.* were filed only six months apart, Becky's case has moved faster through the federal courts. In the summer of 2021, a federal judge granted our request for a preliminary injunction, concluding that Becky was likely to win at trial and that she would be deeply harmed if the law went into effect. Two years later—after Becky had been running with the girls' team for two seasons—he reversed course when deciding the case on its merits. West Virginia, he said, could limit participation in school sports based on sex designated at birth because the "physical characteristics that flow from [sex] are substantially related to athletic performance and fairness in sports." He dissolved the injunction and let the law go into effect.

Disappointed, we asked the Fourth Circuit to reinstate the injunction while we appealed. The court did so, agreeing that Becky was likely to win her appeal. But then West Virginia, working with the ADF, took an unusual step: it asked the U.S. Supreme Court to erase the Fourth Circuit's injunction. Three weeks later, that aggressive effort failed by a 7–2 vote, keeping the injunction in place as the case progresses. As state and federal lawmakers continue their nationwide misinformation-filled grandstanding about athletic fairness, we will be there at Becky's side—and at Luc's side—fighting for the right of all trans kids to participate in an important ritual of childhood: school sports.

"I love running, and being part of a team, and the State of West Virginia should explain in court why they won't let me."

—BECKY PEPPER-JACKSON

(above, left) Harrison County, West Virginia middle school student Becky Pepper-Jackson

(above, right) Becky with her mother, Heather Jackson.

"Four kids, and only one of them playing girls sports. That's what all of this is about. Four kids who aren't dominating or winning trophies or taking scholarships. Four kids who are just trying to find some friends and feel like they are a part of something. Four kids trying to get through each day. Rarely has so much fear and anger been directed at so few. I don't understand what they are going through or why they feel the way they do. But I want them to live."

—FROM UTAH GOV. SPENCER COX'S LETTER EXPLAINING WHY HE VETOED A 2022 BILL THAT WOULD BAR TRANSGENDER STUDENTS FROM PARTICIPATING IN SCHOOL SPORTS CONSISTENT WITH THEIR GENDER IDENTITY. SADLY, THE LEGISLATURE LATER OVERRODE COX'S VETO.

Supporters of equality in Washington, DC, in 2019.

STACK THE DECK AGAINST HATE

03

MACK BEGGS

"I was really looking forward to trying out for the boys' golf team and, if I made it, training and competing with and learning from other boys and improving my game. Then, to have the legislature pass a law that singled out me and kids like me to keep us from being part of a team, that crushed me, it hurt very much. I just want to play, like any other kid."

—LUC ESQUIVEL

(top) Knoxville, Tennessee high school student Luc Esquivel

(above) The "Stack the Deck Against Hate" campaign transformed anti-trans legislation into sports trading cards that celebrated transgender athletes across the country.

BANS ON ACCURATE IDENTITY DOCUMENTS

As discussed in Chapter 1, identity documents are an inescapable feature of modern society. Lambda Legal has prioritized making it possible for trans, nonbinary, and gender-diverse people to obtain accurate identity documents with updated names and gender markers. Our opponents, however, are trying to turn back the clock on equality. Two recent cases illustrate this line of attack.

F.V. v. Jeppesen (2017-2020)

After years of success challenging outdated restrictions, we identified Idaho as among the few remaining states enforcing a categorical ban preventing trans people from correcting the gender marker on their birth certificates. In 2017, we sued in Idaho's federal trial court on behalf of F.V. and Dani Martin, two transgender women who were born in Idaho, and who had both endured public harassment in government agencies as well as other day-to-day difficulties due to their outdated documents. We argued that Idaho was discriminating against them and invading their privacy, liberty, and freedom from compelled speech. In March 2018, the federal court agreed and gave state officials one month to start allowing transgender people born in Idaho to correct the gender markers on their birth certificates.

But that wasn't the end of the matter. First, the health department balked. Then, in early 2020, the Idaho legislature passed a law that effectively reinstituted the ban on gender marker corrections—in direct defiance of the federal court's 2018 order. Governor Brad Little signed the bill into law against the advice of his Attorney General and five previous attorneys general, all of whom cautioned that the law was likely unconstitutional and could subject the state to costly legal challenges. (They were right on both counts.) Within the month, we were back in Judge Dale's court requesting an enforcement order. The judge not only agreed that the new law violated her prior ruling but ordered the state to pay more than $320,000 in attorney fees.

> "When you treat the federal court like a doormat, there are going to be consequences. The rule of law comes to a grinding halt if government officials can act as if they are above the law that the rest of us are expected to follow."

−NORA HUPPERT, ONE OF OUR ATTORNEYS ON *F.V.*

(below) Dani Martin (R) with her wife and members of the legal team (L-R): Peter Renn, Monica Cockerille, and Kara Ingelhart.

Fowler v. Stitt (2022-ongoing)

The reactionary fever that seized GOP state politics following Joe Biden's election was not confined to legislatures. Governors and other state officials often grabbed the spotlight. Oklahoma's Governor Kevin Stitt did so by reversing a 14-year-long state health department policy allowing transgender people to correct their birth certificates to match their gender identity. He issued an executive order in late 2021, proclaiming: "I believe that people are created by God to be male or female. Period." The state legislature soon followed his lead, passing a bill to write the discriminatory policy change into state law.

We sued Governor Stitt in federal district court on behalf of three transgender Oklahomans— a transgender woman, Rowan Fowler, and two transgender men, Allister Hall and Carter Ray. As in *F.V. v. Jeppesen*, we argued that the new ban was discriminatory and an unconstitutional denial of equality, privacy, and liberty. It also violates free speech rights by compelling identification with a sex other than one's actual identity.

Unfortunately, in June of 2023, unlike in *F.V.*, the district judge granted the state's request to dismiss our case. With reasoning that willfully ignored the intentional targeting of transgender and nonbinary people and the lack of any adequate justifications, the decision misapplied the law at every step. Our appeal to the Tenth Circuit was underway as this book went to press.

"...Defendants do not defend the constitutionality of the policy. Instead, they admit it is unconstitutional."

–U.S. MAGISTRATE JUDGE CANDY W. DALE, *F.V.*

"My Social Security card and my birth certificate don't match. I am looking for a job now. It brings up a lot of questions. What genitalia I was born with is no one's business but mine and my doctor's at this point. These are embarrassing questions that no one should have to answer."

–ROWAN FOWLER, LEAD PLAINTIFF IN *FOWLER*

GENDER-AFFIRMING HEALTHCARE BANS

Of all the recent government attacks on transgender people, the barrage of measures attacking gender-affirming care (GAC) are especially frightening. They insert government into the most private realms of intimate decision-making and substitute political for personal and medical judgment at profound, physical and emotional cost to people needing medical care. Measures that target children specifically—as most do—also interfere with parents' right to make informed healthcare decisions to support their children.

Doe v. Abbott (2022-ongoing), *PFLAG v. Abbott* (2022-ongoing), and *Loe v. Texas* (2023-ongoing)

In 2021, Arkansas became the first state in the nation to enact a measure forbidding doctors from providing some or all GAC to trans youth. By the summer of 2023, the number of states with GAC bans had risen to twenty one. Most states have restricted GAC through legislation. But in Texas, Governor Greg Abbott launched the attack personally by issuing a February 2022 directive ordering state agencies to investigate parents who support their children's access to GAC, deeming it a form of child abuse.

Lambda Legal moved quickly to stop Abbott's directive from tearing apart loving families. Together with the ACLU, we filed two lawsuits seeking a halt to the directive while our cases were in progress. Our clients' stories are chilling. In *Doe v. Abbott*, we represent Jane, John, and Mary Doe, who found themselves living a nightmare. (Our clients are anonymous to protect their privacy and safety.) When the order was issued, Jane, an employee of the Texas Department of Family and Protective Services (DFPS), asked her supervisor how the directive would affect DFPS policy. Within hours, she was placed on leave, because her daughter Mary is transgender and receiving GAC to treat her gender dysphoria. One day later, she was told that she and her husband were under investigation for child abuse, because of Mary's medically necessary care. A DFPS investigator then showed up at the family home, interviewed Mary separately from her parents, and tried to get Mary's medical records, which the Does refused to provide.

In *PFLAG v. Abbott*, we represent PFLAG,[78] which is acting to protect all its Texas members, and three additional families directly harmed by Abbott's directive. Like the Does, these three families were investigated by DFPS, solely because their children were receiving medically necessary GAC. The Roes were pulled into an investigation when their son's high school pulled him out of class to meet with a DFPS investigator, who interviewed him without anyone else present and who asked him deeply personal and invasive questions. The Briggles, the only family not using pseudonyms, don't know for sure why they were investigated, but suspect that their vocal advocacy for their son and other transgender youth played a role. The Voes, in contrast, know precisely what happened. Their transgender son tried to commit suicide when he learned of Abbott's letter. He was taken to a hospital and from there to an outpatient psychiatric facility. When the staff at the outpatient facility learned that Antonio was receiving GAC, someone reported the Voes, and one week after their son was discharged, DFPS showed up at their door.

In our requests for immediate injunctions, we argued that Abbott doesn't have the authority to treat GAC as child abuse because doing so goes against extensive medical and scientific evidence establishing its efficacy and puts parents in an impossible position: forcing them to risk losing their children and being branded as criminals in order to provide for the medical needs of the children they love. Abbott's directive, we said, also threatens the health and well-being of the very transgender youth he claims to be protecting, while communicating that transgender people and their families are not welcome in Texas.

The trial court in *Doe v. Abbott* agreed with us and temporarily blocked the directive from being

"Fringe politicians without an ounce of medical training are seeking to override and interfere with the rights of parents to take care of and love their children. These laws, beyond having devastating medical consequences, also have created a hostile climate for trans youth and their families. They send the message that trans and nonbinary lives are expendable."

—SRUTI SWAMINATHAN, ONE OF OUR ATTORNEYS ON *L.W. V. SKRMETTI*, OUR CHALLENGE TO TENNESSEE'S BAN ON GAC FOR YOUTH

(top) Amber and Adam Briggle with their children.

Community members take part in the Trans Pride March in Portland, Oregon on June 16, 2018.

"It really is just affecting these kids and their parents in the most traumatic of ways."

–KAREN LOEWY, ONE OF OUR ATTORNEYS ON THE *ABBOTT* CASES

enforced. The Texas Attorney General's Office appealed all the way up to the Texas Supreme Court, which ruled that DFPS could not investigate the Doe family during litigation but could still investigate other families. We filed *PFLAG v. Abbott* to protect those families. The trial court in *PFLAG* also blocked enforcement of Abbott's directive and ordered that DFPS could not investigate members of PFLAG—who live all across Texas—during the litigation.

When the Texas legislature passed a 2023 law prohibiting GAC for youth, we challenged it as well, working together with the ACLU and the Transgender Law Center (*Loe v. Texas*). Our petition for an emergency injunction was granted by the trial court, which held that our clients "will suffer probable, imminent, and irreparable injury" were the law to take effect. These rulings have prevented Texas from weaponizing its child protection services against transgender youth and their families, at least temporarily.

While we await the next stages in *Doe, PFLAG,* and *Loe,* we have been busy challenging GAC bans elsewhere. As this book goes to press at the close of 2023, we have lawsuits in progress against Louisiana, Missouri, Montana, North Carolina, Oklahoma, and Tennessee.[79] Our movement colleagues are spearheading challenges in many other states.

The legal landscape around GAC bans is evolving rapidly. The first several courts to hear challenges to their constitutionality prohibited states from letting GAC bans take effect during the litigation process, agreeing that they were likely unconstitutional. One federal judge, for example, called Florida's attacks on transgender medical care "an exercise in politics, not good medicine" that engaged in "purposeful discrimination" against transgender people in clear contravention of medical consensus and in blatant violation of their rights.[80] But the Sixth and Eleventh Circuits have both allowed GAC bans to take effect while the litigation plays out, ignoring the profound harms such laws cause to trans youth.[81] By the time this book reaches you, the landscape will surely have shifted yet again.

We cannot know how long this period of attack on LGBTQ+ people will last. We can promise you, though, that Lambda Legal will not back down from this fight. Our mission has been and remains the pursuit of full civil rights for our community through test case litigation, policy development and legislative lawyering, and public education. This is the story of our first half-century. It ends on a cliff-hanger. In doing so, it sets up the first pages of the story of our next fifty years. We cannot know what those fifty years will look like. But we do know that we will meet them with a fierce commitment to securing the freedom, equality, and inherent dignity of our ever-evolving LGBTQ+ community.

"The thing that has impacted me the most and given me the most hope beyond the growing legal protections is the growing acceptance, and frankly, ferocious love and protectiveness demonstrated by parents and families of LGBTQ youth, and especially trans youth. This support has really bloomed in my lifetime and will save and change so many lives."

—SASHA BUCHERT, NONBINARY AND TRANSGENDER RIGHTS PROJECT DIRECTOR

CHAPTER 11

ENVISIONING JUSTICE/ CLAIMING OUR FUTURE

BY KEVIN JENNINGS

Never doubt that a small group of thoughtful committed individuals can change the world. In fact, it's the only thing that ever has.

—MARGARET MEAD

The story of Lambda Legal is simply remarkable. Founded fifty years ago, when homosexuality was deemed a mental illness by the medical profession and same-sex relations were still a crime in forty-five states, an organization that had to sue for its very right to exist has persevered and, in the process, revolutionized life for LGBTQ+ people in the United States. It is an amazing and inspiring story.

But, as I write in 2023, it is self-evident that our work is not finished. Tidal waves of anti-LGBTQ+ legislation have been sweeping the nation, with hundreds of bills being introduced into forty-plus states each of the past few years. A federal judiciary that has been yanked hard to the right has reversed *Roe v. Wade* and dangerously undermined other core constitutional protections, and now threatens to overturn some of Lambda Legal's landmark victories and roll back the hard-won progress we have made over the past five decades. Determined, well-resourced opponents remain relentless in their efforts to relegate LGBTQ+ people to second-class citizenship in America.

So, as we turn our attention to an uncertain future, we must ask: "What's next?"

That is exactly the question we set out to answer in 2020 when we mapped out a strategic plan for Lambda Legal's future. We took a careful look at our work and the world we live in today and prioritized the many distinct buckets of work we do into a rank order list. At the end, we realized we

(page 270) San Francisco Pride 2015

(left) Kevin Jennings

(opposite) Lambda Legal at 2023 New York City Pride.

could summarize our strategy in a single sentence: "Lambda Legal wins new protections for the most vulnerable in the LGBTQ+ community while defending the community from attacks."

Our road map is clear. For far too many people in our community—trans and nonbinary people, LGBTQ+ youth, people living with HIV, LGBTQ+ seniors, BIPOC LGBTQ+ people, LGBTQ+ immigrants, the list could go on—freedom is not a lived reality but a future aspiration. We must be tenacious and determined and do the hard work that remains to earn and win freedom for present and future generations.

Yet at the same time as we fight for new protections, we must be vigilant to prevent the fragile progress we have made in our first fifty years from being reversed. As they have proven with their decades-long, successful fights to undermine voting and reproductive rights, our opponents are also tenacious and determined and will stop at nothing to impose their vision on the rest of America. We remain locked in a struggle for the soul of our nation, a battle over which future will prevail: one where there is freedom, equity, and justice for all Americans or one where we remain a nation that privileges some of its members over others.

Our victory is not guaranteed. Fortunately, we do not start from scratch, as our founders did five decades ago: instead, we have fifty years of history, advocacy, and victories to learn from and to inspire us to continue to do the work that began in 1973. And do it, we shall.

Trevor Wilkinson

AFTERWORD
TREVOR WILKINSON

One of my favorite musicals is *Hairspray*. There's a song titled "I Know Where I've Been," and I think there is a certain beauty in the lyrics of the song that virtually every member of the LGBTQIA+ community can connect to: "There is a struggle that we have yet to win, and there's pride in my heart 'cause I know where I'm going and I know where I've been." We in the queer community have felt these lyrics for decades and still today, we feel these lyrics in our hearts. We know where we have been. We have fought for the rights others take for granted. We rioted at Stonewall. We have fought relentlessly to marry so that the states we live in will recognize our unions as legitimate partnerships. Throughout this book, you have read stories of struggles. You have also read stories of pride thanks to organizations like Lambda Legal who are fighting for our rights every day. That is where we have been, but where are we going in the next fifty years?

The thing I hope most for the queer community is peace. I hope people won't have to come out. Instead, two people can date without there being anything uncommon about it. I hope that we as a society can work to accept others for who they are and not who we want them to be. I hope drag queens dance and do story hours for children without fearing for their safety. I hope our society stops stigmatizing people living with HIV. I hope transgender folks can live authentically and walk downtown without receiving death threats. Most of all, in the next fifty years, I hope everyone in this vast community knows and understands peace in whatever way is true for them. It starts with me, it starts with you, and it starts with us. If we want future generations of queer people to live in peace, we must work together and make our voices heard. We must recognize the state of the world and call out the anti-LGBTQIA+ bigotry dominating legislatures. There is a struggle that we have yet to win. But, together, we can and doing so will pave the way to a world where we queer people are not scared to live our lives authentically. However, this can only be done if we all come together to fight for equality today, tomorrow, and always. So yes, the LGBTQIA+ community knows where we are going because we know where we've been.

---

* Trevor Wilkinson was repeatedly suspended from his Texas high school for refusing to remove the rainbow-colored nail polish he had adopted for Pride. After researching Title IX, which prohibits sex-based discrimination in schools, he launched an online petition against this anti-gay gender stereotype. It went viral, eventually collecting over 400,000 signatures, and bringing national attention to his protest.

ABOUT THE AUTHORS

Jenny Pizer is Lambda Legal's Chief Legal Officer. She is an honors graduate of Harvard/Radcliffe College and received her J.D. from NYU School of Law. Jenny's affiliation with Lambda Legal began in 1985 as a law student intern for Abby Rubenfeld and Roz Richter. She served on Lambda Legal's Board of Directors while in private law practice and has been honored to play many roles since joining the staff in 1996, including Managing Attorney, Marriage Project Director, and Law and Policy Director. She also is honored to serve currently on the Board of Directors of Outright International, which advances the human rights of LGBTIQ+ people globally through research, capacity building, and United Nations advocacy.

Jenny considers herself blessed to have had wonderful teachers, mentors, and friends in school and in her various legal and non-legal jobs. She counts herself especially fortunate to have had nearly forty years of learning from and with Lambda Legal staff, board colleagues, and cooperating counsel who model fierce creativity, compassion, and tenacity in tackling hard problems. It has been her honor to have represented clients who put their trust in our good faith and skill, and to have had so many inspiring movement partners. This book is a tribute to everyone who has believed in Lambda Legal's mission and invested their time, resources, and spirit to help us all advance.

Jenny lives in Los Angeles with her wife, Doreena Wong. They met the first day of law school, waiting in line to get their student ID cards. Since then, they have shared a path of public interest lawyering and movement building. For Jenny, Lambda Legal's work has been both professional and personal. It always has presented intriguing questions and worthy goals. But advocating for the freedom to marry was about love and family. Jenny proposed to Doreena from the West Hollywood rally stage the day of our victory in the California Supreme Court. Luckily, Doreena said yes.

And now Jenny celebrates the lucky accident of crossing paths with a scholar whose expertise is the role of advocacy within our LGBTQ+ movement—a scholar who was steeped in the first three decades of Lambda Legal's history, and who became a treasured partner in telling a half-century version of our story.

(above, middle) Jenny and Doreena at Los Angeles Pride, June 20, 2016.

(above, right) Jon Davidson, Camilla Taylor, and Jenny at the U.S. Supreme Court, March 26, 2013.

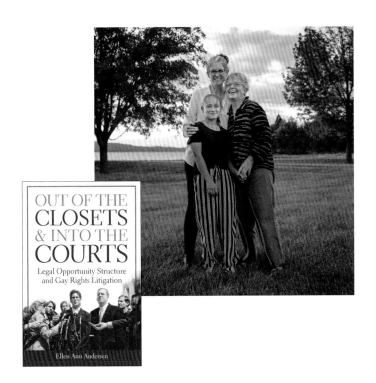

Ellen Ann Andersen is an associate professor of political science and gender, sexuality, and women's studies at the University of Vermont. She holds a Ph.D. from the University of Michigan and teaches classes on the American political system, constitutional law, American political history, LGBTQ+ politics, and social movements. Her research is centered on the intersection of law and politics, especially in the context of LGBTQ+ rights.

She first got interested in studying Lambda Legal when she took a class on sexual orientation and the law at the University of Michigan School of Law in the early 1990s. The course (one of the first of its kind) was taught by the inestimable Paula Ettelbrick—then the outgoing legal director at Lambda Legal. Ellen became fascinated by the way that groups like Lambda Legal used litigation strategically to advance social movement aims. An idea began to form: a study of the role of litigation in the struggle for gay rights (as it was known at the time.) A study of how law and politics collide.

Paula put Ellen in touch with then-Executive Director, Kevin Cathcart, who graciously allowed her to set up camp in Lambda Legal's New York office for weeks at a time over the next several years. The idea eventually blossomed into a book—*Out of the Closets and Into the Courts*—centered on Lambda Legal's first three decades.

Some twenty years later, she is delighted to have the opportunity to work closely with Lambda Legal again. *Making the Case for Equality* is a labor of love: a chance for a practitioner and an academic to bond over a shared passion for LGBTQ+ rights and the role of litigation in achieving them.

Ellen lives in South Burlington, Vermont, with her wife Susanmarie Harrington, and daughter, Sofia. Their life together is a testament to the importance of LGBTQ+ rights litigation. After a religious wedding in 1995, Ellen and Susanmarie entered into a Vermont civil union in 2000, and a legal marriage in 2013. Describing this sequence, Ellen says she married once for love, once for politics, and once for money. They adopted Sofia along the way, in one of Indiana's earliest same-sex adoption cases. Adoption, civil unions, and legal marriage gave their family a level of safety for which they are endlessly grateful.

(above, right) Ellen, Susanmarie, and Sofia at Shelburne Farms in Vermont, 2020.

INDEX

Principal cases are indicated by bolded page numbers.

303 Creative v. Elenis, 97, 244, 282

Abbott, Greg, 10, 266, 268–69
Able, Jane, 78
Able v. United States, **78**
Abrigo, Jose, 66
Adams, Drew, 258–59
Adams v. School Board of St. Johns County, **258–59**
adoption, 124, 126–29, 142, 187, 201, 236, 280
Affordable Care Act of 2010 (ACA), 115, 280
Alexander-Burk, Dani, 95
Alison D. v. Virginia M., **124**, 126, 128
Americans with Disabilities Act of 1990 (ADA), 48, 58, 60, 65
anti-LGBTQ+ attacks, 10–11, 36–37, 176–81, 238–69
Arizona v. United States, **214–15**
Arroyo Pizarro, Yolanda, 157
Asti, Robina, 96, 162–63, 164, 200
asylum, 206–15, 227

B., Brooke, 128–29
Baehr, Ninia, 136–37
Baehr v. Lewin, **136–39**, 167, 281
Bailey, Karen, 156
Baker v. Vermont, 167, 281
Barber v. Bryant, 247
BarbouRoske, Jennifer and Dawn, 142–45
Barrett, Amy Coney, 231
bathrooms, 10, 78, 240, 256–59
Bell, Simone, 34, 247, 257
Benitez, Lupita, 112–13
Benitez v. North Coast Women's Care Med. Grp., **112–13**, 242
Bennett, Jim, 93, 95
Berg, Alex, 96
Berg, Copy, 74–75
Berg v. Claytor, **74–75**
Biden administration, 11, 80, 196, 198, 212, 228, 230, 232, 246, 250, 265
Black LGBTQIA+ Migrant Project, 204, 207, 212–13
Boggan, Cary, 7, 74–75
book banning, 10, 254
Borelli, Tara, 106, 258
Borenstein, Ruth, 157
Bostock v. Clayton Cnty., 82, 89, 115
Bova, Patrick, 157
Bowers v. Hardwick, 22–23, **26–27**, 28, 30–31, 121
Bowman-Cryer, Rachel and Laurel, 243–45
Boy Scouts of America v. Dale, **182–83**
B.P.J. v. West Virginia Bd. of Educ., **260–61**
Bradkowski, Keith, 132–33
Bradley, Bob, 48–49
Bradley, Thomas, 48–49

Bradshaw, Erica and Tevonda, 138–39, 157
Brandon v. Richardson, **32–33**, 99, 216
Bridge v. Oklahoma State Dept. of Educ., 256, 282
Briggle, Amber and Adam, 266–69
Briteramos, Nikko, 60–61
Briteramos v. King of Kuts, **60–61**
Brooke S.B. v. Elizabeth A.C.C., **128–29**
Brown, Margie, 64–65
Buchert, Sasha, 99, 269
Buckel, David S., 176–77
Bufford, Taeko, 192–93
Burbank, Kent, 156
Burger, Warren, 26
Burnett, Lynne, 157
Burns, Richard, 7, 18
Burwell v. Hobby Lobby, 242–43

Calhoun v. Pennington, 32, **34–35**, 216
Cammermeyer, Grethe, 6–77
Cammermeyer v. Perry, **76–77**
Campos, Lillith, 38
Campos v. Cohen, **38**
Carcaño, Joaquín, 256–57
Carcaño v. Cooper, **256–57**
Carter, David O., 175
Castillo, Paul, 39
Castro-Bojorquez, Marco, 97
Cathcart, Kevin, 7, 18, 155, 277
censorship, 174–75, 178–79, 241, 248–55
Cervelli, Diane, 192–93
Cervelli v. Aloha Bed & Breakfast, **192–93**, 242
Chappell, Michelle, 156
Charles, Carl, 33
Chung, Cristy, 156
Civil Rights Act of 1964 (Title VII), 71, 86–89
civil union, 149, 152, 166, 167
Clark, Christopher, 64
Clark, Joanne, 112–13
Clark, Stephen, 231
Clinton, Bill, 18, 78–79, 138–39
Cockerille, Monica, 264
Colín, Anthony, 174–75
Colín v. Orange Cnty. Unified Sch. Dist., **174–75**
Collins, Tracy, 107
Collman, Jeff, 132–33
Cook, Currey, 198, 228, 236
County of Santa Clara v. HHS, 246
courts, bias in, 229–37
Cousins, Jen and Matt, 254–55
Cousins v. Sch. Bd. of Orange Cnty., 170 –71, **254–55**
C.P. v. Blue Cross/Blue Shield of Illinois, **114–15**
criminal legal system, 63–67, 216–22
Cunninghis, Amy, 108–9
Cusick, Matthew, 52–53, 200
Cusick v. Cirque du Soleil, **52–53**

Dale, Candy W., 264–65
Dale, James, 182–83
Danak, Mark, 35
Dancel, Genora, 137
Daniels, Chris, 34
Darby, Jim, 157
Davidson, Jon, 7, 82, 211, 217, 276

Davis, Corey, 157
Davis, Rick, 95
Defense of Marriage Act of 1996 (DOMA), 108, 138–39, 140, 152, 167
"Deploy or Get Out" policy, 54, 56
DeSantis, Ron, 171, 248, 254
Diaz, Joseph, 106–7
Diaz v. Brewer, **106–7**
Dinan, David, 254–55
Dobbs v. Jackson Women's Health Organization, 10, 116
Doe v. A.J. Boggs Co., **62**
Doe v. Abbott, **266–69**
Doe v. Mutual of Omaha, 48
Dohrn, Beatrice, 7, 78
domestic partnership, 103, 106, 126, 130, 132–33, 142, 166, 233
"Don't Ask, Don't Tell" policy (DADT), 74–79
"Don't Say Gay or Trans" laws, 10, 240, 248, 254–55
drag performances, targeting of, 238, 240–41, 250, 275
Dubofsky, Jean, 36
Dueñas, Francisco, 98, 214
Dunbar, Kevin, 84–85
Dunbar v. Foot Locker, **84–85**
Duncan, Kyle, 231

Easter, Kelly, 197
Easter v. HHS, **197**
Ely, Michael, 164
Ely v. Saul, **164–65**
employment discrimination, 52–57, 68–89
Espinoza-Madrigal, Iván, 215
Esplin, Bryn, 194–97
Esquivel, Alec, 110–11
Esquivel, Luc, 260, 263
Esquivel v. Oregon, **110–11**
Ettelbrick, Paula, 124, 136, 277
Everly, Bonnie, 157
Ewert, Pat, 95, 134, 136, 156
Executive Order 13950 (Trump administration), 250–51

Facing Foster Care in Alaska v. HHS, **228**
Fair Housing Act of 1968 (FHA), 58, 187–91
Fields v. Smith, **219**, 281
Fink, Lee, 112–13
Finstuen, Heather, 127
Finstuen v. Crutcher, **126–27**, 280
Fletcher, Brian, 157
Florida Parental Rights in Education Act of 2022, 10, 240, 248, 254–55
Foley, Dan, 138–39
Forrest, Diana, 107
foster and out-of-home care, 187, 194–99, 224–28
Fowler, Rowan, 265
Fowler v. Stitt, **265**
Franke, Michelle, 156
Franke, Robert, 58–59
Franke v. Parkstone Living Center, **58–59**
Fulton v. Philadelphia, 194, 282
F.V. v. Jeppesen, **264**, 265

Gabel-Brett, Leslie, 7, 141
Garcia, Jaime, 156

Garden State Equality v. Dow, **148–49**
Garner, Tyron, 28–31
Gay, Roxane, 9–11
gay marriage. *See* marriage equality
Gay Students Organization v. Bonner, **172–73**
gender-affirming care, 10, 38, 56, 110–11, 114–16, 219–21, 224, 240, 266–69
Glavaris, Will, 157
Glenn, Vandy Beth, 86–87, 95
Glenn v. Brumby, **86–87**
Goldberg, Jackie, 132
Goldberg, Suzanne, 30–31, 210
Golinski, Karen, 108–9
Golinski v. OPM, **108–9**, 152
Gongidi, Vik, 254–55
Gonzalez-Pagan, Omar, 115, 212, 218
Goodridge v. Dept. of Public Health, 167
Gordon, Demoya, 221
Gorenberg, Hayley, 52
Gorsuch, Neil, 89, 231
Gottschall, Joan B., 219, 281
Grant, John, 156
Gray, Vernita, 95, 134, 136, 156
Gregg, Jonathan, 161
Grobeson, Mitch, 82–83
Grobeson v. Los Angeles, **82–83**
Gross, Al, 112–13
Guardianship of Lydia M. Ramos, **122–23**
Guillermo-Togawa, Pauline and Jill, 157

Hall, Allister, 265
Hamm, Thomas, 218
Hamm v. City of New York, **218**
Hardaway, Lisa, 143
Hardwick, Michael, 26–27
Harlow, Ruth, 2, 7, 30–31, 138
Harrison, Nick, 54–55
Harrison v. Austin, **54–55**, 56, 280
Hayes, Thomas, 35
health insurance and medical care, 38, 130, 132, 100–117, 219–21, 224, 266–69
Heath-Toby, Alicia, 156
Hempel, Greg, 127
Henkle, Derek, 178–79
Henkle v. Gregory, **178–79**, 254
Henry v. Hodges. See Obergefell v. Hodges
Hicklin, Jessica, 216-17, 220–21
Hicklin v. Precythe, 216, **220–21**, 280
Hickok, Robert, 157
HIV/AIDS discrimination, 16, 42–67, 222–23, 280
Hively, Kim, 88–89
Hively v. Ivy Tech, 86, **88–89**, 188, 191
Hobby Lobby Stores, 242–43
Hollingsworth v. Perry, 152
housing discrimination, 58–59, 136, 187–93
Humphrey, Keith, 107
Huppert, Nora, 264

identity documents, 23, 38–39, 162–63, 264–65
immigration, 26, 45, 97–98, 160–61, 204–15
Immigration Equality v. DHS, 206–7, **212–13**

In re Marriage Cases, 94, 108, 152, 280
In re Robina Asti, 96, **162–63**
In re Soto Vega, **211**
In re Soul,, **227**
In re Thom, **24–25**, 280
Ingelhart, Kara, 56, 264
Inniss, Christopher, 150–51
Inniss v. Aderhold, **150–51**
Irwin, Patty, 126

Jackson, Ketanji Brown, 231
Jennings, Kevin, 7, 271–73
Jimenez, Ruben, 106–7
Johnson, Stefan, 7, 60, 201
Judkins, Lyn, 157
juvenile justice, 194, 220, 224, 226–27

Kacsmaryk, Matthew, 231
Karnoski, Ryan, 81
Karnoski v. Trump, **80–81**
Katine, Mitchell, 30–31
Kavanaugh, Brett, 231
Kennedy, Anthony, 28, 37, 152, 154–55
Kilian, Maureen, 148–49
Kippins, Kristine, 116, 231
Kiviti, Adiel and Roee, 160–61
Kiviti v. Pompeo, **160–61**
Klay, Robert, 107
Klein v. Oregon Bureau of Labor and Industry, 243–45
Korty, Lee, 156
Kramer, Erika, 96

L.W. v. Skrmetti, 267, 282
Lam, Huong, 203
Langbehn, Janice, 130–31
Langbehn v. Jackson Memorial Hospital, **130–31**
Larkins, Will, 170–71, 254–55
Lavery, Michael, 7, 14
Lawrence, John, 28–31
Lawrence v. Texas, 2, 7, 10, **28–31**, 116, 152
L.E. v. Lee, **260, 263**
Legal Help Desk, 7, 13, 60, 71, 96, 98, 200–203
LeJeune, Andre, 157
Levasseur, Dru, 111, 162
Lewis v. Harris, **148–49**
Littrell, Beth, 35, 130, 247
Loe v. Texas, **266–69**
Loewy, Karen, 165, 191, 268
Logue, Pat, 2, 7, 25, 31, 124–25, 136, 177
López Aviles, Maritza, 157
Lyon, Phyllis, 137, 156

Mackler, Peter, 217
Mackler v. Los Angeles, **217**
Magro, Ann, 127
Majors, Nelda, 156
Majors v. Jeanes, 106, **146–47**
Marouf, Fatma, 194–97
Marouf v. Becerra, **195–96**
marriage equality, 7, 9–11, 16, 92, 106, 121, 126, 132, 134–67, 234–35, 241
Martin, Dani, 264
Martin, Del, 137, 156
Martinez, George and Fred McQuire, 46–47
Martinez, Hector, 157
Masliah, Noemi, 124

Masterpiece Cakeshop v. Colorado Civil Rights Comm., 241, 243–44, 282
Matlovich, Leonard, 74–75
Matlovich v. Secretary of the Air Force, **74–75**
Matter of Dana, **126**
McNamara, Seph, 112–13
McQuaid, Jr., Robert A., 178
McShan, Donisha, 96
medical care and health insurance, 38, 100–117, 130, 132, 219–21, 224, 266–69
Melillo, Joe, 137
Meneghin, Cindy, 148–49
Messina, Gail, 126
military service, 26, 54–57, 72–81
Mitchell, Karrie, 107
Mize, Derek, 161
Mize and Gregg v. Pompeo, **161**
Moore, Roy, **234–35**, 281
Morrison, Jane, 25, 95
Morton, Bert, 156
Murdock, Justin, 157
Murray, Dawn, 180–81
Murray v. Oceanside Unified Sch. Dist., **180–81**

Nabozny, Jamie, 176–77
Nabozny v. Podlesny, **176–77**, 178, 254
Nagarajan, Mala, 156
Nance, W. Mitchell, **236**
Neeley, Scott, 107
Nevins, Greg, 86, 88–89
Newcombe, Mary, 76–77
Nicholson-McFadden, Marcye and Karen, 157
Noriega, Mona, 95
Nonbinary and Transgender Rights Project, 99

Obama administration, 80, 108, 130–31, 154–55, 228, 230
Obergefell, Jim, 155
Obergefell v. Hodges, 10–11, 116, 152, 154–55, 167, 231, 234
Ocampo, Carmina, 146, 209
O'Kelley, Judi, 92
Oliveras Vega, Zulma, 157
Olson, Kell, 255
O'Mara, Robyne, 157
Osaze, Ola, 204, 207, 213
Osborn, Kenneth, 78

parenthood, 121, 122–29, 142–43, 158–61, 194–99
People v. 49 W. 12 St. Tenants Corp. (Sonnabend case), 46, 58
Pepper-Jackson, Becky, 260–61
Perkins, Penny, 124
PFLAG v. Abbott, **266–69**
Pitcherskaia, Alla, 210
Pitcherskaia v. INS, **210**
Pizer, Jenny, 112, 122, 276
police misconduct, 32–35, 82, 216–18, 222–23
Porter, David, 231
Pride parades, 16, 82–83, 94, 116, 162, 186–87, 208, 213
Pritchard, Casey, 114–15
Pritchard, Patricia, 114–15
Proctor, Bob, 157

Proposition 8, 93, 152, 281
Proyecto Igualdad, 98
public accommodations, 60–61, 182, 187, 192–93, 242–245
public education and engagement, 52, 60-61, 90–99, 138, 152

Quasney, Niki, 157
Quon, Myron, 180

Ramos, Lydia, 122–23, 132, 200
Ray, Carter, 265
refugees, 196–97, 204–15
religion-based discrimination, 112–15, 192–99, 242–47
Religious Freedom Restoration Act (RFRA), 115
Renn, Peter, 80, 264
reproductive rights, 116–17, 224
Respect for Marriage Act, 11
Reyes, Daniel, 140
Rhoades, Nick, 63–64
Rhoades v. Iowa, **63–64**
Rice, Ethan, 237
Richter, Roz, 7, 14, 25, 276
Rivera-Rivera, Iris Delia, 157
Rizzo, Daryl, 156
Robinson, Thomas J., 156
Rodrigues, Tammy, 137
Roe and Voe v. Austin, **54**, 56, 280
Roe v. Critchfeld, 256, 282
Roe v. Precythe, 63, **65**, 216
Roe v. Wade, 10, 116
Rogers, Eden, 198–99
Rogers v. HHS, **198–99**
Romer v. Evans, **36–37**, 152, 280
Rubenfeld, Abby, 7, 26, 46, 276
Russell, Stephen, 107
Russo, Nick, 7, 14

Saenz, Richard, 221–22
Sandler, Amy, 157
Santa Cruz Lesbian and Gay Cmty. Ctr. v. Trump, **250–51**
Santos, Mercedes, 156
Sawyer, Heather, 48, 124–25
Schmid, Cathrine, 80
Schoettes, Scott, 58, 61
schools and students, 168–83, 231, 240, 248, 254–63
Scott-Henderson, Daphne, 120–21
Seckinger, Beverly, 106–7
Seemiller, Corey, 107
Seltzer, Michael, 14
sex work, 63, 66–67
Shapcott, Sue, 107
Shutt, Michael, 95
Skeen, Shelly, 95
Smith, Paul, 2, 7, 31
Smith, Rachel and Tonya, 188–89
Smith v. Avanti, **188–89**
Smith-Carrington, Avatara, 251
Sommer, Susan, 31, 128–29
Sonnabend, Joseph, 46, 58
Soto Vega, Jorge, 211
Sotomayor, Sonia, 97, 244
Soul, 227
Spencer, Stephen, 78
Sperling, Carrie, 107
sports bans, 10, 240, 260–63
Stitt, Kevin, 265
Stoddard, Tom, 136
Stonewall, 6–9, 172, 216, 254

Strauss, Karen, 157
Stroman, Shelton, 150–51
Subramaniam, Vega, 156
Sullivan, Colleen, 225
survivor benefits, 146, 158, 162–65
Swaminathan, Sruti, 267
Swaya, Ed, 127
Sweeney, Tim, 7, 45

Talanquer, Vicente, 156
Talmas, Rob, 157
Taunton, Susan, 106–7
Taylor, Camilla, 125, 143, 176, 276
Taylor, Lorenzo, 54–55
Taylor, Spider, 164
Taylor v. Rice, **54–55**
Teena, Brandon, 32–33
Thom, Bill, 7, 14, 18, 24–25, 200, 280
Thomas, Clarence, 10, 116
Thornton, Helen, 164–65
Thornton v. Saul, **164–65**
Tillery, Beverly, 104
Title VII, 71, 86–89
Toby-Heath, Saundra, 157
Torres, Chelsea and Jessamy, 158–59
Torres v. Seemeyer, **158–59**
Torruellas Iglesias, José, 156
Trump administration, 9, 54, 56, 80–81, 161, 196, 198, 207, 212–13, 228, 230–31, 240–41, 246, 248, 250–51

United States v. Windsor, 108, 152, 167
Upton, Ken, 126

Vaid, Urvashi, 18
Vargas, Hector, 235
Varnum v. Brien, **142–45**, 146, 229
Vitale, Joseph, 157
Volpe, Theresa, 156
Von Wohld, Richard, 78

Weiss, Daniel, 156
Welch, Brandy, 198–99
Wetzel, Marsha, 190–91
Wetzel v. Glen St. Andrew Living Community, **190–91**
White, Byron, 27
Wilkerson, Connie Glenn, **233**
Wilkins, Isaiah, 56–57
Wilkins v. Austin, **56–57**
Wilkinson, Trevor, 274–75
Wilson, Pete, 217
Wilson, Phill, 61
Winters, Megan, 81
Wolfson, Evan, 92, 136–41, 183
women living with HIV, 66–67
Woo, Lancy, 156, 287
Wood, Diane, 191
Woolbright, Curtis, 140

Yorksmith, Pam and Nicole, 157
Young, Jessica and Kathy, 156

Zarda v. Altitude Express, 89
Zawadski, Jack, 96
Zawadski v. Brewer Funeral Services, 96, 280
Zehr, Werner, 78
Zetin, Heather, 174–75
Zzyym, Dana, 38–39
Zzyym v. Blinken, **38–39**

ENDNOTES

NOTES FROM CHAPTER 1

1   As noted in "Making the Case," the language used reflects the time under discussion. In the early '70s, Lambda Legal's focus was on the problems facing lesbians and gay men.

2   The completed petition stated that Lambda Legal would engage in a number of activities designed to protect the civil rights of lesbians and gay men. In describing the intended activities of Lambda Legal, Bill Thom took verbatim from the language of the Puerto Rican Legal Defense and Education Fund's successful petition, substituting homosexuals for Puerto Ricans:

"providing without charge legal services in those situations which give rise to legal issues having a substantial effect on the legal rights of *homosexuals;* to promote the availability of legal services to *homosexuals* by encouraging and attracting *homosexuals* into the legal profession; to disseminate to *homosexuals* general information concerning their legal rights and obligations, and to render technical assistance to any legal services corporation or agency in regard to legal issues affecting *homosexuals.*" (emphasis added)

3   Andy Humm, "Remembering How Gay Lawyers Became Legal," *Gay City News* (Chicago, IL), June 21, 2018. https://gaycitynews.com/remembering-how-gay-lawyers-became-legal/.

4   Lambda Legal, *Snapshots from a Civil Rights Movement* (1998).

5   Chad Graham, "Changing History," *The Advocate,* January 20, 2004, 38.

6   Chris Bull, "The *Lawrence* Legacy," *The Advocate,* January 20, 2004, 38.

7   Pooja Lodhia, "Houston lawyer looks back on landmark Lawrence v. Texas case: My kids live 'in a much better world.'" ABC13 News, December 16, 2022. https://abc13.com/president-joe-biden-signs-respect-for-marriage-act-lawrence-v-texas-same-sex/12576332/

8   Col Const, Art II, § 30b. The amendment stated:

"Neither the State of Colorado, through any of its branches or any of its agencies, political subdivisions, municipalities or school districts, shall enact, adopt or enforce any statute, regulation, ordinance or policy whereby homosexual, lesbian or bisexual orientation, conduct, practices or relationships shall constitute or otherwise be the basis of or entitle any person or class of persons to have or claim any minority status, quota preferences, protected status or claim of discrimination. This Section of the Constitution shall be in all respects self-executing."

NOTES FROM CHAPTER 2

9   AIDS (Acquired Immune Deficiency Syndrome) is caused by HIV (human immunodeficiency virus). AIDS is the advanced stage of HIV infection.

10   Centers for Disease Control, "Current Trends Mortality Attributable to HIV Infection/AIDS—United States, 1981-1990," *MMWR. Morbidity and Mortality Weekly Report* 40, no. 3 (January 25, 1991): 41–44.

11   *People v. 49 West 12 Street Tenants Corp.*

12   Centers for Disease Control, "Estimated HIV incidence and prevalence in the United States, 2017–2021." *HIV Surveillance Supplemental Report 28,* no. 3 (2023), http://www.cdc.gov/hiv/library/reports/hiv-surveillance/vol-28-no-3/index.html

13   *Doe v. Centinela Hospital.*

14   *Bradley v. Blue Cross/Blue Shield.*

15   *Doe v. Mutual of Omaha.*

16   The EEOC (Equal Opportunity Employment Commission) is responsible for enforcing federal anti-discrimination laws.

17   Sarah Kaufman, "Fired by Cirque du Soleil, Matthew Cusick Landed on His Feet," *The Washington Post*, October 21, 2004.

18   Rehabilitation Act of 1973, 29 U.S.C. § 701 et seq.

19   At the outset, the case was called *Harrison v. Shanahan*, then became *Harrison v. Esper*, and finally *Harrison v. Austin*. The name changes reflect turnover in the leadership of the Department of Defense.

20   As with *Harrison v. Austin*, *Roe and Voe v. Austin* changed names several times as new Secretaries of Defense took office.

21   Tim Murphy, "Service Member Discusses Historic Win in His Fight Against the Military's HIV Ban," *The Body*, April 18, 2022, https://www.thebody.com/article/sgt-nick-harrison-win-against-military-hiv-ban

NOTES FROM CHAPTER 3

22   David Zurawik, "Close hopes that film about gay Army officer will 'get people talking,'" *Baltimore Sun*, Jan 11, 1995.

23   "Don't Ask, Don't Tell, Don't Pursue," 10 U.S.C. § 654 (1993).

24   General Accounting Office, *Military Personnel: Personnel and Cost Data Associated with Implementing DOD's Homosexual Conduct Policy*, January 20, 2011.

25   Don't Ask, Don't Tell Repeal Act of 2010, Pub. L. 111–321, Dec. 22, 2010, 124 Stat. 3515-3517.

26   Rebecca Ruiz, "Ryan Karnoski is a trans man who sued Trump for the right to serve in the military," *Mashable*, June 2, 2019, https://mashable.com/article/karnoski-v-trump-trans-military-ban

27   You can hear the program at https://beta.prx.org/stories/131544

28   The case was *Zawadski v. Brewer Funeral Services.*

NOTES FROM CHAPTER 4

29   See, for example, Ning Hsieh and Stef M. Shuster, "Health and Health Care of Sexual and Gender Minorities," *Journal of Health and Social Behavior* 62, no. 3 (2021): 318–33.

30   Prior to the passage of the Affordable Care Act in 2010, insurance companies could discriminate against Americans with preexisting health conditions by charging higher premiums or refusing coverage entirely.

31   *In re Marriage Cases.*

32   The acronym TGNCNB stands for Transgender, Gender Non-Conforming, and Nonbinary.

NOTES FROM CHAPTER 5

33   T. Shawn Taylor, "Ties that Unwind," *Chicago Tribune*, November 17, 2004.

34   Scattered lower courts in California were also approving second-parent adoptions at this time, but the California Supreme Court did not bring second-parent adoptions to the entire state until 2003's *Sharon S. v. Superior Court*. We filed an amicus brief in that case.

35   The case was originally called *Finstuen v. Edmundson*. The name change reflects turnover in the Oklahoma Attorney General's office.

36 "Gays can seek parental rights for nonbiological kids, New York's highest court rules," *WABC*, August 30, 2016, https://abc7ny.com/court-parenthood-children-family/1491238/

NOTES FROM CHAPTER 6

37 The case changed names a few times over the course of litigation, from *Baehr v. Lewin* to *Baehr v. Anderson* to *Baehr v. Mi`ike*, reflecting turnover in the leadership of the Hawai`i Department of Health. We continue to call the case *Baehr v. Lewin* because that's how it's widely known.

38 Evan Wolfson, "Crossing the Threshold: Equal Marriage Rights for Lesbians and Gay Men and the Intra-Community Critique," *N.Y.U. Review of Law and Social Change* 21 (1993): 567, 572.

39 Tom Stoddard, "Why Gay People Should Seek the Right to Marry," *Out/Look* 6 (Fall 1989): 13.

40 Paula Ettelbrick, "Since When Is Marriage a Path to Liberation?" *Out/Look* 6 (Fall 1989): 14.

41 The civil union cases were *Baker v. State of Vermont* (VT 1999) and *Lewis v. Harris* (NJ 2006). The marriage equality cases were *Goodridge v. Department of Public Health* (MA 2003), *Kerrigan v. Commissioner of Public Health* (CT 2008), *In re Marriage Cases* (CA 2008), and *Varnum v. Brien* (IA 2009). Our movement partner GLAD brought *Baker*, *Goodridge*, and *Kerrigan*. Lambda Legal brought *Lewis* and *Varnum*. Lambda Legal, NCLR, and the ACLU jointly litigated *In re Marriage Cases*.

42 Proposition 8 amended California's constitution to add: "Only marriage between a man and a woman is valid or recognized in California."

43 In 2011, New York enacted marriage equality, while Illinois, Hawai`i, Delaware, and Rhode Island created civil unions. In 2012, the states of Washington, Maryland, and Maine passed marriage equality laws, all of which were challenged by ballot measures. Voters in all three states approved marriage equality, a striking illustration of how much public attitudes about marriage equality were changing. Then, in 2013, during the months prior to *Windsor*, Rhode Island, Delaware, and Minnesota passed marriage equality laws while Colorado enacted civil unions.

44 The name of the case striking down Wisconsin's discriminatory marriage law was *Wolf v. Walker*. It was brought by the ACLU.

45 "Remembering Robina Asti, 99-year-old pilot, WW II veteran and transgender icon," *CBC* Radio, March 22, 202. https://www.cbc.ca/radio/asithappens/as-it-happens-the-monday-edition-1.5959382/remembering-robina-asti-99-year-old-pilot-ww-ii-veteran-and-transgender-icon-1.5959384

46 Paula Span, "Social Security Opens to Survivors of Same-Sex Couples Who Could Not Marry," *The New York Times*, January 23, 2022, https://www.nytimes.com/2022/01/23/health/social-security-same-sex.html

NOTES FROM CHAPTER 7

47 This quote comes from Heather's courtroom testimony in *Colín*.

48 Masha Gessen, "Remembering David Buckel, the Pioneering Lawyer Who Championed L.G.B.T. Rights," *The New Yorker*, April 16, 2018, https://www.newyorker.com/news/our-columnists/remembering-david-buckel-the-pioneering-lawyer-who-championed-lgbt-rights

49 David Buckel, "Legal Perspective on Ensuring a Safe and Nondiscriminatory School Environment for Lesbian, Gay, Bisexual, and Transgendered Students," *Education and Urban Society* 32, no. 3 (2000): 285–432. https://journals-sagepub-com.ezproxy.uvm.edu/doi/epdf/10.1177/0013124500323007.

50 Sonia K. Katyal, "A Dream Deferred: Disturbing Recent Setbacks for LGBT Rights, and an Older Court Victory that Provides Hope,"

FindLaw, October 5, 2010, https://supreme.findlaw.com/legal-commentary/a-dream-deferred-disturbing-recent-setbacks-for-lgbt-rights-and-an-older-court-victory-that-provides-hope.html

51 *Frontline*, "Assault on Gay America," directed by Claudia Pryor Malis, aired February 15, 2000, on PBS. https://www.pbs.org/wgbh/pages/frontline/shows/assault/interviews/henkle.html

52 "Lesbian teacher pursues harassment case in appellate court," *The Record Courier*, December 20, 2001. https://www.recordcourier.com/news/2001/dec/20/lesbian-teacher-pursues-harassment-case-in-appella/

53 *Curran v. Mount Diablo Council of the Boy Scouts of America*

NOTES FROM CHAPTER 8

54 Reuters. "Federal Judge Rules Fair Housing Law Protects Colorado LGBT Couple," *The Washington Post*, March 20, 2023. https://www.reuters.com/article/us-colorado-lgbt/federal-judge-rules-fair-housing-law-protects-lgbt-couple-idU.S.KBN17731A

NOTES FROM CHAPTER 9

55 The case originally was called *Sundstrom v. Frank* and included five plaintiffs. *Sundstrom* changed to *Fields* when two of the plaintiffs were released from prison and dismissed from the suit. The change from *Frank* to *Smith* reflects, among other things, turnover in the Wisconsin Department of Corrections.

56 The case originally was called *Hicklin v. Lombardi*. The name change reflects turnover in the leadership of the Missouri Department of Corrections.

57 More specifically, the Supreme Court ruled in *Miller v. Alabama* (2012) that juveniles could only be sentenced to life without parole after consideration of the offender's maturity level and the individual circumstances of the case. In *Montgomery v. Louisiana* (2016), the Court further held that *Miller* must be applied retroactively.

58 We changed the report's name slightly from the first to the second edition.

59 The case was *In re D.H. v. H.H.*

60 In 2017, Roy Moore ran for the U.S. Senate. He won the Republican primary but then his campaign went sideways when allegations of sexual misconduct emerged, including three allegations of sexual assault and multiple claims of unwanted sexual advances toward teenage girls. Moore went on to lose the general election to Democrat Doug Jones.

61 Bettina Boxall, "City Settles Police Brutality Suit Over Incident at Gay Rights Protest," *Los Angeles Times*, February 7, 1997. https://www.latimes.com/archives/la-xpm-1997-02-07-me-26465-story.html

62 Although Judge Gottschall was a U.S. District Court judge rather than a U.S. Courts of Appeal Judge, she was sitting on the Seventh Circuit temporarily as a visiting judge. Such appointments are not unusual and help the federal court system to manage its workload.

63 Katie Quinn, "The Missouri Court Case that Expanded Trans Health Care in Prisons," *KBIA*, May 1, 2023. https://www.kbia.org/2023-05-01/the-missouri-court-case-that-expanded-trans-health-care-in-prisons

64 In retention elections, voters determine whether or not a judge should have another term in office. Iowa is one of 20 states that hold retention elections for judges. Justices of Iowa's Supreme Court face a retention election after their first year in office and then again after each eight-year term.

65 The "non-qualified" judges were L. Steven Grasz and Jonathan Kobes, both appointed to the Eighth Circuit, and Charles B. Goodwin and

Holly Lou Teeter, both appointed to federal district courts. Two additional "non-qualified" nominees withdrew their nominations.

66 See Lambda Legal's 2021 report, *Courts, Confirmations, and Consequences: How Trump Restructured the Federal Judiciary and Ushered in a Climate of Unprecedented Hostility toward LGBTQ+ People and Civil Rights.*

67 We submitted friend-of-the-court briefs showing the dangerous stakes for LGBTQ+ people in most of these cases, including *Masterpiece Cakeshop v. Colorado Civil Rights Commission* (whether bakeries can refuse to sell wedding cakes to same-sex couples), *Fulton v. Philadelphia* (whether taxpayer-funded foster care agencies can discriminate against potential foster-parents who are LGBTQ+); *Kennedy v. Bremerton* (whether it is acceptable for a public school coach to engage in after-game prayers with team members at center field); *Carson v. Makin* (whether Maine can deny tuition support to religious high schools if it provides support for non-religious schools), and *303 Creative v. Elenis* (whether a website designer can refuse to design wedding websites for same-sex couples if she creates wedding websites for different-sex couples).

NOTES FROM CHAPTER 10

68 Movement Advancement Project, *Under Fire: The War on LGBTQ People in America* (February 2023), http://www.mapresearch.org/under-fire-report

69 "FIX THIS NOW," *The Indianapolis Star,* March 31, 2015, https://www.indystar.com/story/opinion/2015/03/30/editorial-gov-pence-fix-religious-freedom-law-now/70698802/

70 From her speech at the Georgia Unites Against Discrimination rally, February 9, 2016.

71 Merrit Kennedy, "Controversial Mississippi Law Limiting LGBT Rights Not Heading to Supreme Court," NPR, January 8, 2018, https://www.npr.org/sections/thetwo-way/2018/01/08/576500364/controversial-mississippi-law-limiting-lgbt-rights-not-heading-to-supreme-court

72 Gay, Lesbian, and Straight Education Network. "Laws prohibiting 'promotion of homosexuality' in schools: Impacts and implications (Research Brief)." *New York:* GLSEN (2018).

73 Arizona Revised Statutes § 15-716(C) (1991).

74 S.C. Code Ann. § 59-32-30 (1988).

75 Our case was *Equality Arizona v. Hoffman.* The repeal measure, SB 1346, was enacted on April 11, 2019.

76 Our case was *Gender and Sexuality Alliance v. Spearman.*

77 The cases are *Roe v. Critchfield* and *Bridge v. State of Oklahoma.*

78 PFLAG—originally Parents and Friends of Lesbians and Gays—is dedicated to supporting, educating, and advocating for LGBTQ+ people and their families. Like Lambda Legal, PFLAG turned fifty years old in 2023.

79 The cases are *Soe v. Louisiana* (Louisiana), *Noe v. Parson* (Missouri), *Van Garderen v. Montana* (Montana), *Voe v. Mansfield* (North Carolina), *Poe v. Drummond* (Oklahoma), and *L.W. v. Skrmetti* (Tennessee).

80 The case was *Doe v. Ladapo* (2023), which was brought by GLAD, NCLR, HRC, and Southern Legal Counsel.

81 The Sixth Circuit decision covered two cases, our own *L.W. v. Skrmetti* (brought jointly with the ACLU) and *Doe v. Thornbury,* brought by the ACLU and NCLR. The Eleventh Circuit case is *Boe v. Marshall,* brought by the Southern Poverty Law Center, NCLR, GLAD, and HRC.

PHOTO CREDITS

pp. 146-148:
Lambda Legal

p. 149: © *The Record Sun* – USA TODAY NETWORK

pp. 150-151:
Lambda Legal

p. 152: Jewel Samad/AFP via Getty Images

p. 153: (clockwise from top) © *The Burlington Free Press* – USA TODAY NETWORK; © The Economist Group Limited, London; Lambda Legal; POLITICO LLC copyright 2016. Used with permission; *Newsweek;* © 1994 Jacques Loustal & *The New Yorker*. All rights reserved. Used by permission.; © USA TODAY NETWORK

p. 154: (top left) *The Boston Globe;* (top left inset) Doug Mills/*The New York Times/*Redux; (middle) © *The Des Moines Register* – USA TODAY NETWORK; (top right) Art Lien; (bottom) National Archives & Records Administration

p. 155: (top) Andrew Harrer/Bloomberg via Getty Images; (bottom left) The New Press/Lambda Legal; (right) Lambda Legal

pp. 156-157:
see page 287

p. 158: (left) Lambda Legal; (right) *Star Tribune*

pp. 159-161:
Lambda Legal

p. 162: Courtesy of Dru Levasseur

p. 163: (top) Lambda Legal; (bottom) M.Sharkey

p. 164: (left) Courtesy Michael Ely; (right) Mark Navarro

p. 165: (top) Chona Kasinger/*The New York Times/*Redux; (middle) Courtesy of Helen Thornton; (bottom) Lambda Legal

INTERLUDE: THE LONG ROAD TO MARRIAGE EQUALITY

p. 166-167:
p. 166-167: Design by Brian Rosenkrans. Research by Ellen Andersen

CHAPTER 7

p. 168: Brianna Soukup/*Portland Press Herald* via Getty Images

p. 170: Arielle Bader for *The Hechinger Report*

p. 172-173:
(left) University of Washington Libraries, Special Collections, [PNW04055]; (middle, right) Milne Special Collections & Archives Division, Dimond Library, University of New Hampshire, Durham, N.H.

p. 174: (left) Courtesy of Jason Hinojosa/Sacramento Country Day School; (right) Leonard Ortiz, Orange County Register/SCNG

p. 175: (top) Cover photo by Michele A.H. Smith. Courtesy of *The Advocate* and Stonewall National Museum, Archives & Library; (bottom) Courtesy of United States District Court, Central District of California.

p. 176: Jeff Zelevansky/Reuters

p. 177: Rita Reed

p. 178: Ron Oden/*Reno Gazette-Journal* - USA TODAY NETWORK

p. 179: Suen Wiederholt/Lambda Legal

p. 180: Courtesy of Myron Quon

p. 181: (top) Lambda Legal; (bottom) The ArQuives

p. 182: Courtesy of James Dale

p. 183: (top) *The Advocate*; (bottom) Bob Pileggi/Lambda Legal

CHAPTER 8

p. 184: Michael Moloney/Shutterstock

p. 186: Kenneth Hawk/CC-BY-NC-2.0

pp. 188-191:
Lambda Legal

p. 192: *Honolulu Star Advertiser,* (inset) Eric Risberg/AP

p. 193: Lambda Legal

p. 194: (left, right) © *Austin American Statesman* – USA TODAY NETWORK; (middle) *Fort Worth Star Telegram.* © 2017 McClatchy. All rights reserved. Used under license.

p. 195: Nicole Prescott. Styled by Jason Alba for Vivienne Westwood

p. 196: (left) Library of Congress; (right) Nadia Awad/*Fort Worth Weekly*

p. 197: Matt Andrews

p. 198: © *The Greenville News* – USA TODAY NETWORK

p. 199: Lambda Legal

INTERLUDE: THE LEGAL HELP DESK

p. 200-203:
Design by Brian Rosenkrans; Photos courtesy of Lambda Legal

CHAPTER 9

p. 204: Bryan Schutmaat

p. 206: Paolo J. Riveros

p. 208: (top) Courtesy of Translatina Coalition; (bottom) © M10s/TheNEWS2 via Zuma Press Wire/Alamy

p. 209: (top) Rodrigo Abd/AP

p. 210: (left) Phyllis Christopher; (right) Tom Tyburski/Lambda Legal

p. 211: (left) Jenny Pizer; (middle) ©2007. *Los Angeles Times.* All rights reserved; (right) Michael Chiabaudo/Lambda Legal

p. 212: (top) *The Right Girls*/Woler Productions, L.L.C.; (middle) Lambda Legal; (bottom) Julián Aguilar/*The Texas Tribune*

p. 213: (top) Yakoniva/Alamy; (bottom) Courtesy of Ola Osaze

p. 214: (left) Jenny Pizer; (right) Tomas Abad/Alamy

p. 215: (top left) Tomas Abad/Alamy; (top right) Courtesy of Iván Espinoza-Madrigal; (bottom) Jack Kurtz/ZUMAPress.com

p. 216: (top) Chad Zuber/Shutterstock; (bottom left) Courtesy of Jessica Hicklin; (bottom right) Derek Bacon/Ikon Images

p. 217: (left, right) Courtesy of Peter Mackler

p. 218: (left) Frances Sparkle Davis/Lambda Legal; (right) Leslie Von Pless/Lambda Legal

p. 219: (top) Courtesy of *Seattle Gay News*; (bottom) Courtesy of Judge Gottschall

pp. 220-221:
Courtesy of Richard Saenz/Lambda Legal

p. 221: (bottom right) Courtesy of Demoya Gordon

p. 224: Steve Rhodes/Flickr/CC-BY-2.0

p. 225: (top) Lambda Legal; (middle left) Steve Rhodes/Flickr/CC-BY-2.0; (middle right) Janine Wiedel Photolibrary/Alamy

p. 227: Lambda Legal

p. 228: (top) Alex Wong/Getty Images; (bottom) Lambda Legal

p. 229: Stephen Mally/*The New York Times/*Redux

p. 230: (bottom) Ellen Andersen and Michael Green; (bottom left) Evan Vucci/AP; (bottom middle) Patricia Schlein/STAR MAX/IPx/AP; (bottom right) Susan Walsh/AP

p. 231: (left to right) Joshua Hoover/U.S. Department of Education; Ed Andrieski/AP; Courtesy of U.S. District Court, Northern District of Texas; Stephanie Strasburg Copyright © *Pittsburgh Post-Gazette*, 2023, all rights reserved. Reprinted with permission; (bottom) Courtesy of Kristine Kippins

p. 232: Chris DeCarlo

p. 233: (top to bottom): *Seattle Gay News*; WLOX; *Clarion Ledger*

p. 234: CNN/Warner Bros. Discovery

p. 235: (top) Michelle Lepianka Carter, *The Tuscaloosa News*/AP; (middle) *The New York Times*; (bottom right) Courtesy of Hector Vargas

p. 236: (top right) Courtesy of *Seattle Gay News*; (bottom) Lambda Legal

p. 237: Courtesy of Ethan Rice

CHAPTER 10

p. 238: John Amis/AP Images for Human Rights Campaign

p. 241: Victoria Pickering/CC-BY-NC-ND-2.0

p. 242: Pablo Martinez Monsivais/AP

p. 243: Joe Brusky/CC-BY-NC-2.0

p. 244: (bottom) Steve Petteway/Collection of the Supreme Court of the United States

p. 245: (top) © 2016 Beth Nakamura / *The Oregonian*. All rights reserved. Used with permission.; (bottom) Alexander DG/Shutterstock

p. 246: © *Indianapolis Star* – USA TODAY NETWORK

p. 247: (top left) A.Katz/Shutterstock; (top right, middle) Lambda Legal; (bottom) Jeff Amy/AP

p. 248: (left) Douglas R. Clifford/*Tampa Bay Times* via AP; (right) ArQuives.ca

p. 249: Wilfredo Lee/AP

p. 250: Jon Viscott/City of West Hollywood

p. 251: (top) Lambda Legal; (bottom) Official White House Photo by Tia Dufour

p. 252-253: Erik McGregor/LightRocket via Getty Images

p. 255: Lambda Legal

p. 256: AwakenedEye/istockphoto

p. 257: (top, bottom left) Lambda Legal; (bottom right) Eric Gay/AP

p. 258: (left) Scott Olson/Getty Images; (right) Lambda Legal

p. 259: Lambda Legal

p. 261: (left) ACLU of West Virginia; (right) Raymond Thompson Jr.

p. 262: Ted Eytan/Flickr/CC-BY-SA-2.0

p. 263: (top) Shawn Poynter/ACLU; (bottom) Lambda Legal

p. 264: Lambda Legal

p. 265: (top) Courtesy of District of Idaho, United States Courts; (bottom) Lambda Legal

p. 267: (top) Jillian R McKenzie; (bottom) Courtesy of Sruti Swaminathan

p. 268: (top) Alex Milan Tracy/Sipa USA via AP; (bottom) Lambda Legal

p. 269: Lambda Legal

CHAPTER 11

p. 270: Kenneth Hawk/Flickr/CC-BY-NC-2.0

pp. 272-273: Lambda Legal

p. 274: Courtesy of Trevor Wilkinson

BACK COVER:
(top left) Division of Political and Military History, National Museum of American History, Smithsonian Institution; (top middle) Bettye Lane, Schlesinger Library, Harvard Radcliffe Institute; (top right) Mario Suriani/AP; (middle left) Diana Jo Davies, Manuscripts and Archives Division, The New York Public Library; (middle center) © *The Des Moines Register* - USA TODAY NETWORK; (middle right) Cover photo by Michele A.H. Smith. Courtesy of *The Advocate* and Stonewall National Museum, Archives & Library; (bottom left) Alex Milan Tracy/Sipa USA via AP; (bottom middle upper and lower) Lambda Legal; (bottom right) Bob Pileggi/Lambda Legal

FACES OF MARRIAGE EQUALITY

FACES OF MARRIAGE EQUALITY

See p. 287 for the names of these marriage plaintiffs.

All photos courtesy of Lambda Legal, except as noted below.

P. 156

Top row (L-R):

Karen Bailey and Nelda Majors, Arizona

Michelle Chappell and Michelle Franke, with daughter Rose, Illinois

Phyllis Lyon and Del Martin, California *(Deanne Fitzmaurice/San Francisco Chronicle via Getty Images)*

Second row (L-R):

Theresa Volpe and Mercedes Santos, with children Ava and Jaidon, Illinois

John Grant and Daniel Weiss, New Jersey

Vega Subramaniam and Mala Nagarajan, Washington

Daryl Rizzo and Jaime Garcia, with daughter Siena, Illinois

Third row (L-R):

Vernita Gray and Pat Ewert, Illinois *(Timmy Samuel/Starbelly Studios)*

Bert Morton and Lee Korty, Illinois

José A. Torruellas Iglesias and Thomas J. Robinson, Puerto Rico

Bottom row (L-R):

Vicente Talanquer and Kent Burbank, with sons Daniel and Martin, Arizona

Jessica and Kathy Young, Arizona

Lancy Woo and Cristy Chung, California

P. 157

Top row (L-R):

Pauline (back), Zumi (middle), and Jill (front) Guillermo-Togawa, Hawaii

Joseph Vitale and Rob Talmas with son Cooper Talmas-Vitale, Ohio

Erica and Tevonda Bradshaw and son Teverico, New Jersey

Second row (L-R):

Robert Hickok and Brian Fletcher with their children, Hank, Ellie, and Jack, Illinois

Saundra Toby-Heath and Alicia Heath-Toby, New Jersey

Justin Murdock and Will Glavaris, West Virginia

Lynne Burnett and Robyne O'Mara, Illinois

Third row (L-R):

Zulma Oliveras Vega and Yolanda Arroyo Pizarro, Puerto Rico.

Amy Sandler and Niki Quasney (before Niki's untimely death of cancer in 2015), Indiana

Bob Proctor and Hector Martinez, Illinois

Iris Delia Rivera-Rivera and Maritza López Aviles, Puerto Rico

Fourth row (L-R):

Bonnie Everly and Lyn Judkins, Indiana (Timmy Samuel/Starbelly Studios)

Pam and Nicole Yorksmith, with children Grayden and Orion, Ohio (Sam Greene/SGdoesit.com)

Jim Darby and Patrick Bova, Illinois

Bottom row (L-R):

Ruth Borenstein and Karen Strauss, California

Marcye and Karen Nicholson-McFadden with children Kasey and Maya, New Jersey

Corey Davis and Andre LeJeune, California

By Jennifer C. Pizer and Ellen Ann Andersen

Editor: Carla Sakamoto
Designers: Phil Kovacevich and Shawn Hazen
Photo research and selection by Michael Green
Research by Jamie Farnsworth
Production Director: Michael Vagnetti
Cover design by Phil Kovacevich

Library of Congress Control Number: 2024905691

ISBN: 978-1-58093-614-9

Printed in China

Monacelli
A Phaidon Company
111 Broadway, Suite 301
New York, New York 10006

www.monacellipress.com